MIGRATION AND TRANSNATIONALISM
PACIFIC PERSPECTIVES

MIGRATION AND TRANSNATIONALISM
PACIFIC PERSPECTIVES

EDITED BY HELEN LEE
AND STEVE TUPAI FRANCIS

ANU
THE AUSTRALIAN NATIONAL UNIVERSITY

E PRESS

Published by ANU E Press
The Australian National University
Canberra ACT 0200, Australia
Email: anuepress@anu.edu.au
This title is also available online at: http://epress.anu.edu.au/migration_citation.html

National Library of Australia
Cataloguing-in-Publication entry

Title: Migration and transnationalism [electronic resource] :
              Pacific perspectives / editors, Helen Lee, Steve Tupai Francis.

ISBN: 9781921536908 (pbk.)   9781921536915 (pdf)

Subjects: Transnationalism.
              Migrations of nations.
              Pacific Area--Emigration and immigration.

Other Authors/Contributors:
              Lee, Helen.
              Francis, Steve Tupai.

Dewey Number: 304.80995

Cover design by ANU E Press

Table of Contents

Contributors

Ping-Ann Addo is an Assistant Professor of Anthropology at the University of Massachusetts, Boston. Her research uses Tongan textiles and gift exchange to analyse Tongan women's agency and their communities' ethnic identities in Auckland, New Zealand, and Oakland, California. She teaches courses on the anthropology of art and material culture, multiculturalism, and ethnic expression and has managed a community arts project with Tongan textile artists in Oakland. She has published in the areas of transnationalism, Tongan exchange, ethnicity, and the political economy of contemporary diaspora. Ping-Ann is ethnic Chinese and Ghanaian, and hails from Trinidad and Tobago.

Kalissa Alexeyeff is currently a research fellow in the School of Philosophy, Anthropology and Social Inquiry at the University of Melbourne, seconded from her position as lecturer in the Gender Studies Program. She has written a book *Dancing from the Heart: Movement, Gender and Cook Islands Globalization* (Univeristy of Hawai'i Press, 2009) which explores the significance of dance in the Cook Islands throughout colonial history and in its contemporary manifestations.

Maria Borovnik is a lecturer in the School of People, Environment and Planning at Massey University, New Zealand. She has a PhD from Canterbury University. Her main research area is the social strategies of people living mobile livelihoods and she has studied seafarers from Kiribati and Tuvalu who work on international merchant and fishing ships. Her recent publications on this appear in the *Asian and Pacific Migration Journal* and *Asia Pacific Viewpoint*.

John Connell is Professor of Human Geography in the School of Geosciences at the University of Sydney. He has long been interested in development issues in island states and the role of culture in development. He has written several books on the Pacific, especially focused on Bougainville and Papua New Guinea, and recently edited two books *The international migration of health workers* (Routledge, New York, 2008) and, with Barbara Rugendyke, *Tourism at the grassroots. Villagers and visitors in the Asia-Pacific* (Routledge, London, 2008).

Mike Evans is an Associate Professor at UBC Okanagan. After completing his doctorate at McMaster University in 1996, he taught at the University of Northern BC, and then at the University of Alberta prior to moving to UBC in 2003. His primary research relationships are with people in the Métis community in Northern BC, the Métis Nation of BC, and the Kingdom of Tonga. He has published extensively on Tongan adaptations to globalization, the impact of imported foods on Tongan diets and health, and other issues facing contemporary Indigenous communities in Canada and the Pacific.

Steve Tupai Francis is an Australian-born Tongan with a PhD in Anthropology from the University of Melbourne. Steve is an Honorary Fellow with the School of Anthropology, Geography and Environmental Studies at the University of Melbourne and an Honorary Associate with the Refugee Health Research Centre, School of Social Sciences, La Trobe University. Steve is Manager—Movement Relations and Advocacy for the Australian Red Cross.

Paul Harms did doctoral research at the University of Alberta on the economic and social importance of Tongan migration.

Ingjerd Hoëm is Associate Professor at the Department of Social Anthropology, University of Oslo. She has held the position of Head of Research at the Institute for Pacific Cultural History and Archaeology at the Kon-Tiki Museum, of which she is now a member of the Board of Directors. She is the scientific leader of the research project 'Identity Matters: Movement and Place', funded by the Norwegian Research Council. Among her latest publications are: *Theatre and political process. Staging identities in Tokelau and New Zealand* and 'Stealing the Water of Life: The Historicity of Contemporary Social Relationships', in *History and Anthropology*.

Helen Lee is Associate Professor of Anthropology in the School of Social Sciences at La Trobe University and Visiting Fellow of the ANU Pacific Centre. Since the 1980s her research has focused on the people of Tonga, both in their home islands in the South Pacific and in the diaspora. Her publications include *Becoming Tongan: An ethnography of childhood* (Helen Morton, University of Hawai'i Press) and *Tongans overseas: Between two shores* (University of Hawai'i Press). Her current work is on second generation Tongan transnationalism and her most recent book is the edited collection *Ties to the homeland: Second generation transnationalism* (Cambridge Scholars Publishing, 2008).

Sa'iliemanu Lilomaiava-Doktor was born and raised in Salelologa, Savaii, Samoa. She did her primary and secondary education in Savaii and went on a Samoan government scholarship through ADAB to do her BA at the University of Newcastle, NSW, Australia. She taught at Samoa College (high school) for five years before she went back on a Fulbright scholarship to do her MA in Pacific Islands Studies followed by her Ph.D. in Geography, both at the University of Hawaii. Sa'ili is a lecturer in Hawaiian and Pacific Studies in the Humanities Division at the University of Hawaii-West Oahu. Her publication, 'Beyond Migration: Samoan Population Movement (*Malaga*) and Geography of Social Space (*Va*)' appears in the February 2009 issue of *The Contemporary Pacific* 22 (1): 1-32.

Cluny Macpherson is Professor of Sociology at Massey University at Auckland. **La'avasa Macpherson** is a research associate and orchardist. They have worked in both Samoa and in Samoan diasporic communities over some 35 years. They have written a book *Samoan medical belief and practice (*Auckland University

Press) and numerous journal articles on topics including Samoan migration, the social correlates of suicide, law and dispute resolution, religion and development in Samoa; economic development and the transformation of Samoan kinship and transnationalism. Their interest in transnationalism is personal and professional and they divide their time between family in Samoan and New Zealand.

Camille Nakhid is Senior Lecturer in the Department of Social Sciences at Auckland University of technology. Her research interests include migrant and refugee communities, research methodologies, and Maori and Pasifika student achievement.

Vili Nosa completed his Master of Arts (Hons) in Sociology in 1997. His master's thesis focused on the pull/push influences on Niuean migration. He also has a PhD in Behavioural Science for a thesis entitled: 'The Perceptions and use of alcohol among Niuean men living in Auckland'. He is the first Niuean to gain a PhD. Vili is currently employed as a lecturer in the Section of Pacific Health, School of Population Health, University of Auckland. He lectures on number of health related courses in the certificate, undergraduate, post-graduate, and medical courses within the School of Population health.

Nancy Pollock's interest in transnationalism stems from concerns about Globalisation and its many dimensions, particularly as they affect food access for populations in the Pacific. Her research on local foods and their uses over time has raised concerns about development, particularly poverty and thus food security and the health issues they raise in today's commercial world. She has retired from the Departments of Anthropology and Development Studies at Victoria University in Wellington, but continues her research activities, drawing on Pacific issues for wider concerns such as transculturation. Her latest publication is: 'Sustainability of the Kava Trade', 2009, in *The Contemporary Pacific* 21 (2).

R. Colin Reid, PhD (University of Victoria) is Assistant Professor in Health Studies at the University of British Columbia Okanagan. He is a social gerontologist and demographer, with particular interest in quantitative and mixed methods.

Mark Schubert holds a PhD in Anthropology from the University of Queensland. He grew up in the Pacific Islands in places as varied as Pitcairn Island and Papua New Guinea and spent his fieldwork time in Australia's south-west of New South Wales, among the many Pacific Islander migrants in Griffith town. He is currently lecturer in the School of Population Health at the University of Queensland and in his spare time does social mapping work in Papua New Guinea.

Acknowledgments

We are so grateful to the contributors to this book, who have patiently followed all our editorial requests over the past two years. From their enthusiastic participation in the Pacific Transnationalism conference in November 2006, at La Trobe University in Melbourne, Australia, and through several revisions of their papers, all of the authors have been generous with their time and have enabled us to create a book that is more than simply a collection of conference proceedings. Thankyou also to those who participated in the conference but whose papers are not included here; all of the presentations were of high quality and contributed to lively discussions throughout the sessions. Those discussions continued in the community forum held during the conference, at which members of a number of Pacific communities in Melbourne shared their views about migration and transnationalism; many thanks to them for giving their time and so generously sharing their thoughts and experiences.

We are also grateful to ANU E Press for publishing this collection and to the anonymous reviewers whose reports helped us shape the collection into its final form.

Helen Lee and Steve Tupai Francis

Introduction

Helen Lee

In the context of contemporary globalisation and increasing population mobility, the topics of migration and transnationalism have become the focus of studies in a number of disciplines, including anthropology, sociology, cultural geography and political science, and the contributors to this collection reflect this diversity. They bring a range of perspectives, theories and methodologies to their research, and focus on many Pacific Island states and Pacific populations in the main host nations of New Zealand, the United States and Australia.

Within the vast body of literature on global migration the Pacific is well represented, however within the field of transnational studies the Pacific is virtually absent as there has been a focus on the transnational practices of migrants in the United States and Europe from the Caribbean, Latin America, Asia and Africa. This book provides, for the first time, a collection of papers that unite Pacific migration studies with the field of transnational studies and present a number of detailed case studies of contemporary Pacific populations. The authors focus on transnationalism as a feature of migration, although the term 'transnationalism' can be used more broadly, in relation to global business, finance, governance and so many other aspects of globalisation. The case studies presented in this book show that these broader aspects of transnationalism are often vital to the connections between migrants and their homelands, as when people remit money via financial institutions such as Western Union, or when globalised technologies such as the internet enable them to communicate with friends and family around the world.

Previous work on Pacific migration has focused primarily on migrants' experiences within the diaspora; to a lesser extent this work has examined migrants' ties to their homelands. Within the literature on connections between Pacific migrant populations and their countries of origin the central concern has been remittances and their impact on island economies, and the chapters in this volume acknowledge the importance of remittances as a crucial element of Pacific transnationalism. However, the contributors also seek to go beyond a narrowly economic focus in order to examine the multiple strands of transnational connections that weave a complex web linking the islands and the many parts of the Pacific diaspora. For Pacific Islanders, transnationalism involves the multidirectional movement of people, money, goods of many different kinds, artefacts, ideas and symbols, and involves individuals, families, groups and institutions.

Indeed, it is difficult to discuss Pacific migration without also discussing transnationalism, because Islanders' experiences of migration have always been inherently transnational. People's motivations for migration are diverse but the desire to retain connections to kin 'at home' has long been a feature of Pacific Islanders' mobility. As the chapters in this volume show, kinship may be the strongest thread in the transnational web but is by no means the only one; the authors address other elements of transnationalism as varied as the movement of food around the Pacific and involvement of migrants in homeland politics.

In presenting 'Pacific perspectives' this book does not claim to cover the entire sweep of Oceania. The book's chapters focus on the regions known as Polynesia and Micronesia, although the French territories and former territories of the United States are not represented, nor is the region known as Melanesia, with the exception of Fiji, which has long had an ambiguous position within these European-imposed regional designations. And, while there is a chapter on Fijian migrants, there is little mention of Indo-Fijians, who have migrated in large numbers in recent years. Rather than attempt a broad but inevitably shallow coverage of the entire Pacific region, the chapters instead present a range of case studies that highlight the key themes of Pacific migration and transnationalism: reciprocity and gift-giving, kinship, identity, work and the ideal of a return 'home'.

After a chapter presenting an overview of the history of Pacific migration and transnationalism, and some of the current issues in the literature on these topics, the themes of reciprocity and kinship are highlighted in the next four chapters. Chapter Two, by Ping-Ann Addo, draws on ethnographic research conducted in Auckland, New Zealand and California in the United States, to examine Tongan women's roles in controlling family economics by exchanging *koloa*, traditional wealth in the form of textiles produced by women, across sites of Tongan transnationalism. Addo explores the role that cash has come to play in such exchanges and she uses a Tongan funeral in the diaspora as a case study of how the transnational Tongan economy is transforming as cash enters into ceremonial gift-giving.

Sa'iliemanu Lilomaiava-Doktor brings a *fa`a-Samoa* (Samoan culture and way of life) perspective on transnationalism to Chapter Three, examining how social, cultural, political, and economic practices have changed over time, and the forms that Samoan transnational processes take, with a particular focus on the concept of 'social remittances'. Her chapter continues the themes of reciprocity and kinship by focusing on gift exchanges as a central nexus of transnational activity for Tongans She draws on research in the village of Salelologa on Savai`i, in independent Samoa, and as in Addo's chapter she also focuses on villagers' *'aiga* (family, kin group) in Auckland, New Zealand and California in the U.S. Her chapter exemplifies the importance of considering the transnational engagements of those who remain in the islands, as well as acknowledging the active agency of Samoans in constantly transforming practices such as gift exchanges.

In Chapter Four, Cluny and La'avasa Macpherson describe kinship as the foundation of Samoan transnationalism. They draw on their longitudinal research to examine transformations in 'kin-based activity' in Samoan migrant communities in New Zealand since the 1950s which, they argue, have transformed the nature of Samoan transnationalism and have influenced practices in Samoa itself. Like Lilomaiava-Doktor they focus on the reciprocity of gift exchanges as central to expressions of *fa'a Samoa*, tracing the changes in gift-giving practices over time in the Auckland communities. Their concept of a contemporary Samoan 'meta-culture' which encompasses Samoans at home and abroad could usefully be applied to other Pacific populations and is a new way to imagine the spread of Pacific peoples and their interconnectedness over vast distances.

Kalissa Alexeyeff's Chapter Five on the Cook Islands describes *tere pati*, the movement of large groups of people to visit Cook Islanders in other locations, both within the islands and between the Cook Islands and New Zealand and other diasporic locations. While much of her chapter focuses on the excitement and sociality of *tere pati*, Alexeyeff also reminds us that migration and transnationalism inherently involve experiences of 'loss and dislocation'. Transnational movement means that people experience not only the joy of visiting family and friends but also the sadness of leaving them again and movements such as *tere pati* are constant reminders of the distances between loved ones.

The issue of identity, which is a thread running through each of the preceding case studies, is addressed more directly in Chapter Six, by Nancy Pollock, through a broad comparative approach across the Pacific with a focus on food. Pollock looks at the mobility of 'gastronomies' across the Pacific and describes the centrality of food as means of cultural expression. She traces the movement of foodstuffs into the Pacific from Asia in the original migrations, and the modern influences of Asia on Pacific diets, as well as the influences of European and American cuisines. Pollock also describes the influence of transnational corporations which bring particular kinds of food and drink to the Pacific, and the rest of the world. Her chapter takes us right back to the first migrations into the Pacific then brings us to the present day, to contemporary Pacific migration and transnationalism and the increasingly complex expressions of identity both within the islands and in the diaspora.

Chapter Seven, jointly authored by Mike Evans, Paul Harms and Colin Reid, continues the focus on identity as a key theme in Pacific migration and transnationalism. The authors employ a quantitative approach, using a survey of Tongan adults in Tonga and Auckland. Their survey was designed to ascertain participants' attitudes towards key elements of Tongan identity and to assess whether these are influenced by demographic factors. Their work demonstrates the value of taking a quantitative approach to issues that have previously been researched qualitatively, such as how being 'Tongan' is defined through specific values and practices. Like many of the chapters in this book, it also demonstrates that the home/abroad dichotomy should not be overstated, with people living in transnational households, even transnational villages, rather than in divergent communities.

The importance of employment as motivation for migration is highlighted in Chapter Eight, by Mark Schubert, which presents a case study of Fijians in Griffith, a regional town in Australia. Schubert focuses on the issue of 'overstaying' in order to work (illegally) overseas. He looks at why Griffith is an attractive destination for Fijians who have overstayed their short-term visas and who are seeking unskilled work picking fruit and vegetables, and he examines their interactions with documented, settled Fijians in the town. He also looks at the transnational activities of Fijians which bring visiting relatives, friends and church ministers to the town, or entail trips to Fiji for holidays and family events, and contact via telephone phone and email. For the undocumented Fijians, the options for transnational engagements are more limited and their situations are more tenuous given that they can be apprehended and deported at any time. Schubert's paper is timely, given the introduction in 2009 of short-term labour schemes in Australia, as these may well be a way for Fijians and other Islanders to live and work legally in Australia and more fully engage in maintaining transnational ties to their homelands.

Chapter Nine, by Maria Borovnik, looks at another form of temporary work away from the islands; the seafaring undertaken by people from the Pacific 'microstates' of Kiribati and Tuvalu, formerly colonised by Great Britain. Borovnik traces the history of recruitment of Pacific seafarers onto international merchant vessels since the 1950s and looks at the experiences of modern day seafarers from Tuvalu and Kiribati. She shows that these men, and today some women, are participating in a global system yet retaining ties to home, including remitting money that is now helping to support many of the families remaining in the islands.

John Connell's Chapter Ten, on the return migration of skilled health workers to Fiji, Tonga and Samoa, draws on quantitative data from surveys of nurses and doctors, both those who have migrated and returned and those who have not migrated. Connell explores their reasons for leaving (largely economic) and returning (largely social), and why some have chosen to remain in the islands. He also looks at why some who have returned intend to leave again for overseas. Return migration is a topic generating considerable interest in transnational studies and Connell's paper provides an example of how important it can be to the countries of origin; as he points out, even when health workers who return do not work in the health sector their impact is nevertheless 'significant for both social and economic development'. However, returnees encounter numerous difficulties in readjusting to life 'at home' and may desire to move back overseas; understanding why this is the case can be helpful in the development of policies and programs aimed at encouraging migrants to resettle in their country of origin.

Return migration is also a focus of Chapter Eleven, in which Vili Nosa addresses the situation for Niue, another Pacific 'microstate' and the most depopulated island country of the Pacific. He describes the history of movement from Niue, from the labour trade within the Pacific that began in the mid–19th century to present day movement beyond the Pacific. Nosa describes the rapid decline in population once Niueans gained citizenship in New Zealand in 1974; today far more live outside Niue than remain on the island. In his chapter he explores the various strategies that have been employed to encourage return migration He shows that Niue's environmental, economic and political problems present even greater obstacles than those described in the previous chapter.

Like Niueans, Tokelauns have New Zealand citizenship and many have moved away from the islands while retaining ties to kin at home. Chapter Twelve, by Ingjerd Hoëm, examines the issues of citizenship and governance for Tokelau. She looks at how these issues have changed over time as Tokelau's relationship with New Zealand has changed; and how in turn this has affected patterns of sociality in the atolls. Hoëm describes the debates that have occurred in Tokelau and its diaspora about self-governance, many of which revolved around retaining New Zealand citizenship so that transnational mobility could continue. She shows that the overseas Tokelauan community was very active in these discussions, reminding us of the 'long distance nationalism' that can have a significant influence on the homeland.

The following chapter, by Steve Tupai Francis, complicates the prevailing picture of transnationalism and the study of diaspora and movement out of Oceania by comparing different patterns of transnational movement from three Tongan villages. He demonstrates through the comparison of these villages how movement can differ within island nations, and how variables such as history, origin and socio-economic context can greatly affect how transnational movements are enacted and transacted. Through the case studies Francis also shows how the lives and experiences of individuals and families are shaped by transnationalism, even in remote island villages.

Finally, in Camille Nakhid's concluding chapter, we return to the relationship between Pacific migration and transnationalism and to the wider literature on transnationalism. Nakhid argues that the transnational practices of Pacific Islanders are shaped by the central importance placed on the principle of reciprocity, particularly as it influences cultural identity and the relationship of migrants to the homeland. As her chapter, and so many of the others, makes clear, Pacific migrants are deeply embedded in complex relationships that transcend national borders and create webs of connection spanning the distances between them and their homelands.

The chapters in this book were developed from papers written for a conference on Pacific Transnationalism held at La Trobe University in Melbourne, Australia, in November 2006. This two-day conference drew together for the first time scholars from around the world who are researching aspects of transnationalism among Pacific populations, leading to many lively and exciting discussions. Not all papers presented at the conference could be included, or this volume would be considerably larger, as it would be if every Pacific country was included. A forum was held during the conference, during which members of Pacific communities in Melbourne shared their experiences of migration and transnationalism. Their stories provided a powerful reminder of the profound emotional significance of the interconnections that transcend national borders and sustain a sense of identity and belonging for Islanders wherever they may live.

An element of drama was added to the conference when we heard from Paul Harms, a co-author of Chapter Seven, who arrived mid-conference from Tonga after witnessing the riots that devastated Nuku'alofa on 16 November. Paul's vivid description of the riots and their immediate aftermath, and a passionate address by Don Kennedy about the future of Tuvalu, during the community forum, brought a sombre note to the proceedings, reminding us that the future of Pacific countries is uncertain. As they face political unrest and the impact of climate change, as well as ongoing problems including precarious economies and environmental destruction, the ties between the islands and the diaspora will continue to be crucial and should not be ignored in any discussions of Pacific peoples. The future of the Pacific is inherently tied to Pacific migration and transnationalism.

1. Pacific Migration and Transnationalism: Historical Perspectives

Helen Lee

Introduction: Mobility Within and Beyond the Pacific Islands

The area now known as the Pacific was settled from west to east in surges of movement between island groups over hundreds of years, eventually taking people as far as Hawai'i in the north, Rapanui/Easter Island in the east and Aotearoa/New Zealand in the south. Throughout this process people maintained networks of contact between some of the islands, travelling in various kinds of seagoing vessels. Epeli Hau'ofa (1993a) has described the pre-colonial Pacific, the area he prefers to call Oceania, as a 'sea of islands' within which people moved freely and frequently, created social networks, traded and exchanged goods, and at times engaged in conflict and attempted to exert dominance over one another. His depiction of the Pacific is constructed in opposition to the 'Western' perspective which emerged during the colonial period and emphasises the vastness of the Pacific Ocean and the small size and isolation of the areas of land dotted across it. The worldview Hau'ofa describes suggests a Pacific model of migration and transnationalism in which the ocean connects migrants to their homelands and is not regarded as a hindrance to their ongoing, enduring ties.

The early patterns of inter-island mobility, such as that between Tonga, Samoa and Fiji (Kaeppler 1978), continued and expanded once Europeans entered the Pacific and colonised all but Tonga. The colonial era afforded opportunities for movement within and beyond the Pacific, initially for men working on European and American vessels in the late 18th century. By the mid–19th century a labour trade had emerged in which Islanders, mainly from what had become known as Melanesia, spread across the Pacific to work on plantations and into Queensland, Australia, to work in the sugar cane fields. Other Islanders found their way to port towns like Auckland in New Zealand, and Sydney in Australia, and settled there as the earliest Pacific migrants. Some of this movement was voluntary as people sought new ways to access the goods and money that were rapidly transforming their home economies, while some was part of the notorious 'blackbirding' in which people were taken against their will (Howe 1984). Movement between the islands also involved Islander missionaries, from the late 19th century to mid–20th century, with the mainly east-west flow of these missionaries reversing the direction of the initial migrations into the Pacific. As

Hau'ofa (1993b) has shown, these are just some of many forms of movement within the Pacific in the period before World War II.

The Pacific was the last region of the world to be affected by European and American imperialism and after World War II it was also the last region to undergo the often difficult process of decolonisation. This began in 1962 when Western Samoa (now Samoa) gained independence, and continued throughout the 1970s and '80s, although even today some of the islands are not fully independent. It was during this post-war era that people began to migrate from the Pacific in significant numbers and this movement was influenced by the colonial history of the islands. The USA and New Zealand opened pathways for migration for Islanders with whom they had colonial ties, whereas other nations with colonies in the Pacific, such as England, Germany and Australia, did not follow suit; in the case of French colonies there was significantly more movement of French settlers into these countries than of Islanders to France. To some extent this influenced the predominance of migration from the regions known as Polynesia and Micronesia, with far less movement from the region known as Melanesia in the Western Pacific.

Tonga is an unusual case in the Pacific because it was the only country that escaped colonisation. In the colonial era its main links were with Britain, of which it was a protectorate from 1900 to 1970, but there was no preferential treatment encouraging Tongans to move to England. However, even without any access to migration through colonial ties, Tongans have managed to migrate in significant numbers since the late 1960s, mainly to New Zealand, the United States, and Australia, keeping Tonga's population relatively stable since that time. There are now more Tongans living overseas than in Tonga, if the overseas-born are included, as is the case for many Pacific populations.

One of the most recent developments in Pacific migration has been a rapid increase in the mobility of Fijians and Indo-Fijians. Although Indo-Fijians began migrating to Canada and the USA in the mid–1960s and have also moved in large numbers to Australia and New Zealand, fewer indigenous Fijians migrated internationally until late in the 20th century, when increasing political and economic problems in Fiji led to a surge in migration by both indigenous Fijians and Indo-Fijians (see Schubert, this volume). Migration from Fiji expanded rapidly in the aftermaths of the coups of 1987, 2000 and 2006. For example, Carmen Voigt-Graf cites Fiji's National Planning Office as claiming that 'over half of Fiji's stock of middle to high-level labor was lost over the 10 years following the 1987 coup through emigration' (2007, 149). However, migration from Fiji is not simply motivated by its political crises and Hannan describes the economic problems caused by downturns in the sugar and garment industries that also have motivated migration (2006; see also Stahl and Appleyard 2007).

Mohanty provides a useful overview of the history of migration from Fiji, describing the '"great waves" of outflow of skilled human resources during the 1980s and 1990s and again after May 2000' (2006, 111). This skilled migration has included nurses and other health workers migrating to a range of countries (Brown and Connell 2004; see Connell, this volume), and movement of Fijian soldiers working for the United Nations as peacekeepers and members of the British Army in Iraq (Connell 2006a, Mohanty 2006). Many former Fijian soldiers have found employment as security guards for private companies in the major Iraqi cities and other Fijians are employed in support roles in Kuwait, covering engineering, mechanical and information technologies (Connell 2006a, 67).

There also has been some movement of Fijians within the Pacific, working as temporary skilled migrants in many Pacific countries in a wide range of professions. Rokoduru (2006) provides an interesting case study of Fijians working in the Marshall Islands and Kiribati in 2002, most of whom were indigenous Fijians and most of whom were remitting. She found that they moved 'in order to make the most of better economic and social opportunities elsewhere, and that they have every intention of returning to Fiji' (2006, 184). Rokoduru concludes that 'the success and future of this trend of intra-regional migration in the Pacific rests largely on one crucial aspect of temporary labour migration: that it remains just that—temporary' (ibid, 185).

What follows is a brief overview of the patterns of Pacific Islander migration to the three main destination countries—New Zealand, the USA and Australia.[1] This chapter also introduces the topic of transnationalism and surveys the literature on the Pacific that has addressed the many ties that have now been formed by Pacific peoples at home and abroad since the post-war migrations.

Movement to Aotearoa/New Zealand

New Zealand's role in the Pacific during the colonial era has shaped its history of migration, as have frequent changes in immigration policies over the years (Bedford 1984). In the post-war era New Zealand gave citizenship to people from the Cook Islands and Niue, which it had formally annexed at the beginning of the 20th century, and Tokelau, which it had administered since 1926. The Cook Islands and Niue are now self-governing territories in free association with New Zealand, while Tokelau remains a non-self-governing country. Each of these countries continues to have close ties to New Zealand and so many people have used their citizenship to migrate that the populations remaining in the islands are now considerably smaller than the migrant and overseas-born populations living in New Zealand.

In contrast, Western Samoans did not gain citizenship rights in New Zealand. Samoa was split into Western Samoa and American Samoa during the colonial era and after a period of German rule, New Zealand administered Western Samoa on behalf of the League of Nations then the United Nations from 1918 until 1962, when it gained independence. Nevertheless, many Samoans have migrated to New Zealand, and the Samoan Quota was established in 1970, permitting 1100 Samoans to immigrate each year.

In the 1950s the New Zealand government began actively recruiting labourers from Pacific countries to work in its rapidly developing industrial and agricultural sectors and from the late 1960s formal work-permit schemes were introduced, first for Fijians then for Tongans and Western Samoans, mainly for work in agriculture and forestry. The scheme ended with the 1987 coup in Fiji (Bedford et al 2007, 257). New Zealand also tried a brief period of visa-free entry for some Pacific Islanders in 1986, however, the net migration from Fiji, Tonga and Western Samoa in the late 1980s was 'more than double the number during the previous five years' and this surge of immigrants led to the scheme being abandoned after only a few months (Stahl and Appleyard 2007, 23).

At that point the New Zealand government decided to shift immigration policy to favour skilled migrants, such as teachers, health professionals and others with a range of qualifications, and reduced migration options for unskilled workers. This was a significant change which has had an ongoing impact on the nature of Pacific Islanders' movement into New Zealand. Another shift in policy in 2002 introduced the Pacific Access Category (PAC), which allows 250 migrants from Tonga, 75 from Kiribati and 75 from Tuvalu, and, since 2003, a further 250 migrants from Fiji. These migrants are accepted under certain conditions, and a ballot system is used to decide which applicants are successful. As with the Samoan Quota, the number of applicants through PAC has fluctuated and at times the quotas have not been filled. In late 2006 New Zealand again shifted its migration policies towards the Pacific and reopened access for seasonal agricultural workers, including those from Melanesia, first through the Seasonal Work Permit Policy (Stahl and Appleyard 2007, 35) then most recently the Recognised Seasonal Employer (RSE) scheme, specifically aimed at eligible Pacific Islands Forum member nations and offering 5,000 places per year (Department of Labour, 2007).

In addition to the Pacific Islanders who have entered New Zealand under these various policies and schemes, others have settled in New Zealand as illegal immigrants, or 'overstayers.' This became a contentious issue in the 1970s and although the New Zealand government responded with heavy-handed tactics for removing those that could be found, it also held amnesties that enabled many to gain permanent residence and remain in the country. Today, the many pathways that have led Pacific Islanders to New Zealand have resulted in a 'Pasifika' population in which Samoans are the largest group, followed by Cook Islanders, Tongans, Niueans, Fijians and Tokelauans (Stahl and Appleyard 2007, 22).

Movement to Australia

Australia did not instigate any preferential treatment for Papua New Guineans, despite its colonial ties to that country, nor did it assist migration from the countries of origin of the 'South Sea Islanders' (or 'Kanaks') working in the sugar plantations of Queensland. More generally, Australia tended to discourage migration from the Pacific through its 'White Australia' policy, in place from 1901 to 1973, and an emphasis on skilled migration. Nevertheless, there has been significant migration into Australia from the Pacific by various means, particularly the Trans-Tasman Travel Arrangement (TTTA) which allowed Australians and New Zealanders to move easily between the two countries to visit, live and work. Many pakeha and Maori New Zealanders have taken advantage of this arrangement to move to Australia, as have many Pacific Islanders, who first became citizens of New Zealand.

The TTTA has generated considerable tension between Australia and New Zealand over the years, particularly when New Zealand instituted amnesties for Pacific overstayers and work schemes for unskilled and low-skilled Islanders. Australia was concerned that this would lead to poorly skilled Islanders entering the country and circumventing its stringent, skills-based immigration policies (Bedford et al. 2007, 258). By the end of the 20ᵗʰ century this tension led to a review of the trans-Tasman relationship aimed at restricting access to social security payments to New Zealanders in Australia.

Not all Islanders have entered Australia via New Zealand, however, and many of the early migrants were students who married and settled in Australia then sponsored their relatives to migrate. Australia's family reunion policies have enabled these early migrants to initiate chains of migration in which the later migrants sponsored still more family members. Others have entered on short-term visas and become overstayers, working mainly in rural areas in the eastern states (see Schubert, this volume). In Australia today the largest group of Pacific immigrants are from Fiji, mainly Indo-Fijians who have entered as skilled migrants, followed by Samoans, Tongans and Cook Islanders (Stahl and Appleyard 2007, 40).

Movement to North America

As in the case of New Zealand, the history of Pacific migration into the USA has been shaped by its colonial ties and ongoing political associations (Ahlburg and Levin 1990). The USA controlled American Samoa from 1900 and since 1951 these islands have been an unincorporated territory of the USA, granting American Samoans the status of US Nationals and free entry to the USA, but fewer rights than American citizens. The USA also grants free access to citizens of the Federated States of Micronesia, the Republic of the Marshall Islands and the Republic of Belau (Palau), known collectively as the Compact States since the Compact of Free Association in 1986. In addition, Guam, which has been a US territory since 1898, has the 1950 Organic Act of Guam which gives its inhabitants US citizenship (Levin and Ahlburg 1993, 96).

Other Islanders, particularly Tongans and Samoans, have migrated to the USA by various means such as 'step migration' through American Samoa and Hawai'i. Many others had their moves to the USA facilitated by membership of the Mormon Church (Church of Jesus Christ of Latter Day Saints) and they have settled around Mormon centres in Utah and Hawai'i. Some Pacific Islanders also have been able to migrate through the Green Card lottery system. Today, Samoans are the largest Pacific population in the US, followed by Micronesians, Tongans and Fijians (Ahlburg and Song 2006, 111).[2]

An Expanded Pacific

The populations of Pacific Islanders in these three main destination countries are large relative to the populations remaining in the islands. Attempts to describe this diasporic spread include Gerard Ward's discussion of the 'expanding worlds' of Pacific Islanders (1997) and Hau'ofa's depiction of the 'enlarged world of Oceania' and 'expanded Oceania' (1998, 392). More recently, Manuhuia Barcham has proposed the term 'new Polynesian triangle' to describe the population that stretches beyond the Pacific to North America, New Zealand and Australia (2005; see also Barcham, Scheyvens and Overton 2007). If we extend this idea to include the mobility of people from Micronesia and Melanesia we could speak of a 'new Pacific triangle'. Macpherson and Macpherson (this volume) refer to a Samoan 'meta-culture', an idea that could be applied to other Pacific populations.

However they are described, the diasporic populations of Pacific peoples are so large, relatively speaking, and have maintained such strong links to their island homes, that they cannot be ignored in any discussion of the Pacific. The case studies presented in the remaining chapters of this book explore those ties to the islands: the multiple and complex forms of transnationalism that have developed since the first movements out of the Pacific and continue to shape the lives of Pacific peoples both at home and abroad.

These ties were first established by the early migrants who, for the most part, settled permanently in their new homes. From the start, many expressed an intention to return home, but relatively few have done so, at least not permanently, and there are now second and third generations of these populations established in the destination countries. There also has been some temporary migration, particularly to New Zealand where, as we have seen, various short-term labour schemes have been introduced. In recent years the opportunities for temporary migration have been expanding, as people with different skills—teachers, rugby players, soldiers, health workers, and so on—look globally for opportunities for mobility. Pacific Islanders now live and work in places such as the Gulf States, the Middle East and Japan (Voigt-Graf 2007, 151; see also Voigt-Graf, Iredale and Khoo 2007). This movement of skilled workers and professionals adds to the concerns about 'brain drain' that have also been expressed in relation to longer-term migrants (Connell 2004, 2006b, 2007).

Whether they move away from the islands temporarily or permanently, few Pacific migrants do not maintain ties with their homelands and there is an ongoing flow of people, money, goods, ideas and so on, between those at home and overseas, and across the diaspora. This flow is captured by the term transnationalism, which has become a central preoccupation of scholars of migration worldwide in recent years.

Transnationalism: The Wider Literature

Transnationalism was originally a concern of international economists describing flows of labour and capital but was later applied more broadly, including within the field of migration and diaspora studies. Although even the earliest studies of migration noted that some migrants maintained ongoing connections with their homelands, it was not until the late 1980s that such connections developed to the extent that they became the focus of research and 'transnational' studies came to the fore. Cheaper and faster transport and developments in information and communications technologies have enabled people to move more easily, send money and goods more cheaply and quickly, and maintain personal connections with family and friends. These increasing options for transnational connections have a wide range of implications for the lives of both migrants and those remaining 'at home'.

Since emerging in the 1990s the literature on the transnational practices of migrants has focused primarily on individuals and families: 'how ordinary individuals live their everyday lives across borders and the consequences of their activities for sending—and receiving—country life' (Levitt and Waters 2002a, 8). This focus on the relationship between transnationalism and people's everyday lives has been described by Michael Smith and Luis Guarnizo (1998) as 'transnationalism from below', in contrast to 'transnationalism from above' in arenas such as the global media, political institutions, global financial organisations and transnational business.

Studies of transnational migrants examine aspects of their lives including their complex ties with kin; their economic connections to the homeland, particularly remittances; their citizenship; their involvement in political and ethnic organisations; and their ties through religion and 'cultural' elements such as music, food and art. In addition, research increasingly takes into account 'the national and international policy regimes within which transnational activities take place' (Levitt, DeWind and Vertovec 2003, 568). Thus far, however, the vast majority of this work on transnationalism has focused on immigrants from Caribbean, Asian, Latin American and African countries who live in the USA, Canada and Europe. The contributions to this book redress this imbalance by focusing on Pacific peoples who until now have been largely absent from discussions of transnationalism.

In the relatively short time since transnationalism became a major focus of migration studies, a great deal has been done to refine and redevelop the concepts and terminology employed.[3] Levitt and Jaworsky (2007) provide an excellent overview of the transnational literature and recent developments in research, which include works on the transnational engagements of people who remain in the home country; the process of return migration; how transnationalism impacts on gender, class and race both in host and home countries; and the negative outcomes of transnationalism. This recent focus on negative outcomes is needed to counterbalance a tendency in the earlier transnational literature to celebrate transnationalism as a means for migrants to increase their opportunities, enhance their social networks and cope with the problems they faced in the host country. However, practices such as remitting can have negative outcomes, such as creating and exacerbating poverty amongst remitters, as Dennis Ahlburg (2000) noted for Pacific Islanders in the USA. Transnationalism can also make it difficult for migrants ever to feel completely 'at home' in any one place, which in turn can provoke identity crises and lead to an ongoing sense of being unsettled even among so-called 'settler migrants'. As Kalissa Alexeyeff's contribution to this volume reminds us, a further negative outcome is the 'loss and dislocation' inherent in the movement of people who visit, but then also leave—ongoing connections can also involve disconnections.

Within Pacific studies, even the earliest work on migrants' ties to their homelands considered both positive and negative outcomes. Indeed, as becomes apparent in the discussion below, this became a major focus of Pacific migration research, particularly the impact of remittances and the issue of dependency. The Pacific literature was also ahead of its time in considering both religion and gender, two of the issues that have only recently been highlighted in wider transnational research. Given the strong adherence of most Pacific migrants to churches with close ties to their counterparts in the islands, it would have been impossible to discuss Pacific transnationalism without acknowledging religion, and gender differences in remitting patterns have been noted since Paul Shankman acknowledged that women were the most frequent and reliable Samoan remitters (1976).

Recently there also has been a growing critique of the 'nation' in transnationalism; of the idea that in the context of transnationalism social relations are organised around and shaped by the nation-state (Levitt and Jaworsky, 2007). The idea of 'post-national' is sometimes used to indicate that 'while the nation-state still plays a part in the development options available to individuals and groups in the modern world it is merely one of many 'actors' that impacts on peoples' lives and developmental options available to them' (Barcham 2005, 3). In Pacific studies this idea of looking beyond national borders is not new, as seen in the idea of 'world enlargement' proposed by Hau'ofa (1993a, 1998). Hau'ofa conceptualises Pacific peoples as interacting across national borders and describes their 'informal movement along ancient routes drawn in bloodlines invisible to the enforcers of the laws of confinement and regulated mobility' (1993a, 11). While Hau'ofa's intent was to challenge Western views of the Pacific, it can also serve to challenge models of transnationalism that focus on distance, separation, and the boundedness of nation-states.

Pacific Transnationalism

The process of world enlargement as described by Hau'ofa has created a vast, complex and complicated network of ties between Pacific individuals, groups and institutions which stretches to the triangle formed by the USA, New Zealand and Australia, and far beyond that to the Pacific peoples living in many countries of the world today. Indeed, the movements of some Islanders across multiple national and state borders, with or without the required visas and work permits, inspired the author of one of the chapters in this book to suggest that such people's perceptions of their movements might best be characterised by 'border-irrelevance' (Mark Schubert, personal communication, 10 October 2007). In her critique of Pacific migration studies, Sa'iliemanu Liliomaiava-Doktor has emphasised the need to recognise 'movement as a social or cultural act' (2009, 3) and she discusses recent analyses by Pacific Islander scholars of indigenous concepts of space and movement which focus on social connections (see also her chapter in this volume).

Although there is still much to be done to incorporate such indigenous perspectives into theories of population movement, the concept of transnationalism, with its implied transcendence of national borders, seems more useful in many respects than 'migration' which, as Lilomaiava-Doktor points out, 'might imply severance of ties, uprootedness, and rupture' (2009, 1). Retaining the term transnationalism also reminds us that to some, particularly governments, national borders are highly relevant and well guarded. The transnational movement of people, money and goods is regulated and controlled, and the borders involved often also represent 'cultural' borders to be encountered and negotiated as part of population movement. The form of transnationalism with which Pacific peoples typically engage is shaped by this awkward relationship between state-imposed borders and cultural differences, and their own perceptions of social relatedness that transcend national boundaries and emphasise reciprocity, kinship and cultural identity; themes that are discussed in the following chapters of this book. The case studies presented in the chapters highlight the multidirectional nature of Pacific transnationalism and its influences, which result in populations in both home and host nations undergoing continual processes of cultural transformation.

The literature on Pacific migration comprises two main bodies of work. The first is concerned with the experiences of migrants in the destination countries, with a particular focus on identity issues and giving only limited consideration of migrants' ties to their homelands. The other body of work addresses the twin issues of remittances and aid as factors in the economies of Pacific nations, and so is interested in migrants primarily as remitters. As Barcham has noted:

> The problem lies, however, in the sad fact that these two bodies of literature talk past each other and so do not engage with their common concern—the impact of migration and movement on the well-being and welfare of Polynesian individuals and communities. In a sense, each body of literature is discussing part of the issue and in doing so they are missing many of the positive and dynamic developments occurring in Polynesian communities across the Pacific (2005, 2).

There have been some exceptions in recent years, which are discussed later in this chapter, but for the most part Barcham's observation still holds true. Clearly, there is a need not only to draw these two bodies of work together but also to expand our understanding of Pacific transnationalism beyond remittances, given that it takes such diverse forms and occurs in such a wide range of contexts. The papers in this book do just that, providing a more detailed picture of Pacific peoples' transnational practices and the impact of these practices on their experiences both 'at home' and abroad.

Pacific transnationalism certainly fits descriptions of transnationalism as influencing migrants' everyday lives and involving individuals, groups, institutions and even governments. People move between their host nations and countries of origin, and within the diaspora, for many different reasons: to visit family; to attend special family events such as weddings, funerals and the birth of children; to attend church events or national celebrations; to visit different overseas communities to raise funds for various purposes; for sporting events; for employment; or for education. Money and goods circulate within these webs of connections and people also maintain transnational ties through phone calls, letters, email, internet forums and networking sites, video and DVD recordings of events, and in many other ways. The extent of engagement in transnational practices varies between individuals and each engages differently according to their life-stage, particular life experiences and circumstances, and the situation of the people, groups and institutions with whom they are connected.

A common finding in the Pacific literature is that as more members of an individual's family migrate and as elderly kin in the islands pass away, transnational connections can dwindle. However, if what I have called *intradiasporic transnationalism* (Lee 2007a) is taken into account, transnational ties can continue across the diaspora even if ties to the homeland diminish. Within the broader literature on transnationalism these kinds of connections have only recently been discussed and some researchers have moved beyond simply looking at links between country of origin and country of settlement to look at 'other sites around the world that connect migrants to their conationals and coreligionists' (Levitt and Jaworsky 2007, 131). More research is needed on this issue for Pacific Islanders if the full breadth of their transnational engagements is to be taken into account.

It is important to note that not all migrants maintain transnational connections and there are certainly Pacific migrants who make conscious decisions not to participate in transnational activities. However, given the central importance of kin to Pacific peoples it is difficult to withdraw completely from the transnational networks that have been developed. Such withdrawal would entail refusing to uphold obligations to kin, which could in turn lead to exclusion from the kinship group and local community, and therefore from the social networks that not only make demands on members but also provide important sources of support. For most Pacific migrants the very process of migration is motivated in part by a desire—or sense of obligation—to support kin in the homeland, so, in a sense, transnationalism is perceived as an inherent element of migration.

In the case of migrants' children, the 'second generation', there is more scope for withdrawing from transnational activities and, as will be discussed below, many do not maintain direct ties to their parents' homelands. Nevertheless, I have identified processes of *indirect transnationalism*: if migrants or their children retain any involvement with members of their ethnic group in the host nation they are likely to be part of a web of transnational ties even without direct involvement with the home nation (Lee 2007a). For example, they may participate in and contribute to ceremonial events in the diaspora, such as weddings and funerals, at which gift exchanges occur that involve the transnational movement of people, money and goods. They may donate money to their church, which sends some of the collected donations to a church in the islands, or funds volunteers to travel to the islands to help build a new church or otherwise contribute their labour, or raises money to send youth groups 'home'. They may attend social events at which money is donated through various activities, such as performances from fundraising groups visiting from the homeland and that money is also channelled back to the islands. In the case of the second generation, another common form of indirect transnationalism is when older family members request money from junior members and send it 'home' as part of the family's collective remittances. Again, more research is needed to ascertain the forms and extent of indirect transnationalism and whether in some cases we could perhaps consider it as *involuntary transnationalism*.

Remittances and the MIRAB Model

Remittances have been the primary preoccupation of studies of Pacific migration and transnationalism for many years as part of a widely-expressed concern about the economic futures of many island countries. The focus has been on remittances of money and goods, and to a lesser extent on what have been referred to in the broader literature on transnationalism as 'social remittances', that is, the ideas, values, practices and even identities that move between diaspora and homeland (Levitt and Jaworsky 2007, 132). A range of factors including limited domestic resources, small land masses and geographical isolation, declining commodity prices, limited opportunities to generate income, environmental problems, government policies that create obstacles to change and the rising expectations of the population have all been cited as factors in the creation of a reliance on remittances and foreign aid in order for the small island countries to remain economically viable. This led to a focus in the 1970s on the issue of dependency, generating considerable debate about the role of remittances in the home country (Bedford 1984). A key argument was that remittances were used primarily for consumption and therefore acted as a disincentive to investment and local production, hindering development and creating a dependent relationship between those at home and the migrants (Connell 1980; and see below).

The issue of remittances has recently become a key concern in studies of transnationalism, as shifts in the world economy create increasing opportunities for labour mobility and the generation of remittances. Steven Vertovec, for example, says of remittances:

> The money [that] migrants send not only critically supports families, but may progressively rework gender relations, support education and the acquisition of professional skills and facilitate local community development through new health clinics, water systems, places of worship and sports facilities. Remittances may also undermine local labour markets, fuel price increases, create new status hierarchies and generate patterns of economic dependence (2001, 575).

These are all issues discussed in the literature on Pacific migration and remittances from the late 1960s, and this same tension between the cost and benefits of remittances has been debated in much of the subsequent work. In the mid–1980s some of this work on the Pacific began to draw on the 'MIRAB model' developed by Geoff Bertram and Ray Watters, based on the elements of MIgration, Remittances, Aid and Bureaucracy that characterised some Pacific states. Bertram and Watters originally developed the model to describe the island states with colonial links to New Zealand (1985, 1986; Bertram 1986) and as the model gained currency it was used to describe other Polynesian and Micronesian countries with similar economic situations, even countries beyond the Pacific (Bertram 1999).

The MIRAB model emphasises the integration of island economies with 'the mainland' (New Zealand in the initial model) and how this process 'turned the Islands from resources-based into rent-based economies' (Bertram and Watters 1986, 57). An essential element in this process was migration from the islands so that remittances could be sent to support those at home. Bertram and Watters argued that migration from the Pacific was shaped by the collective decision making of family units in order to maximise benefits to the whole group. Drawing on earlier work on Tonga by George Marcus (1974, 1981) they used the term 'transnational corporations of kin' to describe this process (Bertram and Watters 1985, 499). They argue that remittances are sustainable as long as 'kin corporations' continue to operate and there is a continuing flow of new migrants.

A substantial literature now exists discussing the pros and cons of the MIRAB model and the question of whether MIRAB economies are sustainable over time. Despite various critiques of the model it continues to be applied and developed to take into account changes within Pacific economies and the importance of social relationships and personal agency (e.g. Bertram 2006; Evans 1999, 2001; Fraenkel 2006; Stahl and Appleyard 2007).

Remittances: Other Perspectives

It is understandable that remittances became the central preoccupation of the literature on Pacific migrants and their ties to their homelands, given that many of the Pacific economies have been significantly bolstered by this income. Tonga and Samoa, for example, have been among the top remittance earning countries of the world for some years and their economies would be in danger of collapse if there were any drastic decline in remittance income. For this reason, debates on the sustainability of remittances continued to dominate the literature on Pacific migration throughout the 1990s. This work was concerned with a number of questions, including:

- Who sends remittances?
- What kinds of remittances are sent?
- To whom are remittances sent?
- How much do individuals and families send?
- How reliant on remittances are the Pacific nations?
- What channels are being used to send remittances?
- What purposes do remitters have for the money and goods they send?
- How are remittances actually used?
- What is the impact of remittances on the receiving nations?
- Do remittances decline over time?
- What kinds of policies relevant to remittances should be in place in home and host nations?

A substantial body of work now exists that addresses these questions and a report by John Connell and Richard Brown, *Remittances in the Pacific* (2005), provides a useful overview of the findings to date in relation to the questions listed above. In their conclusion they return to the broader context of migration, in which transnational ties such as remittances play a key role, and they argue

> that maximising the benefits of international migration is crucial since it is highly valued throughout the region for social and economic reasons. As long as considerable economic challenges face island states, as their population growth rates remain above world averages, as development prospects are few, as the possibility of declining aid becomes more apparent, and as expectations rise, the ability to migrate will be crucial (Connell and Brown 2005, 55).[4]

The kinds of issues that have been discussed in the literature on Pacific remittances for many years are now affecting Fiji, which is rapidly moving towards the situation in countries like Tonga and Samoa, where a large proportion of households have members living overseas who send remittances home (Stanwix and Connell 1995). As Mohanty (2006) points out, this has been occurring only since the late 1990s, so this has been a remarkably rapid transformation of Fiji's economy. Fiji is now dealing with including increasing reliance on remittances and how they are being used, as well as the issues of 'brain drain' and associated slowing of the 'development' processes.

The Uses of Remittances

An ongoing debate in the literature on Pacific migration, over whether remittances help or hinder economies, has led to a body of research into how remittances are used. As we have seen, on one side of this debate is the view that remittance-dependence is unsustainable and hinders the expansion of the local economy; on the other is the position characterised by the MIRAB model, which sees these economies as sustainable so long as migration, remittances and aid continue but views self-sustainability as impossible. Associated with the debate is the question of whether remittances are used for 'unproductive' purposes or contribute to savings and investment in the island economies (Poirine 1998; Ward 1997).

In the Pacific today, remittances are being used for a wide range of purposes that go well beyond simple consumption, although consumption certainly remains significant, particularly for families entirely reliant on remittances for income. Remittances are used for purposes as varied as paying debts, purchasing airfares, paying school fees and church donations, building homes and business premises, contributing to the costs of events such as weddings and funerals, and facilitating investment in businesses. In addition, it has become clear that remittances are not sent simply to 'help the family' but also for migrants' own benefit: to maintain land rights, for personal investment and to support their plans for retirement. Remittances are also used in status building, as when money that is sent to kin is presented to institutions such as churches, schools and sports groups, to signal that the family is generous and prosperous (James 1997).

Remittances are also facilitating a growing informal economy; for example, goods are sent by migrants for resale through second-hand markets. Brown and Connell (1993) studied Tongan flea-markets and found that they have opened up new ways for individuals to generate income and are a means of contributing to the domestic economy through investment. Some who were selling in the markets were developing business-like arrangements with their overseas kin, sending and receiving goods to build up profits (see also Besnier 2004; James 2002). Similarly, Ward has reviewed studies that 'proved support for the argument that the emergence of trans-national families as economic units can be a very effective form of business organisation for the Pacific Islands' (1997, 193). Ward points out that the arrangements between migrants and kin at home are made through the informal remittance system; for example, sending goods for local businesses in the islands and return trade of agricultural products for niche markets of Pacific Islander communities overseas. Such arrangements are not recorded in formal trade statistics, making it difficult to assess how island economies are actually faring. The informal economy also makes it impossible to ascertain the full extent of remittances. Brown and Foster found for Tongan and Samoan migrants in Australia in the early 1990s that their unrecorded remittances comprised 57 per cent of total remittances (1995, 32), and Ken'ichi Sato's survey of other studies from the 1980s and 1990s shows estimates of unrecorded remittances as percentages of total remittances varying from 23–41 per cent (1997, 174).

The Sustainability of Remittances

The question of remittance decline has been of concern to researchers whether or not they use the MIRAB model, but there has been considerable disagreement about whether this is likely to occur. A key issue that has been identified is the economic situation in the destination country; for example, in his research on Samoans in New Zealand Cluny Macpherson (1990, 1992) has shown that a decline in the national economy and the effects of government policies favouring skilled migrants can contribute to a decline in remittances. Connell also argues that remittances are likely to decline if migration levels drop, adding:

> However, if the economies of the metropolitan countries are restructured to reduce employment opportunities for unskilled labour, if unemployment increases or there is political opposition to increased migration levels, the tasks of sustaining migration and remittances will be extremely difficult (1990, 11).

Decreasing migration levels can have a significant impact; Ahlburg points out that 'the continued flow of new migrants is critical to the continued growth of remittances' (1991, 3). Ahlburg also sees the aging of current migrants and increasing migration of entire families as potentially contributing to remittance decline. He discusses the difficulty of home governments instituting policies to encourage remittances and suggests:

> Perhaps the best the home country can do is create a good macroeconomic environment where domestic investment opportunities can develop. Such an environment is supportive rather than regulative. Political stability also seems to be important if funds are to flow to the home country (1991, 53).

A further factor that must be considered in relation to the sustainability of remittances is the willingness of migrants to continue to contribute financially to their homelands (Spoonley 2001). As Paul Spoonley points out, migrants may decide to prioritise investment in their own welfare and success over their obligations to kin and community. A decade earlier, Kerry James questioned the MIRAB model's assumption that 'transnational family enterprises' would help sustain remittances, arguing that kin networks could continue without remittances, by obligations being met through 'trading partnerships, overseas hospitality to migrant workers, and other forms of help' (1991, 2).

Although some studies have shown that many individuals and families maintain remarkably high levels of remittances even 20 years after migration (e.g. Brown and Foster 1995), there are other factors involved in the overall picture of remittance sustainability. The demand for remittances is increasing as the cost of living in the islands increases and people desire more consumer goods, while at the same time communities in the diaspora are growing and local demands on people's resources are increasing, creating a tension between obligations to local community and people in the islands. Some migrants' remittances decline or even cease as family members migrate and if migrants themselves do not plan to return to live in the islands this can also reduce their tendency to remit. The literature on the sustainability of remittance shows that all of these factors and more combine to influence the remittance practices of migrants, making it difficult to predict with any accuracy the future of remittances in any of the island countries.

Overall, the general consensus tends to be that remittances could be maintained for some time if current migration levels are sustained or increased, but even that will not guarantee an indefinite flow of remittances to the islands. Cathy Small sums this up in relation to Tonga:

> Remittances will eventually both slow and transform in kind, and both of these processes will have to do with the larger demographic and

economic factors in which the global family has come to be embedded. Neither emphasizing Tongan traditions nor bolstering Tongan identity will keep remittances flowing or family ties strong, for the foundations of Tonga's transnational families and economies lie elsewhere—in global processes occurring outside Tonga (1997, 198).

The long term sustainability of remittances must also be considered in relation to the second generation, who, when they remit at all, tend to do so at significantly lower levels than their parents' generation, as discussed later in this chapter. Another factor is whether temporary worker schemes are continued, as these can generate ongoing remittances. As mentioned above, these have been in place for some time in New Zealand and a similar scheme was introduced in Australia in 2009, but they are subject to the whim of changing government policies.[5]

A final point to be made in relation to remittances is that most of the literature on this topic for the Pacific is concerned only with money and goods sent from the diaspora to the homeland. However, as Connell and Brown remind us:

> In almost every context remittances are bi-directional, and the remittances sent from home countries are most likely to be composed of goods of various kinds, usually foods and handicrafts…In some cases these represent altruistic gifts associated with the essential element of reciprocity; in others they stem from self-interest, pump primers for continued remittances from destination countries (1995, 11).

James observes that among Tongans, 'the contraflows of goods continually remind migrants of their economic and social obligations toward the home-based members of family networks' (1997, 3). Tongan goods are used within the migrant population, including as gifts to widen the support network and help them with opportunities for social mobility, and so, in a sense, reciprocate the money and goods sent by that population (see Addo this volume, Evans 2001). These 'contraflows' are not insubstantial and in a study of Tongan migrants in New Zealand, David McKenzie estimated that the flow of goods, and even some cash, from Tonga to these migrants equalled an average of 43 per cent of the value of their remittances to Tonga (2006).

Beyond Remittances

Little of the existing literature on Pacific migrants' transnational practices looks beyond remittances. An early exception is Evelyn Kallen's *The Western Samoan kinship bridge* (1982) which examines the kinship networks sustained by Samoan migrants, mainly in the USA, with Samoans remaining in the islands. Like much of the literature on the Pacific diaspora it is particularly focused on the issues of kinship and identity, but unlike many other authors, Kallen is interested in the role of transnational ties in shaping diasporic identities and experiences.

Small's *Voyages: from Tongan villages to American suburbs* (1997) has a similar focus, in this case tracing the ties of a particular extended family group between members in different locations in the USA and their village in Tonga. My own work on the Tongan diaspora (Lee 2003, 2004b) also shares Kallen's concern with kinship and identity and examines how transnational ties affect migrants and their children as they negotiate the challenges of life as members of a minority 'ethnic group' in the host nations.

Another exception is the work by Macpherson on Samoan migrants in New Zealand. Over the years he has traced the changes within the Samoan community in New Zealand, particularly Auckland, describing how continued migration and ongoing ties to the homeland have gradually transformed aspects of *fa'a Samoa* (the Samoan way) in the migrant communities (1984, 1991, 1994, 2002, 2004; Macpherson and Macpherson 1999 and this volume). Macpherson has shown that over time there has been a significant shift from the early years of migration in which there were 'expatriate nodes' sending remittances and maintaining other ties with 'the center, which was, of course, the village of origin in which the family's landholdings, its chiefly title, and the core of its members resided' (Macpherson 2004, 168). Now, he argues, 'the nodes have become centers and Samoan culture has become a global one' (ibid, 179; see also Lilomaiava-Doktor this volume).

Beyond such case studies there has been little discussion of transnationalism in relation to the Pacific as a whole. Spoonley has addressed this broader issue from the perspective of transnationalism's challenge to the nation-state:

> Transnational communities by their very nature further contribute to what some interpret as the destabilisation of the nation and the state. They transcend national boundaries by their activities, and their members typically have divided loyalties between their country of residence and their ethnic community, or between the countries of origin and current location. The movement of people and goods across borders, especially when those movements are undocumented and part of informal networks, confirm the increasing permeability of borders and emphasise the significance of multiple loyalties—to place of residence, place and culture of origin, to diasporic communities, and to evolving identities…We can add that the communities also change the nature of the metropolitan societies in which they reside by virtue of their transnational activities. They are one further and important element in the subdivision of the nation and the declining sovereignty of the state (2001, 84–85).

In a later paper, Spoonley, Bedford and Macpherson discuss the transnationalism of Pacific Islanders in New Zealand and conclude: 'The state in New Zealand has yet to grasp the significance of the transnationalism of Pacific peoples' (2003, 43). They argue that this is partly because Islanders themselves have not engaged fully with the possibilities of transnationalism, such as political mobilisation, and partly because of New Zealand's 'openness in both immigration and economic access' (ibid, 43). There have been changes even since their article was written, such as the response of Tongans in New Zealand to ongoing political problems in their homeland, including the public servants' strike in 2005 and a riot in Tonga's capital, Nuku'alofa, the following year. Not only did Tongans mobilise to stage public protests in New Zealand but they also rallied to pressure the New Zealand government to intervene. Nevertheless the argument that New Zealand has not grasped the significance of Pacific transnationalism holds true and could be extended to both the Australian and American governments. To give just one example, a detailed Senate report on Australia's relationship with the Pacific produced in 2003, *A Pacific engaged* (Foreign Affairs, Defence and Trade References Committee), did not mention the Pacific communities dwelling in Australia or their role in maintaining ties with the island nations.

There is clearly a need for more work on Pacific Islanders' 'long distance nationalism' (Fouron and Glick Schiller 2002) to explore migrants' involvement in the processes of nation-building in their countries of origin.

> Long distance nationalists may vote, demonstrate, contribute money, create works of art, give birth, fight, kill, and die for a 'homeland' in which they may never have lived. Meanwhile, those who live in this homeland will recognize these actions as patriotic contributions to the well-being of their common homeland (Fouron and Glick Schiller, 2002, 173).

Pacific migrants may have not had reason to die for their countries, but they have been active for many years in a range of contexts including politics, business and the churches (see the chapters by Hoëm and Nosa in this volume). Hau'ofa pointed out that 'from their bases abroad they are exerting significant influences on their homeland' (1994, 423). He cites their use of media and information and communications technologies to share information and maintain contact. 'National issues are internationalized through transnational networks of a highly mobile population, making it difficult for the powers that be to keep track of, let alone contain, any social movement with tentacles spread across the globe' (1994, 423).

Studies of Pacific people's use of the internet support Hau'ofa's argument. The work by Alan Howard and Jan Rensel on Rotumans (2004; Howard 1999), Marianne Franklin's work on Pacific internet discussion forums (2001, 2003, 2004), and my own work on Tongans online (Morton 1999, Lee 2003, 2006b), has revealed the many ways in which Pacific Islanders scattered across the globe share information and create and maintain transnational networks. This cyber-transnationalism is constantly expanding and changing and the emergence of social networking sites such as MySpace, Facebook and Bebo, and video-sharing sites such as YouTube have opened up new ways for ties to be established and for networks of connections to become increasingly complex.

Transnationalism and Problems in the Diaspora

As noted earlier in this chapter, much of the literature on Pacific migration has focused on the diaspora and the issues facing migrants and their children in their new homes.[6] Although much of this work acknowledges the ties that Pacific migrants maintain with their homelands, little of it examines these transnational ties in any detail, or attempts to explore in any depth the ways in which transnationalism impacts on people's lives and identities in the host countries. As yet, we know little of how people's transnational ties affect their engagements with the wider society, their interactions with others within their own communities, their family lives, or their economic situation. Ahlburg has observed that few studies have investigated the impact of remittances on the sending households and he claims that 'at least in the US, many Pacific Islander households live close to the poverty line. The payment of average remittances can force many of them into poverty and those already in poverty even deeper into poverty' (2000, 65). Ahlburg and Song (2006) later showed that overall, Pacific Islanders in the USA experienced an improvement in their economic situation in the 1980s and 1990s, which they attribute in part to gains in 'human capital' through education and employment.

Spoonley has observed problems associated with poverty in New Zealand:

> there are growing pressures on communities which contain a significant proportion of work—or education—poor, and benefit-dependent households with the negative statistics that accompany such conditions. This disadvantage is now intergenerational as the costs of accessing education, housing and health increase. With a declining ability to pay, future generations are locked into a poverty cycle which even collective strategies are unable to reverse in any significant way…The growing pressure impacts particularly on the children and women of transnational communities (2001, 94).

Further research is needed to ascertain the relationship between economic status and transnational practices: one would assume that living in poverty reduces people's ability to remit, to travel between home and host countries, and otherwise engage transnationally, but anecdotal evidence suggests that this is not necessarily the case. There appears to be a growing disparity between those who have managed upward mobility and those living in poverty, but how does this affect their transnational ties? Or, to pose the question in reverse, how do transnational ties impact on migrants' socio-economic status? Ongoing research will be needed to assess the effects of the global economic crisis that began emerging in 2008 and which could have significant and multiple impacts on migrants' transnational practices. Even before this crisis there was evidence of economic status affecting mobility; for example, Spoonley (2001) reports Pacific Islanders moving to different parts of the diaspora to find work.

Return Migration

Another form of movement that can be motivated by low socio-economic status is return migration. Connell has found that there is generally a low level of return migration in the Pacific and that 'return migration is often an admission of failure' (1990, 19; see also Connell 2009). He observed that those who do return often have problems readjusting and tend to remain in urban areas. Macpherson (1985) also noted problems of readjustment for the few Samoans who return, particularly younger people who had spent most of their lives overseas. He argues that the low rate of return is due to migrants' desire to remain near their adult children and their families overseas and financial considerations such as lack of jobs and low wages. Shankman (1993) concludes that Samoan return migration has been insignificant when compared with movement out of the islands. He adds that if many migrants did decide to return it would create significant problems for Samoa's economy, a point that rings true for other Pacific countries that have experienced emigration and rely on remittance income.

In a recent paper on Samoan return migration Macpherson and Macpherson (2009) note that more migrants began returning to retire in Samoa when New Zealand allowed them to draw on their New Zealand pensions from the islands. However, they also show that many return migrants do not settle permanently in Samoa, but go back to New Zealand after a period living in Samoa, or move between the two locations at intervals. This tendency to re-migrate was also found by Maron and Connell (2008), in their study of returnees in a village in Tonga which showed that half of the return migrants interviewed intended to return overseas.

Ahlburg and Brown (1998) investigated migrants' intentions to return home in a study of Tongans and Samoans in Australia in 1994. Previous studies had shown that those intending to return home tend to remit more and this was confirmed by their study, although intention to return does not necessarily lead to actual return. Overall they found that only around 10 per cent intended to return, and another group (23 per cent for Tongans and 38 per cent for Samoans) were undecided. Ahlburg and Brown conclude that 'the return of overseas migrants is not a major channel for the acquisition of human capital for Tonga and Samoa' (1998, 131). The issue of human capital return is also discussed in the work on health professionals by Connell and Brown mentioned earlier in this chapter, and by Connell in his paper in this volume. Connell's paper shows that even for returning professionals, re-migration is a common outcome.

The practice of returning children and adolescents to their parents' homelands for periods of time is a particular form of return migration that has received only limited attention in Pacific studies and the wider literature on transnationalism (Lee 2009). Macpherson (1985) observed this for Samoa and Kerry James first reported the practice in Tonga in the early 1990s. She argued that it was a way to confirm kinship ties and 'an attempt to sustain future remittances' (1991, 17). However, she expressed a concern about this practice, reiterated in her study of fostering on a small island in Vava'u:

> Some relationships appeared to be so highly subject to change and so peripatetic that I came to wonder where the loyalties of the young will ultimately lie, and whether the children will feel called upon to support either set of parents. Thus, while children are sent as remittances, to ensure social security for themselves through confirming kinship bonds and also possibly to become effective second-generation remitters because of those bonds, I doubt in many cases that the Tongan notion of *'ofa* (love, generosity) will be successfully instilled into the younger generation of migrants. Instead, they are likely to get more clearly the message of self-interest, of economic individualism, which also underlies the actions of their parents (James 1993, 369–370).

James also acknowledges the strain on people in Tonga, particularly older people, who have to take on these children and youths 'in a situation where many of the older forms of social control have been removed or rendered increasingly ineffective' (1991, 22).

Some of the children who are sent to Tonga from the diaspora are requested by family in Tonga and may stay for long periods and be welcomed into the household; most commonly these are grandchildren. Others, such as teenagers sent home because their parents are concerned about their behaviour overseas, may be accepted only because the family in Tonga feels obliged, and they can be resented (Lee 2009). Their time in Tonga is another case of what could be described as involuntary transnationalism. James has noted that 'among the data lacking from studies of Tongans overseas is an estimation of the degree of loyalty to people in Tonga that exists among second-generation migrants who have lived in Tonga for a time' (James 1997, 21). My own research indicates that the experience of being sent to Tonga for periods of time can have diverse outcomes in terms of the transnational ties maintained on return overseas, but that few who do experience this wish to live in Tonga permanently (Lee 2009).

The Second Generation

Beyond these few studies of migrants' children being returned the parents' countries of origin there is very little work on the transnational ties of the second generation. Most of the work on the children of Pacific migrants has been within the body of work mentioned above, which focuses on issues of identity and adaptation in the diaspora. In the broader literature on transnationalism there also has been a neglect of the second generation until recently (Lee 2008). The first collection of papers on this topic, edited by Peggy Levitt and Mary Waters (2002b) focuses on migrants in the USA, mainly from Asian and Caribbean countries, and the authors agree that transnational ties tend to be weaker in the second generation. In a review of the literature on transnationalism, Levitt and Jaworsky conclude that 'transnational activities will not be central to the lives of most of the second or third generation, and they will not participate with the same frequency and intensity as their parents' (2007, 134).

James' work on the return of children to Tonga, discussed above, is largely concerned with the impact of this practice on the sustainability of remittances. In another study that mentions remittances in relation to migrants' children, Loomis found that in 1985 between 55 and 82 per cent of Cook Islanders born in the islands regularly remitted, but only 20 per cent of New Zealand-born did so (1990 cited in Ahlburg 1991, 7). Similarly, Brown and Walker (1995) found for a small sample of New Zealand-born Samoans that on average their remittances were only about 30 per cent of average first generation levels. In general, however, the literature on Pacific remittances ignores the second generation, or simply assumes they will remit at lower levels than their parents but does not pursue the implications of this.

My own recent research on second generation Tongan transnationalism has confirmed that, at least in the Tongan case, remittances and other transnational ties are much weaker for migrants' children (Lee 2004a, 2006a, 2007a, 2007b). Macpherson and Macpherson (this volume) report a similar weakening of ties for the second generation of Samoans in New Zealand. Although they are weaker, some ties do remain, and focusing on remittances can detract from the bigger picture of second generation transnationalism, which is more likely to involve visits, phone calls, and electronic communication than sending money or goods. It is also more likely to involve intradiasporic ties, particularly since online discussion forums and networking sites have facilitated easy communication with Pacific Islanders anywhere in the world.

Much is yet to be learned about the transnational activities of members of the second generation of Pacific peoples overseas, including how their ties may change throughout their life-cycle and in response to events both in their parents' homelands and their country of birth. Most Pacific populations have been established overseas for long enough that there are now more members who were born in the host country than in the home islands, so it is increasingly important to include them in discussions of Pacific transnationalism.

Conclusion

The transnational ties established by Pacific migrants during their post-war migrations to New Zealand, the USA, Australia and elsewhere remain strong today. Cheaper, faster transport and developments in information and communications technologies have intensified these ties but they are still largely kin-based connections, with additional links through institutions such as churches and schools, and assorted other connections through villages, businesses, political groups and so on.

Over a decade ago, Ward observed: 'how relations between the home and expatriate communities of different groups will develop in future decades remains a matter for speculation' (Ward 1997, 192). Since then we have learned a great deal more about those relations, although as I have shown there has been a predominance of research into remittances rather than other forms of transnational ties. Even so, the literature on Pacific transnationalism was ahead of its time in some ways: paying attention to issues of class, gender and religion from the outset, recognising the more negative outcomes of transnationalism, and addressing the role of remittances. Yet the wider literature on transnationalism rarely mentions the Pacific and until recently scholars of Pacific migration made little use of the concept of 'transnationalism' except in the context of 'transnational kin corporations'. More engagement with the broader literature on transnationalism will bring new approaches and insights to the work on the Pacific, and raise the profile of Pacific transnationalism within that broader literature.

Pacific transnationalism is a topic of growing importance, tied as it is to the very future of Pacific countries. Early in the 21st century many of those countries face an uncertain future, with growing economic woes, political tensions, the impact of climate change, continuing depopulation in some cases and shifts in international relations, including changes to immigration policies in destination countries. Any issues facing Pacific peoples must be discussed in the context of both the islands and their diasporas, taking the processes of 'world enlargement' and transnationalism into account. Research on remittances will remain salient in the Pacific and while much has already been achieved there is still more to learn about issues such as the impact of remittances on the senders, the relationship between socio-economic status in the diaspora and the practice of remitting, and 'contraflows' from the home countries. In addition, a broader focus is needed to take into account the many other elements of transnationalism; issues to be explored include individuals' fluctuations in transnational engagements, intradiasporic and indirect forms of transnationalism, return migration and the transnationalism of the second generation. The chapters that follow address some of these issues and open up even more possibilities for future research.

References

Ahlburg, D. 1991. Remittances and their impact: A study of Tonga and Western Samoa. *Pacific Policy Paper 7*. Canberra: National Centre for Development Studies.

—. 2000. Poverty among Pacific Islanders in the United States: Incidence, change and correlates. *Pacific Studies* 23 (1/2): 51–74.

Ahlburg, D. and R. Brown. 1998. Migrants intentions to return home and capital transfers: A study of Tongans and Samoans in Australia. *Journal of Development Studies* 35 (2): 125–51.

Ahlburg, D. and M. Levin. 1990. The north east passage: A study of Pacific Islander migration to American Samoa and the United States. Canberra: National Centre for Development Studies

Ahlburg, D. and Y. N. Song. 2006. Changes in the economic fortunes of Pacific Islanders in the USA in the 1990s. *Asia Pacific Viewpoint* 47 (1): 109–21.

Barcham, M. 2005. Post-national development: The case of the 'new Polynesian triangle'. *CIGAD Briefing Notes*. Palmerston North: Centre for Indigenous Governance and Development.

Barcham, M., R. Scheyvans, and J. Overton. 2007. Rethinking Polynesian mobility: A new Polynesian triangle. *Centre for Indigenous Development Working Paper Series*. http://cigad.massey.ac.nz/publications.htm (accessed 14 December 2007).

Basch, L., N. Glick Schiller, and C. Szanton Blanc. 1994. *Nations unbound: Transnational projects, postcolonial predicaments, and deterritorialized nation-states*. Pennsylvania: Gordon and Breach.

Bedford, R. 1984. The Polynesian connection: Migration and social change in New Zealand and the South Pacific. In *Essays on urbanisation in South East Asia and the Pacific*, ed. R. Bedford, 131-41. Christchurch: University of Canterbury.

Bedford, R., E. Ho, V. Krishnan and B. Hong. 2007. The neighborhood effect: The Pacific in Aotearoa and Australia. *Asian and Pacific Migration Journal* 16 (2): 251–69.

Bertram, G. 1986. 'Sustainable Development' in Pacific Micro-economies. *World Development* 14 (7): 809–22.

—. 1999. The MIRAB model twelve years on. *The Contemporary Pacific* 11 (1): 105–38.

—. 2006. Introduction: The MIRAB model in the twenty-first century. *Asia Pacific Viewpoint* 47 (1): 1–13.

Bertram, G. and R. Watters. 1985. The MIRAB economy in South Pacific microstates. *Pacific Viewpoint* 26 (3): 497–519.

—.1986. The MIRAB process: Earlier analyses in context. *Pacific Viewpoint* 27 (1): 47–59.

Besnier, N. 2004. Consumption and cosmopolitanism: Practicing modernity at the second-hand marketplace in Nuku'alofa, Tonga. *Anthropological Quarterly* 77 (1): 7–45.

Brown, R. 1994. Migrants' remittances, savings and investment in the South Pacific. *International Labour Review* 133: 347–67.

—.1995. Hidden foreign exchange flows: Estimating unofficial remittances to Tonga and Western Samoa. *Asian and Pacific Migration Journal* 4 (1): 35–54.

—.1997. Estimating remittance functions for Pacific Island migrants. *World Development* 25 (4): 613–26

—.1998. Do migrants' remittances decline over time? Evidence from Tongans and Western Samoans in Australia. *The Contemporary Pacific* 10 (1): 107–51.

Brown, R. and J. Connell. 1993. The global flea market: Migration, remittances and the informal economy in Tonga. *Development and Change* 24: 611–47.

—. 2004. The migration of doctors and nurses from South Pacific Island nations. *Social Science and Medicine* 58: 2193–210.

—. 2006. Occupation-specific analysis of migration and remittance behaviour: Pacific Island nurses in Australia and New Zealand. *Asia Pacific Viewpoint* 47 (1): 135–50.

Brown, R. and J. Foster. 1995. Some common fallacies about migrants' remittances in the South Pacific: Lessons from Tongan and Western Samoan research. *Pacific Viewpoint* 36 (1): 29–45.

Brown, R., J. Foster, and J. Connell. 1995. Remittances, savings and policy formation in Pacific island states. *Asian and Pacific Migration Journal* 4 (1): 169–86.

Brown, R. and B. Poirine. 2005. A model of migrants' remittances with human capital investment and intrafamilial transfers. *International Migration Review* 39 (2): 407–38.

Brown, R. and A. Walker. 1995. Migrants and their remittances. Results of a household survey of Tongans and Western Samoans in Sydney. Sydney: Centre for South Pacific Studies.

Chand, S. 2005. Labour mobility for sustainable livelihoods in Pacific Island states. *Pacific Economic Bulletin* 20 (3): 63–76.

Connell, J. 1980. Remittances and rural development: Migration, dependency and inequality in the South Pacific. In *National Centre for Development Studies Occasional Paper No. 22*. Canberra, The Australian National University.

—. 1990. Modernity and its discontents: Migration and Change in the South Pacific. In *Migration and Development in the South Pacific. Pacific Research Monograph No. 24*, ed. J. Connell, 1-28. Canberra: The Australian National University.

—. 2002. Paradise left? Pacific Island voyagers in the modern world. In *Pacific diaspora: Island peoples in the United States and across the Pacific*, ed. P. Spickard, J. Rondilla, and D. Hippolite Wright, 69-86. Honolulu: University of Hawai'i Press.

—. 2004. The migration of skilled health professionals: From the Pacific Islands to the World. *Asian and Pacific Migration Journal* 13 (2): 155–77.

—. 2006a. Migration, dependency and inequality in the Pacific: Old wine in bigger bottles? (Part 1). In *Globalisation and governance in the Pacific Islands*, ed. S. Firth, 59-80. Canberra: ANU E Press.

—. 2006b. Migration, dependency and inequality in the Pacific: Old wine in bigger bottles? (Part 2) In *Globalisation and governance in the Pacific Islands*, ed. S. Firth, 81-196. Canberra: ANU E Press.

—. 2007. At the end of the world: Holding onto health workers in Niue. *Asian and Pacific Migration Journal* 16 (2): 179–98.

—. 2009. Bittersweet home? Return migration of skilled workers in the South Pacific. In *Return migration of the next generations: twenty-first century transnational mobility*, ed. D. Conway and R. Potter, 139-60. Aldershot: Ashgate.

Connell, J. and R. Brown. 1995. Migration and remittances in the South Pacific: Towards new perspectives. *Asian and Pacific Migration Journal* 4 (1): 1–33.

—. 2004. The remittances of migrant Tongan and Samoan nurses in Australia. *Human Resources for Health* 2 (2): 1-21.

—. 2005. Remittances in the Pacific: An overview. Manila: Asian Development Bank.

Connell, J. and G. McCall. 1989. South Pacific Islanders in Australia. *Research Institute for Asia and the Pacific Occasional Paper 9*. Sydney: University of Sydney.

Department of Labour. 2007. The recognised seasonal employer work policy. New Zealand Department of Labour.

http://www.dol.govt.nz/initiatives/strategy/rse/index.asp (accessed 2 May 2008).

Evans, M. 1999. Is Tonga's MIRAB economy sustainable? A view from the village and a view without it. *Pacific Studies* 22 (3/4): 137–66.

——. 2001. *Persistence of the gift. Tongan tradition in transnational context*. Waterloo Wilfred Laurier University Press.

Foreign Affairs, Defence and Trade References Committee. 2003. A Pacific engaged: Australia's relations with Papua New Guinea and the island States of the south–west Pacific. Canberra: Australian Government

Fouron, G. and N. Glick Schiller. 2002. The generation of identity: Redefining the second generation within a transnational social field. In *The changing face of home: The transnational lives of the second generation*, ed. P. Levitt and M. Waters, 168–208. New York: Russell Sage Foundation.

Fraenkel, J. 2006. Beyond MIRAB: do aid and remittances crowd out export growth in Pacific microeconomies? *Asia Pacific Viewpoint* 47 (1): 15–30.

Franklin, M. 2001. Postcolonial subjectivities and everyday life online. *International Feminist Journal of Politics* 3 (3): 387–422.

——. 2003. I define my own ethnicity: Pacific articulations of 'race' and 'culture' on the internet. *Ethnicities* 3 (4): 465–90.

——. 2004. *Postcolonial politics, the internet, and everyday life: Pacific traversals online* Abingdon: Routledge.

Glick Schiller, N., L. Basch, and C. Szanton Blanc. 1992. *Towards a transnational perspective on migration: Race, class, ethnicity, and nationalism reconsidered*. Vol. 645. New York: Annals of the New York Academy of Sciences.

——. 1995. From immigrant to transmigrant: Theorizing transnational migration. *Anthropological Quarterly* 68 (1): 48–63.

Hannan, K. 2006. Fiji: Sugar and sweatshirts, migrants and remittances. In *Globalisation and governance in the Pacific Islands*, ed. S. Firth, 189-215. Canberra: ANU E Press.

Hau'ofa, E. 1993a. Our sea of islands. In *A new Oceania: Rediscovering our sea of islands*, ed. E. Waddell, V. Naidu and E. Hau'ofa, 3-16. Suva: University of the South Pacific.

——.1993b. A beginning. In *A new Oceania: Rediscovering our sea of islands*, ed. E. Waddell, V. Naidu and E. Hau'ofa, 126-39. Suva: University of the South Pacific.

——. 1994. Thy kingdom come: The democratization of aristocratic Tonga. *The Contemporary Pacific* 6 (2): 414–27.

—.1998. The ocean in us. *The Contemporary Pacific* 10 (2): 392–409.

Howard, A. 1999. Pacific-based virtual communities: Rotuma on the world wide web. *The Contemporary Pacific* 11 (1): 160–75.

Howard, A. and J. Rensel. 2004. Rotuman identity in the electronic age. In *Shifting images of identity in the Pacific*, ed. T. van Meijl and J. Miedema, 219-36. Leiden: KITLV Press.

Howe, K.R. 1984. *Where the waves fall: A new South Sea Islands history from first settlement to colonial rule.* Sydney: George Allen and Unwin.

Hughes, H. and G. Sodhi. 2006. Should Australia and New Zealand open their doors to guest workers from the Pacific? Costs and benefits. *CIS Policy Monograph* 72. Canberra: The Centre for Independent Studies.

James, K. 1991. Migration and remittances: A Tongan village perspective. *Pacific Viewpoint* 32 (1): 1–23.

—. 1993. Cash and kin. Aspects of migration and remittance from the perspective of a fishing village in Vava'u, Tonga. In *A World Perspective on Migration: Australia, New Zealand and the USA*, ed. G. McGall and J. Connell, 359-74. Sydney: Centre for South Pacific Studies, University of New South Wales.

—. 1997. Reading the leaves: The role of Tongan women's traditional wealth and other 'contraflows' in the processes of modern migration and remittance. *Pacific Studies* 20 (1): 1–27.

—. 2002. Disentangling the 'grass roots' in Tonga: 'Traditional enterprise' and autonomy in the moral and market economy. *Asia Pacific Viewpoint* 43 (3): 269–92.

Janes, C. 1990. *Migration, social change and health: A Samoan community in California.* Palo Alto, CA: Stanford University Press.

—. 2002. From village to city: Samoan migration to California. In *Pacific diaspora: Island peoples in the United States and across the Pacific*, ed. P. Spickard, J. Rondilla and D. Hippolite Wright, 118-32. Honolulu: University of Hawai'i Press.

Kaeppler, A. 1978. Exchange patterns in goods and spouses: Fiji, Tonga, and Samoa. *Mankind* 11 (3): 246–52.

Kallen, E. 1982. *The Western Samoan kinship bridge: A study in migration, social change and the new ethnicity.* Leiden: Brill.

Lee, H. 2003. *Tongans overseas: Between two shores.* Honolulu: University of Hawai'i Press.

—. 2004a. 'Second generation' Tongan transnationalism: Hope for the future? *Asia Pacific Migration Journal* 45 (2): 235–54.

—. 2004b. All Tongans are connected: Tongan transnationalism. In *Globalization and culture change in the Pacific Islands*, ed. V. Lockwood, 133-48. New Jersey: Pearson.

—. 2006a. 'Tonga only wants our money': The children of Tongan migrants. In *Globalisation, governance and the Pacific Islands*, ed. S. Firth, 121–35. Canberra: ANU E Press.

—. 2006b. Debating language and identity online: Tongans on the net. In *Native on the net: Indigenous and diasporic peoples in the virtual age*, ed. K. Landzelius, 152–68. Abingdon: Routledge.

—. 2007a. Generational change: The children of Tongan migrants and their ties to the homeland. In *Tonga and the Tongans: Heritage and identity*, ed. E. Wood-Ellem, 203–17. Melbourne: Tonga Research Association.

—. 2007b. Transforming transnationalism: Second generation Tongans overseas. *Asian and Pacific Migration Journal* 16 (2): 157–78.

—. 2008. Second generation transnationalism. In *Ties to the homeland: Second generation transnationalism*, ed. H. Lee, 1-32. Newcastle: Cambridge Scholars Press.

—. 2009. The ambivalence of return: Second-generation Tongan returnees. In *Return migration of the next generations: Twenty-first century transnational mobility*, ed. D. Conway and R. Potter, 41-58. Aldershot: Ashgate.

Levin, M. and D. Ahlburg. 1993. Pacific Islanders in the United States census data. In *A world perspective on Pacific Islander migration: Australia, New Zealand and the USA*, ed. G. McCall and J. Connell, 95-144. Sydney: Centre for South Pacific Studies, University of New South Wales.

Levitt, P. 2001. *The transnational villagers*. Berkeley: University of California Press.

Levitt, P., J. DeWind, and S. Vertovec. 2003. International perspectives on transnational migration: An introduction. *International Migration Review* 37 (3): 565–75.

Levitt, P. and B. N. Jaworsky. 2007. Transnational migration studies: Past developments and future trends. *Annual Review of Sociology* 33: 129–56.

Levitt, P. and M. Waters. 2002a. Introduction. In *The changing face of home: The transnational lives of the second generation*, ed. P. Levitt and M. Waters, 1–30. New York: Russell Sage Foundation.

—. (eds). 2002b. *The changing face of home: The transnational lives of the second generation*. New York: Russell Sage Foundation.

Lilomaiava-Doktor, S. 2009. Beyond 'migration': Samoan population movement (*malaga*) and the geography of social space *va*. *The Contemporary Pacific* 21 (1): 1-32.

Maclellan, N. and P. Mares. 2006. Labour mobility in the Pacific: Creating seasonal work programs in Australia. In *Globalisation and governance in the Pacific Islands*, ed. S. Firth, 137-71. Canberra: ANU E Press.

—. 2007. Pacific seasonal workers for Australian agriculture: A neat fit? *Asian and Pacific Migration Journal* 16 (2): 271–87.

Macpherson, C. 1984. On the future of ethnicity in New Zealand. In *Tauiwi: Racism and ethnicity in New Zealand*, ed. P. Spoonley, C. Macpherson, D. Pearson, and C. Sedgewick, 107-27. Palmerston North: Dunmore Press.

—. 1985. Public and private views of home: Will Western Samoan migrants return? *Pacific Viewpoint* 26 (1): 242–62.

—. 1990. Stolen dreams: Some consequences of dependency for Western Samoan youth. In *Migration and development in the South Pacific*, ed. J. Connell, 107-19. Canberra: The Australian National University.

—. 1991. The changing contours of Samoan ethnicity. In *Nga Take: Ethnic relations and racism in Aotearoa/New Zealand*, ed. P. Spoonley, D. Pearson, and C. Macpherson, 67–86. Palmerston North: Dunmore Press.

—. 1992. Economic and political restructuring and the sustainability of migrant remittances: The case of Western Samoa. *The Contemporary Pacific* 4 (1): 109–35.

—. 1994. Changing patterns of commitment to Island homelands: A case study of Western Samoa. *Pacific Viewpoint* 17: 83–116

—. 2002. From moral community to moral communities: The foundations of migrant social solidarity among Samoans in urban Aotearoa/New Zealand. *Pacific Studies* 25 (1/2): 71–93.

—. 2004. Transnationalism and transformation in Samoan society. In *Globalization and culture change in the Pacific Islands*, ed. V. S. Lockwood, 165-81. Upper Saddle River, NJ: Pearson Prentice Hill.

Macpherson, C. and L. Macpherson. 1999. The changing contours of migrant Samoan kinship. In *Small worlds, global lives: Islands and migration*, ed. R. King. and J. Connell, 277–91. London: Pinter.

—. 2009. It's not quite what we expected: Some Samoan returnees' experiences of Samoa. In *Return migration of the next generations: twenty-first century transnational mobility*, ed. D. Conway and R. Potter, 19-39. Aldershot: Ashgate.

Macpherson, C., B. Shore, and R. Franco (eds). 1978. *New neighbors: Islanders in adaptation*. Santa Cruz Center for South Pacific Studies, University of California.

Macpherson, C., P. Spoonley, and M. Anae (eds). 2001. *Tangata o te moana nui: The evolving identities of Pacific peoples in Aotearoa/New Zealand*. Palmerston North: Dunmore Press.

Marcus, G. 1974. A hidden dimension of family development in the modern kingdom of Tonga. *Journal of Comparative Family Studies* 5 (1): 87–102.

——. 1981. Power on the extreme Periphery: The perspective of Tongan elites in the modern world system. *Pacific Viewpoint* 22: 48–64.

Maron, N. and J. Connell. 2008. Back to Nukunuku: Employment, identity and return migration in Tonga. *Asia Pacific Viewpoint* 49: 168-184.

McCall, G. and J. Connell (eds). 1993. *A world perspective on Pacific Islander migration: Australia, New Zealand and the USA*. Sydney: Centre for South Pacific Studies, University of New South Wales.

McKenzie, D. 2006. Remittances in the Pacific. In *Immigrants and their international money flows*. 2005–06 Werner Sichel lecture-seminar series, Western Michigan University.

Millbank, A. 2006. A seasonal guest-worker program for Australia? *Research Brief no. 16*. Canberra: Parliament of Australia.

Mohanty, M. 2006. Globalisation, new labour migration and development in Fiji. In *Globalisation and governance in the Pacific Islands*, ed. S. Firth, 107-20. Canberra: ANU E Press.

Morton, H. 1999. Islanders in space: Tongans online. In *Small worlds, global lives. Islanders and migration*, ed. R. King and J. Connell, 235-53. London: Pinter.

Parliament, of Australia. 2006. Perspectives on the future of the harvest labour force. Senate Standing Committee on Employment, Workplace Relations and Education. Canberra: Commonwealth of Australia. http://www.aph.gov.au/Senate/committee/EET_CTTE/contract_labour/report/report.pdf (accessed 11 November 2007).

Pitt, D. and C.Macpherson. 1974. *Emerging pluralism: Samoan migrants in New Zealand*. Auckland: Longman Paul.

Poirine, B. 1998. Should we hate or love MIRAB? *The Contemporary Pacific* 10 (1): 65–105.

Portes, A. 1999. Conclusion: Towards a new world—the origins and effects of transnational activities. *Ethnic and Racial Studies* 22 (2): 463–77.

—. 2003. Conclusion: Theoretical convergences and empirical evidence in the study of immigrant transnationalism. *International Migration Review* 37 (3): 874–92.

Rokoduru, A. 2006. Contemporary migration within the Pacific Islands: The case of Fijian skilled workers in Kiribati and Marshall Islands. In *Globalisation and governance in the Pacific Islands*, ed. S. Firth, 173-186. Canberra: ANU E Press.

Sato, M. 1997. Structure and dynamics of MIRAB societies in the South Pacific: An economic study. In *Contemporary migration in Oceania: Diaspora and network. JCAS Symposium Series 3: Population movement in the modern world.*, ed. K. Sudo and S. Yoshida, 165-77. Osaka: The Japan Center for Area Studies.

Shankman, P. 1976. *Migration and underdevelopment: The case of Western Samoa.* Boulder: Westview.

—. 1993. The Samoan exodus. In *Contemporary Pacific societies: Studies in development and change*, ed. V. Lockwood, T. Harding and B. Wallace, 156-70. Englewood Cliffs, NJ: Prentice Hall.

Small, C. 1997. *Voyages: From Tongan villages to American suburbs.* Ithaca: Cornell University Press.

Smith, M. and L. Guarnizo (eds). 1998. *Transnationalism from below.* New Brunswick: Transaction Publishers.

Spickard, P., J. Rondilla, and D. Hippolite Wright (eds). 2002. *Pacific diaspora: Island peoples in the United States and across the Pacific.* Honolulu: University of Hawai'i Press.

Spoonley, P. 2001. Transnational Pacific communities: Transforming the politics of place and identity. In *Tangata O te Moana nui: The evolving identities of Pacific peoples in Aotearoa/New Zealand*, ed. C. Macpherson, P. Spoonley, and M. Anae, 81-96. Palmerston North: Dunmore Press.

Spoonley, P., R. Bedford, and C. Macpherson. 2003. Divided loyalties and fractured sovereignty: Transnationalism and the nation-state in Aotearoa/New Zealand. *Journal of Ethnic and Migration Studies* 29 (1): 27–46.

Spoonley, P., C. Macpherson, D. Pearson and C. Sedgewick (eds). 1984. *Tauiwi: Racism and ethnicity in New Zealand.* Palmerston North: Dunmore Press.

Spoonley, P., D. Pearson, C. Macpherson (eds). 1991. *Nga take: Ethnic relations and racism in Aotearoa (New Zealand)*. Palmerston North: Dunmore Press.

—. (eds). 1996. *Nga Patai: Racism and ethnic relations in Aotearoa/New Zealand*. Palmerston North: Dunmore Press.

Stahl, C. and R. Appleyard. 2007. Migration and development in the Pacific Islands: Lessons from the New Zealand experience. Canberra: Australian Agency for International Development.

Stanwix, C. and J. Connell. 1995. To the Islands: The remittances of Fijians in Sydney. *Asian and Pacific Migration Journal* 4 (1): 69-87.

Vertovec, S. 1999. Conceiving and researching transnationalism. *Ethnic and Racial Studies* 22 (2): 447–62.

—. 2001. Transnationalism and identity. *Journal of Ethnic and Migration Studies* 27 (4): 573–82.

—. 2003. Migration and other modes of transnationalism: Towards conceptual cross-fertilization. *International Migration Review* 37 (3): 641–65.

Voigt-Graf, C. 2007. Pacific Islanders and the rim: Linked by migration. *Asian and Pacific Migration Journal* 16 (2): 143–56.

Voigt-Graf, C., R. Iredale, and S. Khoo. 2007. Teaching at home or overseas: Teacher migration from Fiji and the Cook Islands. *Asian and Pacific Migration Journal* 16 (2): 199–224.

Walker, A., and R. Brown. 1995. From consumption to savings? Interpreting Tongan and Western Samoan sample survey data on remittances. *Asian and Pacific Migration Journal* 4 (1): 89–115.

Ward, G. 1997. Expanding worlds of Oceania: Implications of migration. In *Contemporary migration in Oceania: Diaspora and network. JCAS Symposium Series 3: Population movement in the modern world*, ed. K. Sudo and S. Yoshida, 179-96. Osaka: The Japan Center for Area Studies.

World Bank, The. 2006. Pacific Islanders at home and away: Expanding job opportunities for Pacific Islanders through labour mobility. http://www-wds.worldbank.org/external/default/WDSContentServer/WDSP/IB/2006/11/15/000090341_20061115095505/Rendered/PDF/377150EAP.pdf (accessed 12 December 2007).

ENDNOTES

[1] More detailed overviews of Pacific migration can be found in Connell (1990, 2002, 2006a, 2006b), McCall and Connell (1993) Stahl and Appleyard (2007) and, for Australia and New Zealand, Bedford et al (2007).

[2] In the 1990s there was a surge in Samoan migration to the US, 'increasing 70% in the 1990s compared with 22% in the 1980s' (Ahlburg and Song 2006, 110). Shankman provides a useful overview of migration from Samoa, showing the fluctuations in numbers migrating and shifts in favoured destinations as host countries changed their immigration policies (1993; see also Janes 2002).

[3] Key scholars who helped to establish and shape this field of research include Linda Basch, Nina Glick Schiller and Cristina Szanton Blanc (1994; see also Glick Schiller, Basch and Blanc 1992, 1995). Contributions from scholars such as Peggy Levitt (2001) Alejandro Portes (1999, 2003) and Steven Vertovec (1999, 2001, 2003) further refined the concepts and delineated the scope of transnational research.

[4] Connell and Brown also edited a special issue of the *Asian and Pacific Migration Journal* (1995) on 'Migration and remittances in the South Pacific'. In recent years Connell and Brown have investigated the migration of skilled health professionals from the Pacific and their remittance practices (Brown and Connell 2004, 2006; Connell 2004, 2006b; Connell and Brown 2004). Connell has also looked at the return migration of these workers (2009; this volume). Richard Brown and various colleagues have also contributed a body of work on remittances since the early 1990s examining factors such as unofficial remittances and the informal economy in the islands (Brown 1995; Brown and Connell 1993); the sustainability of remittances (Brown 1997, 1998; Brown and Foster 1995; Brown and Walker 1995; Walker and Brown 1995); and the relationship between remittances and investment (Brown 1994; Brown, Foster and Connell 1995; Brown and Poirine 2005).

[5] The issue of temporary labour schemes has been discussed in Chand (2005), Hughes and Sodhi (2006), Maclellan and Mares (2006, 2007), and a report by the World Bank (2006). There have also been briefing papers for the Australian government on the topic (e.g. Millbank 2006) and a Senate inquiry into Pacific Region seasonal contract labour (Parliament of Australia 2006).

[6] One of the first collections of papers was Macpherson, Shore and Franco (1978). Since then there have been several more: see, for example, the work on New Zealand in Spoonley et al (1984); Spoonley, Pearson and Macpherson (1991, 1996); and Macpherson, Spoonley and Anae (2001). The collection of papers edited by McCall and Connell (1993) looks at Pacific populations in New Zealand, Australia and the US, as does *Pacific diaspora* (Spickard, Rondilla and Wright 2002). There also have been studies of particular Pacific populations, with a predominance of work on Samoans, as in the work of Macpherson, mentioned above (and see Janes 1990; Pitt and Macpherson 1974; Shankman 1976).

2. Forms of Transnationalism, Forms of Tradition: Cloth and Cash as Ritual Exchange Valuables in the Tongan Diaspora

Ping-Ann Addo

Introduction: Tongan Tradition and Transnational Economy

Robin Cohen begins his list of the features of diaspora with following: 'dispersal from a traditional homeland … [and] the expansion from a homeland in search of work, in pursuit of trade or to further colonial ambitions' (Cohen 2008,161). Labor for money is often cited as a main reason for emigration of Tongans overseas and to nodes in the Tongan diaspora. A decidedly transnational economy has resulted for members of this ethnoscape with Tongans traveling overseas from their homeland to earn and remit cash, thus enabling themselves and their families to purchase Western goods and other trappings of modernity. Because most remittances are sent directly to relatives in the homeland, I would add that the desire to fulfill abiding duties towards kin regardless of where they are located is an equally salient feature of modern diaspora. For people from the Kingdom of Tonga who have family ties connecting them to large diasporic communities like that dwelling in Auckland, New Zealand, the idea of laboring for money cannot be divorced from 'on-the-ground' efforts to maintain good social relations in communities in which social interactions are often public and usually highly scrutinized.

The transnational Tongan economy is intricately intertwined with the Tongan kingdom's economy through sending remittances, informal export of local goods which include ritual foods and textiles, and through the movement of people between communities in the Tongan ethnoscape (Lee 2004). Members of the Tongan diaspora remit cash and goods valued between 40 and 50 per cent of Tonga's GNP. These valuables are primarily categorised between family members as gifts (Brown 1998; Lee 2004). Indeed gifts that Tongans present to one another at ritual events such as funerals, weddings, and to other life crisis events generally constitute some combination of food, modern wealth (cash) and textiles (known as *koloa* and constituting traditional wealth). Sometimes, one kind of wealth is deemed more desirable than the other. Recent ethnography of Tongan exchange emphasizes the increased use of cash as gifts in ritual exchange (Addo 2004; Evans 2001; James 2002). This paper examines the case study of a funeral held by diasporic Tongans, members of a family who requested that condolence gifts brought to the event be only in the form of cash—textiles were not preferred. My analysis of the case reinforces Cohen's statement: the reality that Tongan families have made a practice of venturing from the homeland into diaspora in order to increase their access to cash. It also illuminates the extra-monetary expenditures which transnational Tongans (those who travel regularly or maintain active social and economic ties between homeland-based and diasporic communities) have to bear in order to perform rituals and otherwise 'be Tongan'. Moreover, it highlights how diasporic Tongans, as well as homeland Tongans interacting with each other negotiate modernity, the value of wealth and their social status.

Life crisis moments like funerals are times when the reputation of family is brought to the fore and it can be affected by how the family deals with gifts presented at the ritual. During my fieldwork in Tonga (2000–01), a family with whom I had grown very close tragically lost a daughter and her infant child in a car accident in Auckland, New Zealand, the city with the largest Tongan diasporic community. This was a difficult time, not least because of the death of a close relative, but also because travelling to host a funeral in New Zealand, a country where most of the deceased's immediate family did not live, would be costly in terms of time and money and could thus adversely affect the family's ability to maintain its reciprocal social relations. To circumvent the need to spend time reciprocating traditional wealth items like textiles, the family spread the word that they would be accepting no textile gifts, only cash gifts. The reason for their anomalous request was that they anticipated their time in Auckland would be limited, thus preventing them from reciprocating the textiles properly; cash would, and could, be reciprocated later, in accordance with modern customs. Their sentiments were made known via Tongan radio announcements and by word-of-mouth in both Tonga and in Auckland. One widely-held perception was that the family was trying to shirk tradition; another was that it was just inevitable that, with the increasing use of cash in gift exchange, in both Tonga and in the diaspora, money was finally beginning to show signs of replacing *koloa faka-Tonga* (women's valuables) in ritual presentations in diaspora. While this latter concern cannot be accurately answered—Tongan women's practice of *koloa*-making shows no trends toward either boom or bust (Addo 2007)—it is important to engage with analyses of traditional wealth with those of state currencies and their roles in contemporary Pacific societies. To this end, I address the question raised a decade ago by Melanesianists: why does cash seem to be replacing traditional gifts in the Tongan diaspora, but never eclipsing them (Akin and Robbins 1999, LiPuma 2000)? I ask: what can we learn from observing cultural practices in which exchange of traditional wealth incorporates money such that the gifting of cash throws intangible wealth, such as social relations, into relief?

Cloth and Cash

In my experiences conducting fieldwork in Tongan communities in the Kingdom of Tonga and in Auckland, New Zealand, Tongans often discursively liken cash to cloth. For example, my informants frequently used the statement 'our *koloa* are like your money' when trying capture, for me—a Westerner—the value of their *koloa*. Such statements mask both the role koloa is made to play as a key symbol and the cultural knowledge that money is ranked below *koloa* as a ritual valuable. Money is a form of wealth, but *koloa* is 'what one treasures' (Herda 1999). *Koloa* constitute plaited mats, painted barkcloths, machine-made quilts and lengths of store-bought coloured fabric. Moreover, *koloa* are said to regenerate people culturally after the emotional and social rifts caused by life crisis moments and family disputes (Kaeppler 2000). *Koloa* also have long-standing meaning in Tongan society as bodily adornment, the spoils of war and the social possessions to which only highly ranked people had access (ibid.). They continue to constitute durable forms of wealth with which rule is legitimated and with which unions and unity of high-ranking lineages through weddings and births are cemented (Herda 1999; Kaeppler 1978a; Schneider and Weiner 1989). *Koloa* are quintessential gifts and marketable commodities: they can be exchanged as gifts at rituals, or sold or pawned for quick cash in both Tonga and abroad (see Addo and Besnier 2008). *Koloa* sent overseas constitutes important 'contraflows' to cash and other valuables sent from the diaspora to Tonga (James 1997).

Traditional wealth production and exchange embody gendered knowledge. *Koloa* connect key aspects of *'ulungānga faka-Tonga*, knowledge of Tongan culture and traditions, which are among the things that Tongan women, especially, are charged with teaching children (Young Leslie 2004). In a brilliant discussion of the genealogical link to Pulotu, 'the world of the spirits' and the 'source of life and death', Filihia states: 'When women fabricate *koloa*, the *mana* of Pulotu is woven into their mats and hammered into their barkcloth, thus making these goods valuable items to be treasured' (Filihia 2001,387).

Men produce and gift objects called *ngāue* (Kaeppler 2000) or *ngoue* (Churchward 1959) that are the products of their farming activities. These include yams and other root crops, as well as livestock, especially pigs. In ceremonial exchange at life crisis events, *koloa* and *ngāue/ngoue* (today, often replaced by store bought luxury foods like tinned corned beef and bottled soft drinks) are reciprocated similarly with respective gifts of *koloa* or food. Probably because they are drawn from other families' valuable daily provisions, the practice is to reciprocate these gifts of food or of cloth in kind, and to do so soon after the ritual. Typically, whether in diaspora or homeland, *koloa* is reciprocated within days of a funeral. In ritual exchange, gifts of money are usually reciprocated in close to equivalent amounts, but during a later ritual at which the recipient in the former exchange is also involved.[1] Money became associated, very early, with male activities since men were the first to engage in cash-related trade with Westerners (Addo and Besnier 2008). However, cash money is not a traditional wealth item for men; it remains a *palangi* (foreign) valuable.

Just as *koloa* itself belongs to two transactional orders (or types of economic exchange)—that of the gift and of the commodity—so too, money straddles the traditional economic sphere of the gift. To use Akin and Robbins' terms, money is regularly deployed in relationships defined by modes of sharing, as well as modes of equivalent exchange (Akin and Robbins 1999).[2]

Money and Tradition

Tongans use money today for daily modes of equivalent exchange, including financing staples (buying food and paying school fees, as well as purchasing clothes and household supplies). In modalities of sharing, or gift-exchange, cash is employed in ritual presentation at life crisis occasions (birthdays, christenings, weddings, funerals); for weekly and annual church donations; and as rewards for well-rendered artistic performances (dancing and singing at celebratory events or at fund-raising concerts). Cash gifts are always given in the local state currency of the country where the ritual is taking place, regardless of where the giver lives, works, or has travelled from. The money must therefore have the appropriate local form to be immediately useful. When a composite gift of cloth, cash and *ngāue*—or just of cloth and cash—is made, men and women are both implicated in the labour and love required to prepare the gift. Composite gifts indicate that members of a family—even those not present at the ritual—as invested in maintaining tradition as well as their family's reputation.

Among Tongans, having money is extremely important for being seen as able to uphold tradition. However, having money with no respect for tradition is considered antithetical to the most basic Tongan ideals of *'ofa* (love) and *faka'apa'apa* (respect). An important aspect of tradition is making regular church donations and also gifts to clergymen. Adherents of the Free Wesleyan Church of Tonga, as well as other Tongan Methodist denominations in the ethnoscape, present annual donations known as *misinale* by gifting cash bills in a competitive and public forum (Decktor-Korn 1978).[3] These cash gifts, amounting to a sum of between a few hundred and several thousand dollars, are a primary way in which large amounts of cash are remitted from diaspora to homeland (Lee 2004). There is a proper aesthetic to the formal gifting of money: it is enclosed in an envelope—usually white—called *sila pa'anga*, often resting atop a folded textile, and is presented with prayers and other gifts of food and drinks. When gifted during a dance, money is conspicuously tucked inside performers' necklines, waistbands, thrown into the air above their heads, or strung around their necks in a prepared garland. Wrapping or draping the body in things of beauty and of value predates the introduction of money to Tongan culture (Addo 2003), and to gift money in this way is to honour tradition.

Gifts and Funerals

Tongan gift-givers and recipients are usually related as extended kin, or *kāinga*; branches of the *kāinga* normally constitute an immediate family (called a *fāmili*) related to the deceased through one member. In diaspora, funerals are a time to re-assemble far-flung kin, and people regularly travel between Tonga and diasporic communities to pay their last respects. A person's funeral is often the last time that s/he is physically surrounded a by a large number of kin and the last event at which s/he will be honoured by the exchange of gifts in her/his name and memory. Thus, funerals are as much moments for reunion and pride as they are moments for grieving. The esteem for the entire *kāinga* rests on all constituent *fāmili* groups to perform their appropriate ranked roles correctly (Kaeppler 1978b).

Gifts of food and cloth are long-standing material relations through which families help one another to sustain themselves in times of life crises. A gift of textiles, called a *teu*, is typically presented by a group of women, usually members of a *fāmili*. As a representative of the gifting family makes an impassioned speech about the departed, the grieving family and the humble gifts the latter have brought, each piece of *koloa* is brought in and laid at the feet of a male representative of the receiving family, with cash in a *sila pa'anga*. Once presented, the cash and cloth gifts are removed to another room of the funeral venue, to be counted and noted along with the name of the givers. Friends, co-workers and kin members often bring gifts of food before the funeral; these are presented with prayers and sometimes with cash and cloth gifts. Traditionally, these gifts are considered necessary provisions for doing culture and, although they are wealth items, are also immediately useful.

Gifted food may be used to feed the mourners who come to pay their respects on the night of the wake or to sustain the bereaved family during its many days of preparation of and recuperation from the funeral; during this time, very little farming or fishing—and certainly no textile production—would be performed on estates and villages in Tonga. Because of the symbolism which *koloa* and feast foods maintain, to refuse a gift of cloth or food is seemingly to leave unrecognised another family's sacrifice and generosity and a refusal to do tradition. In addition, requesting money in lieu of *koloa* can be read as a preference for non-traditional ways over engaging in acts that honour both the dead and Tongan notions of tradition. Even when the grieving family in my case study explained that they still believed in Tongan traditions, their actions may have spoken (more loudly) of their attempting to eschew it.

Cash, Death and Diaspora: The Persistence of Gift-giving

With high expectations of performing a funeral to honour society's expectations, this family's pride was also at stake. Nunia, the younger sister of the deceased woman, stated:

> Dad stands to lose a lot of face from this funeral…but we have no choice. We can't afford to fly Malia ['s body] back [to Tonga] and have the funeral here. It would cost so much. We would even have to get people coming from New Zealand and Australia to bring some of the food if we were going to have it at home [in Tonga]. It's better to do it [in New Zealand]…and Mum and Dad decided last night not to take any *teu*…any *koloa*…because it would just be too hard for us to have to do the [reciprocal presentations] after the funeral. And we will be lucky if we get a month on our visas to stay [in New Zealand]. If we bury Malia in New Zealand…[my sister] Sona can look after her and visit her. We'll all visit her when we can. I know I will want to.

Nunia's father later told me that his *fāmili* was willing to take risk 'losing face' in order to minimise the logistical challenges, and the monetary and cloth wealth costs of doing a traditional reciprocation, i.e., one involving the presentation of cloth, food and prayers, for each *teu*. Furthermore, the funeral was for both Malia and her young child, each of whom belonged to their respective fathers' lineages and therefore, ritually speaking, to a different *fāmili*. Accepting only cash gifts would mitigate Nunia and Malia's family's obligations to immediately reciprocate numerous and costly gifts to two kin groups.

However, on the night of Malia and her baby's wake, Malia's *fāmili* was gifted with several traditional presentations of *koloa*. In the dim basement of an Auckland Methodist church, I listened and watched intently as the spokesperson for Nunia's family announced his thanks for one *teu* and subsequently relayed the grieving *fāmili*'s decision not to accept *koloa* on this occasion. On hearing this, one member from the gifting family picked up the envelope of money and handed it to the representative, then the women visitors picked up the *koloa* they had already laid down in front of him and left. I had also noticed one woman leaving the wake with her arms laden with *koloa*. Her *koloa* had obviously been refused. After hearing that the gift would not be accepted, she returned to her car, opened the trunk and practically dumped the *koloa* into it. Other visiting mourners would not be so easily deterred. Despite such obvious signs of distress about the refusal of *koloa*, another woman mourner found a way for the *kāinga* to accept her *fāmili*'s gift of *koloa*. I present an excerpt from my fieldnotes:

> A relative of [Nunia's] mother's brother, a[nother] woman named Teuila who lived in Auckland and who, like the other visitors at the wake, had come in carrying part of a *teu* consisting of three pieces of [barkcloth],

two decorated…mats, and several pieces of printed, store-bought fabric. After her *fāmili* had been thanked with a short, formal speech by [Nunia's] family representative and asked to remove their *teu*, she stood and took each of the *ngatu* with the mats folded up in them, and presented these to the three men from Malia's *kāinga* who were seated in front of her, thereby making them the token gift recipients. The men all showed their acceptance of the gifts by saying '*māl* ' (thank you), and then Teuila and her [*fāmili*] group stood and left.

Two of Malia's sisters who had been seated nearby took Teuila's textiles into another room and they later analysed Teuila's motivations this way: 'She was being generous. It's like she just wanted someone to take the *koloa* from her, like if you offered me [some] chocolate and I didn't want to accept it, but you were going to give it away anyway, so you offer it to the person sitting next to me…' Another sister said: 'She was showing that she was *liongi* [in mourning] to the [family members] and the others with him.'[4] This second response revealed that the sister was well aware of the operation of roles at the funeral, rank being the principle governing who must gift and thus who receives and must reciprocate. Sensitivity to her own role and ritual ranked status permeated Teuila's sense of right and proper actions at this funeral and so she proceeded with her gift presentation. Similarly, Rupp reports on *kokorozukai*, a category of Japanese gifts generally given out of gratitude, for example to doctors for healing a sick family member or for delivering a healthy baby. According to Rupp: 'it is not possible to bring these gifts to the hospital, where there is a sign that reads: 'We humbly ask that you refrain from kokorozukai' [so] patients simply send their gifts directly to the doctors' residences' (Rupp 2003:163). In Rupp's example, presumably, the gifts are not refused.

In Tonga, just as in Japan, gifts already refused in one context may be accepted in another to save face for both givers and recipients. So, by ensuring that the gift moved on to another person at the ritual, Teuila fulfilled her duty in commemorating Malia's death. The counter-gift would have to be embodied in future gifts given by Nunia's famili members. The anthropology of Tonga is quite rich in analysis of Tongan gifts and countergifts (Addo 2004; Evans 2001; Gifford 1929; James 1997, 2002; Small 1997; van der Grijp 1993). These authors concur that, once accepted, an appropriate material gift must be reciprocated. To gift koloa is often termed '*mole [lose] koloa.*' Even though the family did not reciprocate, they still engaged in exchange and were thus indebted to others. As Nunia said, they risked 'losing face'. They risked 'paying' for an easier funeral process with the esteem one would otherwise have in others' eyes following the ritual event. As a member of their *kāinga*, extended family, Teuilia might have been trying to dispel any negativity associated with Nunia's famili's anomalous exchange practices.

Friends and relatives also presented *ngāue*—food mostly in the form of store-bought frozen meat and root crops—to Nunia's *fāmili* in Auckland on the night before the wake. Some of this food went towards a light meal prepared for visitors at the wake. In all, Nunia's *fāmili* received NZ$8,800 in condolence gifts from visitors to the Auckland funeral. This sum did not even begin to cover their initial outlay for their plane tickets from various parts of Tonga and Australia to Auckland, the expense of feeding the hundreds who attended, and the cost of countergifts (constituting cloth and store-bought food) to the six or seven Methodist ministers who visited during the night of the wake and the one who officiated at the burial. Still consumed by grief, Nunia's *fāmili* returned to Tonga indebted monetarily, yet grateful for the great amount of spiritual and monetary support they received for dealing with their sudden double loss.

Money as Tongan Gifts

A gift of *koloa* remains a feature of diasporic ceremonial exchanges because its immediate reciprocation underscores the faith of those who also gave money. They believe that they can trust the receiving family to reciprocate cash in the future. As Kaeppler has suggested, *koloa* does indeed assure others of the continued sustenance and renewal of the kin group (Kaeppler 2000). Maintaining good social relations with *kāinga* members who live in close proximity can be challenging, but trying to do so over the many miles between homeland and diaspora, or even between diasporic sites, can be daunting. If, like Nunia's family, the initial recipients of a gift are living far from Auckland when other families celebrate their next ritual, temporal and physical distance between rituals can make balanced and timely reciprocity of cash gifts almost impossible.

Thus, in diaspora, both gifts of money and cloth become fraught with much anxiety for both givers and recipients. The long-standing prescription of answering gifts with appropriate countergifts, even after costly and often sudden events such as funerals, is thrown out of sequence if only cash gifts are accepted. When people who give gifts receive no reward or material recognition for their material expenditure, the givers' feel disrespected and their family economics may also be adversely affected. In material terms, lay people—friends and other kin members who are not professionals like ministers and undertakers—receive no substantial public recognition for their material show of support. By accepting only cash Nunia's *fāmili* upset the sense of on-going, long-term, culturally-salient reciprocation, hence their fear of censure. A great deal more than *koloa* may be lost by refusing a gift that a diasporic dweller has taken pains to prepare and present to a homeland-based Tongan family; as Nunia said, 'a lot of face' is lost. A decision to reciprocate only some or even none of the gifts brought to a funeral is said, by some Tongans, to be the prerogative of oneself and one's family (Decktor-Korn 1978; James 2002; Kaeppler 1978b). Whether in diaspora or homeland, there seems to be little historical precedent for not succumbing to established pressures to gift cash, *koloa* and food at life crisis rituals.

Making gifts of cash in the context of times of ritual crises constitutes a symbolically important aspect of a generalized modality of sharing. It also assures continued prosperity for kin groups.[5] Sharing money, helping a close relative to meet the costs of a child's education, or giving cash at a kinsperson's life crisis event is also a basic performance of *tauhi vaha'a* which Poltorak describes as a cultural value shared by Tongans and which emphasises the importance of caring for the 'space between' or the 'relatedness' of people (Poltorak 2007, 12). Explaining a dialectical variant of the same concept, Ka'ili describes the same phenomenon, which is also known as *tauhi vā,* as operating transnationally and involving 'reciprocal exchange of economic and social goods' (Ka'ili 2005, 92). Sending money primarily from diasporic branches of the family to relatives in the homeland, is thus an important aspect of *tauhi vaha'a /tauhi vā* for it demonstrates willingness to support family materially. To upset this long-standing convention of Tongan exchange, whereby respect for kin and tradition is shown through the obvious and public bi-directional flow of gifts, is to challenge the very notion of Tongans constituting a common culture. It also engages Tongans in a dialogue about how Tonganness can be expressed given the challenges and possibilities presented by living in diaspora. As Matory cautions diaspora scholars to recognise: 'selective reproduction, meaning transformation, and meaningful reinterpretation of past cultural forms' involves '*commemoration* [which] is always strategic in its selections, exclusions and interpretations' (Matory 2006: 163)

It remains to be seen how Tongan families will continue to finance and provide for each other through ritual exchange in the diaspora if the immediate reciprocations demanded by gifts of *koloa* are slowly made obsolete. Writing about Maori *tangi,* funerals, Sinclair states that such rituals are inevitable, yet regulating and familiar (Sinclair 1990). Funerals give life in an (immigrant Tongan) ethnic community in New Zealand a sense of spatial and temporal continuity because participants must perform roles, revisit the history of their social relations and consciously perform *tauhi vā* or *tauhi vaha'a*. No Tongan can control his or her rank, but the esteem within which a *fāmili*, and consequently a *kāinga*, is held can be positively or negatively affected through shared public assessments of an individual's attention to kinship matters like funerals (Kaeppler 1978b).

Tradition, in the form of kinship matters, will always concern families who are dispersed throughout the Tongan ethnoscape and for whom money makes staying connected—by phone, internet, courier mail and plane trips—increasingly manageable. However, as things that regenerate people culturally, cloth remains the symbolically potent material value with which many modern Tongans navigate the waters between upholding tradition and experimenting with modernity in the diaspora. As Tongan families continue *koloa* exchange, they construct these navigations as performances of *anga faka-Tonga*, even while money remains an important medium of Tongan daily and ceremonial exchange.

Conclusion

This paper has discussed the politics of money being made to stand in place of traditional wealth, textile *koloa*. Yet, the argument has also been presented that *koloa* continue to be indispensable to ritual and their role in connecting families. *Koloa* can only stand for themselves, and money is an inadequate stand in. As reflected on above, *koloa* are integral to the aesthetics of gifting cash. As explained earlier, *sila pa'anga* are often formally presented resting on a folded bed of *koloa*. Thus, money requires *koloa* in order to be gifted in ways that provide a further visual index for *anga faka-Tonga*. Perhaps this is one reason why gifts of cloth, as well as composite gifts of cloth and cash, have persisted almost 200 years into the existence of the monetised Tongan economy and with the increasing global spread of Tongan transnationalism.

For analytical neatness, I have presented a somewhat dichotomised view of cash and cloth wealth in the diasporic Tongan economy. In lived reality, however, cash and cloth are far more intertwined forms of wealth, bleeding into each other, but never fully eclipsing one another. Likewise, I have also separated the diaspora from the homeland as nodes of social experience, knowing full well that these practices are dialogic—mutually-constituting and carried out by social agents who negotiate the performance of traditions in their interactions and confrontations (Matory 2006). Tongan ceremonial culture in diaspora probably will continue to strongly affect ceremonial culture in the homeland. With this in mind, I have examined how a homeland-based *fāmili* sought to make the politics of their own grieving process more bearable in material terms by vying for one form of value in a now thoroughly mixed economy of cash and cloth wealth.

Seen in an ethnographically nuanced light, we might re-think Cohen's second major feature of diaspora. Where Cohen cites 'expansion from a traditional homeland in search of work, in pursuit of trade' (Cohen 2008:161), I suggest we consider both permanent and temporary expansions from a homeland as well as the obvious intensification of relationships of emigrants with people still resident in that home land. Another feature of diaspora might also be the rights that emigrants maintain to negotiate a sense of tradition with their homeland-based counterparts. The (extra-local) search for work and the transnational performance of tradition have become basic features of Tongan modernity as well as basic assumptions about how diaspora contributes to the longevity of Tongan culture writ large.

In concluding, I make no predictions about how Tongan diaspora and notions of modernity will affect the intertwined roles of cash and cloth in Tongan exchange. For example, no one can accurately predict if cash gifts will indeed replace cloth gifts in the future. While the relationship of these two categories of valuables has been historically established in Tongan culture, my discussion here has shown that the relationship is subject to much negotiation, especially as life crisis rituals, and decisions around them, may be bi-territorially planned and executed. To see cash and cloth as equivalent forms of value such that one form (money) might replace the other (*koloa*) in ritual exchange, would be to ignore just what is at stake in contemporary transnational identities: good social relations.

This chapter is dedicated to the loving memory of the late Henry Kilifi Quensell and his entire fāmili. Na'a ne haka he langi, Māl .

References

Addo, P-A. 2003. God's kingdom in Auckland: Tongan Christian dress and the expression of duty. In *Clothing the Pacific*, ed. Chloe Colchester, 141–63. Oxford: Berg Press.

—. 2004. Kinship, cloth, and community in Auckland, New Zealand: Commoner Tongan women navigate transnational identity using traditionally-styled textile wealth. PhD thesis, Yale University.

—. 2007. Tongan women authenticate *ngatu pepa* in New Zealand. *Pacific Studies*, New Series 3:60–73.

Addo, P-A. and N. Besnier. 2008. When gifts become commodities: Pawnshops in Tonga and the Tongan diaspora. *Journal of the Royal Anthropological Institute* 14 (19): 39-59.

Akins, D. and J. Robbins. 1999. *State and local currencies in Melanesia*. Pittsburgh: University of Pittsburgh Press.

Brown, R. 1998. Do migrants' remittances decline over time: Evidence from Tongans and Western Samoans in Australia. *The Contemporary Pacific* 10 (1): 107–52.

Churchward, C. 1959. *Tongan dictionary*. London: Oxford University Press.

Cohen, R. 2008. *Global diasporas: An introduction*. New York: Routledge.

Decktor Korn. S. 1978. After the missionaries came: Denominational diversity in the Tonga Islands. In *Missions, church, and sect in Oceania*, ed. J. A. Boutilier, D. T. Hughes, and S. W. Tiffany, 395–422. Ann Arbor, MI: University of Michigan Press.

Evans, M. 2001. *Persistence of the gift: Tongan tradition in transnational context*. Waterloo, Ontario: Wilfred Laurier University Press.

Filihia, M. 2001. Men are from Maama, women are from Pulotu: Female status in Tongan society. *Journal of the Polynesian Society* 110 (4): 377–90.

Gifford, E. W. 1929. *Tongan society*. Bernice P. Bishop Museum Bulletin, no. 16. Honolulu: Bishop Museum.

Herda, P. 1999. The changing texture of textiles in Tonga. *Journal of the Polynesian Society* 108 (2): 149–67.

James, K. 1997. Reading the leaves: The role of Tongan women's traditional wealth and other 'contraflows' in the processes of modern migration and remittance. *Pacific Studies* 20 (1): 1–27.

—. 2002. The cost of custom: A recent funeral in Tonga. *Journal of the Polynesian Society* 111 (3): 223–38.

Kaeppler, A. 1978a. Exchange patterns in goods and spouses: Fiji, Tonga, and Samoa. *Mankind* 11 (3): 246-252.

—. 1978b. *Me'a faka'eiki:* Tongan funerals in a changing society. In *The changing Pacific: Essays in honour of Henry Maude*, ed. Neil Gunson, 174–202. Melbourne: Oxford University Press.

—. 2000. *From the stone age to the space age in 200 years: Tongan art and society at the eve of the millennium*. Tofoa, Kingdom of Tonga: Tonga National Museum.

Ka'ili, T. 2005. *Tauhi vā:* Nurturing Tongan sociospatial ties in Maui and beyond. *The Contemporary Pacific* 17 (1): 83–114.

Lee, H. 2004. 'Second generation' Tongan transnationalism: Hope for the future? *Asia Pacific Viewpoint* 45 (2): 235–54.

LiPuma, E. 2000. *Encompassing others: The magic of modernity in Melanesia*. Ann Arbor: University of Michigan Press.

Matory, J. 2006. The New World surrounds an ocean: Theorizing the live dialogue between African and African American cultures. In *Afro-Atlantic dialogues: Anthropology in the diaspora*, ed. K.A. Yelvington, 151-192. Santa Fe: School for American Research Press.

Poltorak, M. 2007. Nemesis, speaking, and *tauhi vaha'a*: Interdisciplinarity and the truth of mental illness in Vava'u, Tonga. *The Contemporary* Pacific 19 (10): 1–38.

Rupp, K. 2003. *Gift-giving in Japan: Cash, connections, cosmologies*. Stanford: Stanford University Press.

Rutherford, N. 1977. George Tupou I and Shirley Baker. In *Friendly islands: A history of Tonga*, ed. Noel Rutherford, 154–72. Melbourne: Oxford University Press.

Schneider, J. and A. Weiner. 1989. *Cloth and human experience*. Washington: Smithsonian Institution Press.

Sinclair, K. 1990. *Tangi*: Funeral rituals and the construction of Maori identity. In *Cultural identity and ethnicity in the South Pacific*, ed. J. Linnekin and L. Poyer, 218–36. Honolulu: University of Hawai'i Press.

Small, C. 1997. *Voyages: From Tongan villages to American suburbs*. Ithaca, NY: Cornell University Press.

Van der Grijp, P. 1993. *Islanders of the south: Production, kinship, and ideology in the Polynesian kingdom of Tonga*. Leiden: KITLV Press.

Young Leslie, H. 2004. Pushing children up: Maternal obligation, modernity, and medicine in the Tongan ethnoscape. In *Globalization and culture change in the Pacific Islands*, ed. V. Lockwood, 390–413. Upper Saddle River, New Jersey: Prentice Hall.

ENDNOTES

[1] Just as Rupp explains for Japanese gifts of money I suggest that, among Tongans, returning equivalent amounts immediately might be considered 'too calculating' (Rupp 2003).

[2] Akin and Robbins (1999) use this term to indicate that the significance of money shifts depending on whether it is deployed in a modality of equivalence (most commonly as a commodity) or sharing (as a gift), which contextualise the relevant social relations.

[3] Money entered the world of Tongan exchange alongside Christianity and was eventually localised through gifting money in the manner of traditional valuables. *Fakamisinale* (making missionary) was a financial mainstay of the local church, with donations at first being accepted in the form of commodities such as copra and coconut oil. Peruvian and Chilean coin—again, introduced through the copra trade—were the first state currencies Tongans used, after the Australian-based London Missionary Society (LMS) church administration decreed that Tongans should pay their annual church donations in modern cash (Rutherford 1977). The silver coins were shiny and showy, just the thing for distinguishing one's family and honoring a generous God, from whom all other blessings flowed.

[4] *Liongi* is a state of ritual mourning usually physically characterised by the wearing of large and tattered waist mats over black clothes.

[5] The form and timeliness of a countergift delivers a message about one's regard for social rules and kin-based roles (James 2002). In the 1920s Gifford recorded the lengths to which Tongan families would go to ensure that they reciprocated gifts appropriately. Citing an example of wedding gifts exchanged between bride and groom's sides in Nuku'alofa, Tonga, he says: 'In accomplishing [a] return the distributor often stripped his own house of all its possessions, counting the social prestige of his family of greater value than his material property. If he should fail to complete the traditional remuneration to all concerned, his unmarried sons and daughters and the progeny of his married children lost face and might consequently fail to contract desirable marriages' (Gifford, 1929, 193).

3. Samoan Transnationalism: Cultivating 'Home' and 'Reach'

Sa'iliemanu Lilomaiava-Doktor

Declaring the need to rethink conceptions of international migration, anthropologists Basch, Glick Schiller and Blanc defined their understanding of transnationalism:

> We define 'transnationalism' as the processes by which immigrants build social fields that link together their country of origin and their country of settlement. Immigrants who build such social fields are designated 'transmigrants.' Transmigrants develop and maintain multiple relations—familial, economic, social, organizational, religious, and political that span borders. Transmigrants take actions, make decisions, feel concerns, and develop identities within social networks that connect them to two or more societies simultaneously (1994, 1–2).

Issues which have dotted the field in recent years include arguments about the intensity and relevance of transnationalism in certain migrant communities, the significance of investigating the logic of transnationality, and the methodologies to be employed in transnational studies. Transnationalism has not come without its critics. Much transnational scholarship in geography has focused on economic globalisation, particularly the growing international flows of commodities, services, money, and information of the last two or three decades. In analysing the effects of political forces at both international and national scales, numerous geographers have focused in particular on the contemporary geopolitics of the nation-state (Baia 1999; Mitchell 1997; Vertovec 1999). Advances in technology have facilitated globalisation processes and further enabled the presence of global restructuring.

While this 'new vision' is welcome, analysis of the mobility of goods and services and the general capitalist expansion worldwide often relies on a homogeneous vision of global processes. As Mitchell points out:

> Assumptions and hegemonic narratives of modernity are assumed as standards—standards which are, of course, transformed in various ways upon contact with local regions, but which nevertheless contain a form and explanatory potential that is inviolate. The origin of these processes recedes from view, and their power and ability to expand and diffuse take on the characteristic of the self-evident (1997, 104).

The assumption that dominates these narratives is that of nation-states as places of containment with borders. So far, research on transnationalism has focused on documenting evidence of material exchanges between sending and receiving communities (Faist 2000; Gorges 1990; Grasmuck and Pessar 1997; Smith and Guarnizo 1998). Although earlier studies collected data on the transfer of money, goods and resources, scholars are beginning to move beyond this more tangible traffic to uncover ties, links and movements based on ideas, beliefs, and values.

In part, transnationalism began as a critique of globalisation, much of the discussion of which is theoretically rather opaque (Featherstone 1990). If there is ethnography, and there rarely is, it usually involves forays into secondary sources to embellish a particular point. Gardner (1995, 15) writes, 'Without analyzing local responses to wider global processes in far more detail, we are in danger of either recreating the generalisations of earlier, homogenising macro-theories, or simply substituting obsolete notions of modernisation with the more trendy 'globalisation', thus simply reducing it to a code for westernization.' The mechanisms of globalisation—and implicitly, transnationalism—are usually identified as world capitalism, so that in some versions, 'globalisation' becomes a modified version of world-system theory (Wallerstein 1990).

Reflecting on how globalisation is conceived, Amin (1997) argues that the dualistic thinking pervasive in academic discourse misses the point of globalisation. He writes against the bipolar boundaries of state and capitalism, emphasising the meaning of globalisation as an 'intermingling of 'in here'; and 'out there' processes resulting in heterogeneity, shifting identities and multipolarity consistent with contemporary urban reality' (Amin 1997, 123). Much of what Amin discusses is still framed in the context of 'globalisation from above', emanating from a city, or a core in the west. By talking in terms of 'in here' (as the centre) and 'out there' (backstage and invisible), his conception remains tied to the very structures he critiques.

So far, most literature on globalisation has only touched upon local interpretations of the flows of people, goods and meanings distilled in the idea of transnationalism. The ways in which diversity is created locally and how the homogenising tendencies of late 20th century capitalism are resisted, have yet to be integrated with these more general discussions of 'global flows' (Gardner 1995). Clearly, what is missing from these dominating macro-analyses are more grounded, cultural interpretations and a deeper understanding of the social, economic and political processes involved.

This paper brings a *fa`a-Samoa* (Samoan culture and way of life) perspective on transnationalism, examining how social, cultural, political and economic practices have changed over time, and the forms these transnational processes take. It draws on my doctoral research of more than 18 months in the village of Salelologa on Savai`i, Samoa's big island, with members of villagers' `aiga (family, kin group) in Auckland, New Zealand and Santa Ana, California. I use the concept of transnationalism in examining how *fafo* (abroad, overseas) or 'reach' and *i`inei* (here, Samoa, local) or 'home' are linked in Salelologa, Auckland and Santa Ana (see also Lilomaiava-Doktor 2009). Emphasis is given to the interplay between 'home' and 'reach' a twin-metaphor used by the humanist geographer Anne Buttimer (1980) to apprehend the ongoing negotiations of meaning in places of origin and destination. In using these cultural metaphors *fafo* and *i`inei,* I make explicit how they engage power within and between spaces and places arrayed in opposition to each other.

Transnationalism and Social Remittances

How is transnationalism enacted in the Salelologa case? The transnational framework is especially useful in delineating the importance of linkages between home and host countries. Basch, Glick Schiller and Blanc (1995, 48) write that many migrants are now transmigrants, 'whose daily lives depend on multiple and constant interconnections across international borders and whose public identities are configured in relationship to more than one nation-state.' They describe post-World War II migratory patterns among migrants who can no longer be considered 'uprooted'. Because they neither cut the ties to their countries of origin nor fully absorb the new culture offered by host nation, these immigrants are considered transnational. This concept acknowledges that links to the home country are maintained from the host country as immigrants strengthen ties with frequent travel and the sending of goods, resources and funds (remittances, investments).

In a study of Brazilian immigrants in New York city, Margolis (1995, 29) expands the concept by noting that immigrants 'establish and maintain familial, economic, political, and cultural ties across international borders, in effect making the home and the host society a single arena of social action.' Scholars like Levitt have moved beyond this more tangible traffic to uncover ties based on ideas, beliefs and values. She calls this 'social remittance' recognising that transnationalism need not be limited to tangible exchanges but also can include ideational and attitudinal linkages (Levitt, 1999, 927).

Strong components of 'social remittance' found in Salelologa made it possible to explore this sense of transnationalism and in so doing, to move far beyond the dichotomy of receiving and sending countries still found in the literature. As important as those who move are, those who 'stay put' have just as much influence on diasporic processes and the two populations cannot be separated. The Salelologa case involves both tangible and intangible aspects of shared information, trust, contacts and values that members travelling back and forth absorb from and release into the process and dynamic of movement.

Salelologa has ceased to be the only core and centre for its `aiga; there are now multiple centres, but this does not mean the nu`u (village) has been abandoned. Rather, the transformative force of movement fafo has been incorporated into local social and economic processes, forever altering them in the long run. While it is true that members of Salelologa are now physically dispersed from their households and village, such mobility does not deny the value of i`inei. Instead, mobility is involved in its reproduction; mobility strengthens rather than weakens the links between family and home.

Blurring Boundaries: *Matai* and *Tautua* Redefined

How is indigenous knowledge maintained and reproduced in the diaspora? If metaphors and metonyms define Salelologa movements and ongoing interactions in new contexts, what are the implications for matai (chiefly system) and tautua (service)? The discussion below is based on data collected in the field from 1999 to 2002.[1]

The matai system has been described in detail by many authors (Franco 1985; Freeman 1984; Holmes 1957; Liu 1991; Va`a 2001) but in recent decades, it has undergone many changes including a decline in authority over production by the extended family. As matai titles have proliferated and matai have lost their authority and former economic role, families have become smaller and the pool of potential servers limited. Young men can no longer be sure they will be able to command the service of the next generation in their old age (Maiava 2001; O'Meara 1990). Overseas movement and investment in formal education are some of the important ways in which `aiga have dealt with these changes. In turn, parents rely more on their own children and the parent-child relationship has become increasingly emphasised. Similar conclusions have been reached about Fijian population movements, where nuclear family relationships are becoming more central (Young 1998).

Interviews and discussions carried out in Salelologa, Auckland and Santa Ana between 1999 and 2002 also indicate that sibling relationships are becoming more relevant to the orchestration of movement and remittances, although this shift is gradual and subtle, not abrupt. This is because the actual composition of individual households is but a superficial indicator of reciprocities that exist or may be potentially reactivated at some future time. Some families in Auckland have no surviving parents but an eldest cousin has become their matai. For example, despite living in Sydney, one matai, Mulitalo Sefo, has taken on the leadership role for all his cousins and siblings in times of crisis, and mobilises this extended family to collect resources for fa`alavelave (life-cycle events including weddings, births, funerals, graduations) whether they are held in Samoa or overseas.

One of the basic criteria for receiving a title is the imperative to provide *tautua* (service) as expressed in the proverb, *'O le ala 'i le pule 'o le tautua* (the way to authority is through service). Formerly, untitled men lived in the community and served their *matai* and village *fono* (council) until it was their turn to be *matai*, often upon the death of a senior titleholder. But with mobility, the bestowing of titles based on *tautua* has changed and *matai* conferment happens more often overseas. As already discussed, 'place' is an important factor in retaining Samoan values but change is also negotiated and contested in different places. It is possible to invest in the *'aiga* not only through movement abroad and educational achievements but also by conferring *matai* titles overseas. Despite the decline in the traditional economic role of *matai*, their social and political roles remain intact. The village *fono* retain the political power to sanction unacceptable behaviour. It is the *matai* who organises the pooling of resources from immediate and extended family members, combining their contributions to hold *fa'alavelave* and then redistributing the gifts. Skilful organisation of these institutionalised rituals enables *matai* to reposition their power base in society.

Traditionally, certain *matai* titles (chief or orator) came with the right to confer other titles (Meleisea 1987; Va'ai 1998). These can be conferred based on service to the *matai* and *'aiga* by those related by *toto* (blood), *tino* (by adoption) or service connections and usually assumes that the conferment is done in Samoa on the *malae* where *maota* (chiefly house site) and *laoa* (orator house site) are located, for this adds legitimacy and authenticity to titles. During investiture, the *matai* receives recognition through the presence/attendance of the village *fono*. Recently, however, *matai* titles have been conferred overseas, not only by the *matai* of Salelologa to other village members, but, sometimes by *matai* from other villages. Samoans express concern that this is making a 'chop suey' of *fa'a-Samoa* and some question the legitimacy of these new *matai* holders. Most, however, say legitimacy depends on context and describe the creation of new *matai* as pragmatic and sensible.

Samoans draw upon traditional cultural principles to justify the changes they are making to their own practices. On many occasions, *matai* titles conferred overseas are given as reward for family generosity to the resident *matai*. Conferring titles expands the circle of economic and political obligations of support. These are not limited to the untitled and those in Samoa, but also to *matai* living *fafo*. The power of *i'inei* (*matai* resident in Samoa) to bestow titles provides another avenue for receiving *tautua*. The size of Samoan communities and growing number of Samoan churches *fafo* have combined to push *matai* investiture overseas. Some people argue that a *matai* title adds depth, history and status to an individual's educational achievements or his or her economic wealth. Insofar as this conservative sentiment is shared by everyone in Salelologa, it works to bond the community, for *matai* titles are intangible links which hold together the members of the group.

One of the most obvious forms of symbolic capital, a key sign of prestige and household advancement in Salelologa is modern education. Tutai, a woman in her mid-50s, has six children and with her husband, Luamanuvae Taylor, an entrepreneurial chief, owns a store at the wharf. When interviewed in September 2000, four of their children had obtained government scholarships, graduated from overseas universities and today work for the government in Apia. Tutai argues:

> I suppose people can live without doing *fa`a-Samoa* and that is because when you are economically independent you don't need the support of the `*aiga*, I guess. But in reality we have so many of our upwardly mobile Samoans both here and overseas who still participate, when in theory they don't need to. For example, a rich `*afakasi* [half-caste] or a highly educated Samoan could be the director of a department, but when he or she goes to the villages or their `*aiga* they are not readily recognised, that is, given full recognition of their education credentials or the economic wealth they might possess without a *matai* title. So many of them take up *matai* titles. It seems without a title your other attributes, like intelligence, strength, and wealth are insignificant.

The same argument is made by those overseas who have a role in the church. They say it is necessary to have a *matai* title because they need the recognition and respect that comes with it, in the process acknowledging that traditional status thus complements modern achievements. However, it also is a way for *matai* to reassert their authority in overseas contexts where the church minister's authority is becoming quite hegemonic. This illustrates how local idioms and international processes interrelate to shape the dynamics of modern Samoan chieftainship. Indigenous institutions have been assumed in development theory as barriers to modernisation, yet we see here that they have been adapted by Samoans to suit their needs.

Although Samoans think of Samoan chieftainship as timeless, it has changed to suit modern socioeconomic conditions. Since Samoa's independence in 1962, only *matai* could vote and campaign for a seat in the parliament. This means only a small fraction of the population could vote through *matai* suffrage. In the 1970s–80s, new titles that had been created for election purposes not only saw an increase in titles, but just about anybody was given a title, which resulted in what is known as *matai palota* (ballot *matai*). People saw the *matai palota* as rapidly eroding the integrity of chieftainship, which had been based upon *tautua* (service) and the selection of titleholders through consensus. The concern to preserve the integrity of *fa`a-Samoa* prompted universal adult suffrage in 1990, allowing all men and women over 21 years of age to vote but have to be *matai* to run as candidates in the country's general elections.

Among overseas Samoans, family and community provide the social basis for the occupation of urban space and symbolic resources for cultural regeneration. This is not to deny that neither the material nor symbolic conditions for the regeneration of cultural practices are stable. The explanation for the renewed interest in *matai* and the conferment of *matai* on members *fafo*, I suggest is twofold. First, many overseas Samoans have accumulated 'real' power by virtue of their economic positions relative to those in Salelologa, therefore their desirability as potential *matai* has been enhanced. It is also a sign that indigenous Samoan institutions remain paramount, as Tutai said in her interview. The prestige that a *matai* title can bring constitutes, in Bourdieu's terms, 'symbolic capital'. It adds weight to status.

The reassertion of indigenous institutions also counters the secular power of *fafo* society. Senior *matai* conferring titles make some money while at the same time promote redemptive, emotional, perhaps nostalgic, ties with Samoans *fafo*. The institution of *matai* is being used by Samoans to maximise their accumulation of wealth and enhance personal and `*aiga* status. In so doing, they are redefining yet again the concept of *tautua*. Thus, the politics of the *matai* is inextricably linked to economic and social power. The ability to influence *matai* and events is often couched in terms of tradition and seniority, while cultural meanings are often renegotiated, and none too politely.

The process of conferring *matai* titles in Samoa has also changed. In the not so distant past, gifts given during *matai* ceremonies reflected the productive capacity of a family–in the form of pigs, taro, breadfruit, yams and fine mats. Most of the gifts during *matai* ceremonial events are now given as cash. While it appears that modernity is eclipsing tradition, this issue is not so simple. When I asked some *matai* the reason for this change, they responded that it was to lighten the burden of the provision of gifts by the hosts of *saofa`i* (investiture ceremonies), this way, family members are not burdened with the task of providing all the food and doing all the cooking for these events; it is a more efficient use of time.

Others question the integrity of the *matai* system when investitures are conducted through the medium of cash gifts. While village council members can benefit, certain individuals may take advantage of the Samoan propensity for conspicuous distribution. The traditional role of the *tulafale* (orator) prescribes that they act as negotiators speaking on behalf of the *ali`i* (chief). This usually justifies their share of food or money in the redistribution process, but discretion is advisable—the *va fealoa`i* (social space) of both the host and guest, *tulafale* and *ali`i*, must be considered. Excessive demands at a *saofa`i* by some *tulafale* during a matai investiture at the village council is a clear breach of tradition

(Tuimaleali`ifano 2002). Certain individuals have overstepped the mark by demanding more money for their *lafo* (gift from the host), which some call an abuse of the system. The 'commodification' of the *matai* system can be seen in a *saofa`i* which took place in early December 2002. While I was in Samoa, an older sister of a relative of mine had received a *matai* title in Salelavalu, a village near Salelologa. A few weeks later, the relative wrote in an email (8 January 2003):

> Well the saofa`i was alright except that we hardly got any rest with the work and preparations. We just stayed at the family house. There were no fine mats or fa`aaloaloga [i.e., *sua*, exchange of gifts] since Salelavalu was only after the money, so that was like thousands of tala [Samoan dollars]. There were in fact 39 matai altogether that had saofa`i on my dad's side, it made me sad to think that it was not the real way of getting titles.

This example gives a sense of the historical and sociopolitical transformations the *matai* system or chieftainship has been through in everyday life in Samoa. People are negotiating tradition and the modernising effects of a globalising politico-cultural economy. Tradition and modernity are not simple binary opposites, however. Resourceful individuals and collective opportunism interact, producing in some ways radically changing *fa`a-Samoa*.

For Samoans *fafo*, traditional ceremonies remain important and participating in them establishes their status within the `aiga. Returning home with gifts and attending ceremonies important to Samoan culture not only enhances personal status but also achieves a certain prestige for the `aiga. Those who travel to Samoa and back to their *fafo* communities return with their cultural values reaffirmed. Extensive circulation reinvigorates ethnic Samoan identity and its presence everywhere manifests a transnational Samoan social structure.

Increased mobility in the past 20 years between `aiga in Samoa, New Zealand and America has educated families about how to travel less expensively. Life cycle and cultural events sometimes shift overseas when that provides a common ground for dispersed members to meet more quickly, easily and at less cost. These kinds of decisions emphasise the embeddedness of family and `aiga relationships and indicate a strong sense of connectivity and shared goals, irrespective of location. The transnationality of kinship structures, activities, identities and subjectivities are clearly apparent. In short, social position and identity are constructed simultaneously within local and global contexts.[2]

As Koletty (2002, 146) reports in his study of Samoan movement in Southern California, 'For Samoans, migration and circulation are not the disparate processes that such categorisation implies. They are part of the dialectic and a different conception of place.' In short, a recognition of 'all reciprocal flows irrespective of purpose or duration while still emphasizing the dialectic between the centrifugal attractions of wage employment, commercial and administrative forces and the centripetal power of village obligations, social relations and kin ties' (Chapman and Prothero 1985, 4). Today, with nearly half the population of Samoa living overseas, mobility continues to be necessary to fulfil social and economic functions that maintain status within the `aiga and affirm Samoan culture. Chapman and Prothero (1985) point out that modernisation in developing countries has reinforced these customary circuits of mobility and added new ones. Circulation has taken on greater significance because despite the distances involved, it invigorates fa`a-Samoa by linking overseas Samoan communities with each other and the homeland. Although population mobility and remittances have caused fundamental social changes in Samoa, the direction, character and nuances of those changes have been culturally determined through family connections and the relationships among `aiga.

Transactions between *I`inei* and *Fafo*

The sacred power of i`inei can be seen in the case of fa`alavelave (weddings, funerals, graduations) held fafo, at which someone coming from Samoa and bearing gifts is indispensable. The attendance of those i`inei at a wedding, funeral or graduation is a symbol of family pride and social identity. As sisters of a household now living in Auckland said, 'We had our uncles come for our weddings and one of them was the master of ceremony. He handled the `aiga, guests, visitors, and all the protocols of fa`a-Samoa. They brought a special fine mat from Samoa.' The presence of Samoan relatives bringing traditional gifts to overseas fa`alavelave is seen as adding authenticity to the occasion. The exchange of gifts symbolises the importance of genealogical links to the past. As Howard and Rensel (1997, 147) put it, discussing status and power in Rotuma, 'Without chiefs ceremonies of all kinds—births, marriages, welcomings, village and district fetes—would lose their significance, for it is the presence of chiefs that lends dignity and historical depth to such occasions.' The Rotuman case highlights a comparable understanding of the importance of ritual status for Samoan communities. It remains integral to their ethnic identity in overseas communities, while at the same time it reproduces the power of Samoa as a place.

The importance of gift exchange and remittances in the maintenance of socioeconomic and sociocultural relations has also been described by Werbner (1989) in her study of Pakistanis in Great Britain. She argues that British earnings are always converted into inalienable gifts, bringing permanent debt and indelible reciprocity to those exchanging them. While gifts and exchange are key to the creation of social networks in Britain, they are also a 'metonymic exchange of substance between South Asia and Britain' (Werbner 1989, 204). Subedi's (1993) study of remittances and exchange in two rural communities in Nepal shows similar behaviours. Exchange between places does more than reproduce social relationships and surpasses gifts of goods or money at *fa`alavelave*. Exchange carried from Samoa and members *fafo* seeking a Samoan healer and medicines to cure *ma`i* (Samoan illness) demonstrate the reproductive power of places, goods, and people.

Particular goods express notions about the places from which they come. Consumption of *i`inei* (here and local) produce is also a social statement of its spirituality and ability to sustain its inhabitants. In contrast, goods from abroad link their consumers with the economic and political force of *fafo*, the object of desire. Goods thus carry ideas about power which are exchanged between people in Salelologa and overseas. Beside the usual remittances, gifts sent by Samoans abroad tend to symbolise the essence of *fafo*: economic power, industrial production and popular Western culture. Electronic goods, videos, TV sets, DVDs, microwave, refrigerators and lawn mowers all feature in Salelologa households.

During my interviews, one *`aiga* member who had been given a lawn mower when visiting New Zealand transformed it from a personal use to an informal business, charging $20–30 Samoan tala to mow lawns in Salelologa. This demonstrates people's creativity, but such small subtle changes sometimes produce contradictory effects on the community. While the lawn mower effectively cuts the grass in less time and thereby frees young girls and boys of the *`aiga* for other responsibilities, it also means that families must find the money for this service. Furthermore, just as the European style houses have become ubiquitous, so *`aiga* members will put pressure on their children working locally or overseas to provide these kinds of goods. As home appliances have gradually found their way into Salelologa homes, so too will lawn mowers and other agricultural equipment.

Overseas relatives wish to share their wealth with those at home, because hard work and generosity are core social values by which one is evaluated. At times, the desire to provide such goods produces intra and inter-family competition that motivates heightened productivity. At other times, it sets off individualism, jealousy, and dissatisfaction. Part of the balancing act of being Samoan is the reconciliation between the implacable Euro-American demands of the individual with those of the often hegemonic and Island collective self. How can the seemingly irresistible be fused with the seemingly immovable? Indigenous Pacific Island scholars and writers such as Albert Wendt, Epeli Hau`ofa, Konai Thaman, and Sia Figiel explore and question this throughout their work. Ambivalence, the holding of two opposing views or emotions at the same time, is a way of dealing with these contradictions.[3] Ambivalence and ambiguity provide opportunities to explore the costs and benefits of moving, the decisions of what to keep and what to discard. Paradoxical as they appear, ambivalence and ambiguity are an essential part of the dynamic process of culture. In the mobility process, these countervailing views or emotions are usually resolved by appropriating them into *fa`a-Samoa,* although many people are not always aware of this.

When migrants die overseas, their bodies are flown back to Salelologa for the funeral. This further represents the continuing primacy of the *'aiga* and its material roots in the land. While I was conducting the mobility survey and related interviews, a son described how his deceased father was brought back from California in 1991 and in 1997, a deceased aunt was accompanied back by relatives for burial in Samoa. Family is still attached to its community of origin, because the *nu'u* (village) defines one's identity and status overseas. There are also instances where a parent or child is buried overseas when family members recognise that those important to a particular individual are there. The interaction between *i'inei and fafo,* specifically the importance of *fafo* and *i'inei* to the group, shows the inappropriateness of theorising village-metropolitan dichotomies in an increasingly transnational world.

Conclusion

This paper has brought a *fa'a-Samoa* perspective on transnationalism examining how social, cultural, political, and economic practices have changed over time, and the forms these transnational processes take. *Fa`a-Samoa* frames work within local idioms, which in turn feed into and influence change. Local culture is not simply acted upon by external agents, as many accounts of change in Samoa suggest, for people are dynamic, proactive, and perpetually creative. As we have seen in previous accounts, while *i'inei* has been transformed through contact with *fafo* the relationship is reciprocal. Not only is *fafo* imagined and constructed through *i'inei* idioms, but more practically, it too is transformed through the ideological, economic, and physical exchanges which take place in movement. At times, the 'periphery' (*fafo*) becomes a central source of meaning and identity, as overseas *`aiga*, Samoan churches, and *matai* councils are established. *Fafo* (overseas, abroad) has become more like the 'core' Samoa (*i'inei*) over time. Places of the 'periphery' including Auckland, Los Angeles and Sydney are increasingly becoming 'cores'. Core and periphery are therefore always in flux. Home is not only multi-local but trans-local. In population movement, *fafo* and *i'inei* have become part of the inextricably transnational character of Samoan identity.

`Aiga need population movement for economic, social and cultural development; migrants need spiritual and emotional nourishment themselves. This replenishment of the soul is fulfilled in the exchange of gifts and especially by the deliverance of delicacies from home such as *umu* package (taro, breadfruit, and palusami), *fai`ai pusi* (eel in coconut cream) *fai`ai fe`e* (octopus in coconut cream), *fagu sea* (bottle of sea cucumber) or *koko* Samoa (Samoan cocoa). Salelologa people produce the essence of *i'inei* for kin in diasporic spaces and places to consume but themselves consume modernity through the goods sent back to

them from *fafo*. Gifts exchange is thus as much about social relationships and the respective power of givers and receivers as it is about the hegemony of places.

Through negotiations made possible by population movement, `aiga* and *i`inei* have changed, become multi-local and trans-local. Households neither simply expect 'expatriates' to send remittances and receive partially symbolic gifts of taro, sea cucumber, *koko* Samoa or handicrafts in exchange; nor are these transactions purely bilateral between the island home and one or another rim country. Instead, Samoa, New Zealand, the United States and Australia are sites of transnational, triangular, and circular exchange. As Hau`ofa (1993, 11) emphasises, 'the resources of Samoans, Cook Islanders, Niueans, Tokelauans, Tuvaluans, Rotumans, I-Kiribati, Fijians, Indo-Fijians, and Tongans are no longer confined to their national boundaries. They are located wherever these people are living, permanently or otherwise.' In short, envisioning a 'world enlargement' and considering social and cultural meanings of transnationalism (Hauofa 1993). In Salelologa, multi-local families are becoming increasingly dominant. None of this dynamic is captured by the twin images of emigration and depopulation formerly theorised in the mobility literature.

References

Amin, A. 1997. Placing globalization. *Theory, Culture and Society* 14 (2): 123–37.

Baia, L. R. 1999. Rethinking transnationalism: Reconstructing national identities among Peruvian Catholics in New Jersey. *Journal of Inter-American Studies and World Affairs* 41 (14): 93–105.

Basch, L., N. Glick Schiller, and C. Szanton Blanc. 1994. *Nations unbound.* Langhorne PA: Gordon and Breach.

—. 1995. From immigrant to transmigrant: Theorizing transnational migration. *Anthropology Quarterly* 68 (1): 48–64.

Buttimer, A. 1980. Home, reach and sense of place. In *The human experience of space and place*, ed. A. Buttimer and D. Seamon, 166–87. New York: St Martins Press.

Chapman, M. and R. M. Prothero (eds). 1985. *Circulation in population movement: Substance and concepts from the Melanesian case.* London: Routledge and Kegan Paul

Faist, T. 2000. Transnationalization in international migration: Implications for the study of citizenship and culture. *Ethnic and Racial Studies* 23 (2): 189–222.

Featherstone, M. (ed.) 1990. *Global culture: Nationalism, globalization, and modernity.* Newbury Park: Sage Publications.

Franco, R. 1985. *Samoan perceptions of work: Moving up and moving around*. PhD thesis, University of Hawai'i.

Freeman, D. 1984. *Margaret Mead and Samoa: The making and unmaking of an anthropological myth*. Canberra: Australian National University Press.

Gardner, K. 1995. *Global migrants, local lives: Migration and transformations in rural Bangladesh*. London: Oxford University Press.

Georges, E. 1990. *The making of a transnational community: Immigration, development, and cultural change in the Dominican Republic*. New York: Columbia University Press.

Grasmuck, S. and P. Pessar. 1991. *Between two islands: Dominican international migration*. Los Angeles: University of California Press.

Hau`ofa, E. 1993. Our sea of islands. In *A new Oceania: Rediscovering our sea of islands*, ed. E. Waddell, V. Naidu and E. Hau'ofa, 2–16. Suva: School of Social and Economic Development, University of the South Pacific.

Holmes, L. 1957. Ta'u: Stability and change in a Samoan village. *Journal of the Polynesian Society* 66: 301–38.

Howard, A. and J. Rensel. 1997. Ritual status and power politics in modern Rotuma. In *Chiefs today: Traditional Pacific leadership and the postcolonial state*, ed. G. White and L. Lindstrom, 120–49. Stanford: Stanford University Press.

Koletty, S. 2002. The Samoan archipelago in urban America. In *Geographical identities of ethnic America: Race, space, and place*, ed. K. Berry and M. Henderson, 130–48. Reno: University of Nevada Press.

Lee, H. 2003. *Tongans overseas: Between two shores*. Honolulu: University of Hawai'i Press.

Levitt, P. 1999. Social remittances: A local level, migration-driven form of cultural diffusion. *International Migration Review* 32 (124): 926–49.

——. 2001. *Transnational villagers*. Berkeley: University of California Press.

Lilomaiava-Doktor, S. 2009. Beyond 'migration': Samoan population movement (*malaga*) and the geography of social space (*vā*). *The Contemporary Pacific* 21(1): 1-32.

Liu, D. 1991. *Politics of identity in Western Samoa*. PhD diss., University of Hawai'i.

Maiava, S. 2001. *A clash of paradigms: Intervention, response and development in the South Pacific*. Burlington: Ashgate.

Margolis, M. 1995. Transnationalism and popular culture: The case of Brazilian immigrants in the United States. *Journal of Popular Culture* 29 (1): 29–42.

Meleisea, M. 1987. *The making of modern Samoa*. Suva: Institute of Pacific Studies, University of the South Pacific.

Mitchell, K. 1997. Transnational discourse: Bringing geography back in. *Antipode* 29 (2): 101–14.

O'Meara, T. 1990. *Samoan planters: Tradition and economic development in Polynesia*. Holt, Rinehart and Winston.

Pessar, P. 1997. *Caribbean circuits: New directions in the study of Caribbean migration*. New York: Center for Migration Studies.

Small, C. A. 1997. *Voyages: From Tongan villages to American suburbs*. Ithaca: Cornell University Press.

Smith, M. and L. E. Guarnizo (eds). 1998. *Transnationalism from below*. New Brunswick, New Jersey: Transaction Publishers.

Subedi, B. P. 1993. *Continuity and change in population movement: From inside a rural Nepali community*. PhD thesis. Department of Geography, University of Hawaii.

Tuimaleali`ifano, M. 2002. The root of modern corruption in Samoa. Paper presented at the Annual Meeting of Association of Social Anthropology in Oceania, Auckland, February.

Va`a, L. F. 2001. *Saili Matagi: Samoan migrants in Australia*. Suva: Institute of Pacific Studies, University of the South Pacific and Apia: Iunivesite Aoao o Samoa.

Va`ai, S. 1998. *Samoa Faamatai and the rule of law*. Apia: National University of Samoa Press.

Vertovec, S. 1999. Conceiving and researching transnationalism. *Ethnic and Racial Studies*, 22 (2): 447–62.

Wallerstein, I. 1990. Societal development, or development of the world system? In *Globalization, knowledge, and society*, ed. M. Albrow and E. King, 157–71. Newbury: Sage Publications.

Werbner, P. 1989. *The migration process: Capital, gifts and offerings among British Pakistanis*. Explorations in Anthropology Series, Oxford: Berg.

Young, R. 1998. *Pathways as metaphors of movement: A study of place, mobility and embodiment in Fiji*. PhD thesis, Victoria University of Wellington, NZ.

ENDNOTES

[1] Participant observation and interviews both at 'home' and 'reach' were done to understand these issues. Funding for this research was provided by the American Association of University Women, Honolulu and University of Hawaii Globalization Research Center.

[2] This is the 'transnational space' (Small 1997, 193), where personal and social identities are simultaneously constructed in a transnational social field by those in *fafo* and those *i`inei*.

[3] Helen Lee (2003) in her study of identity construction among diasporic Tongans shows similar attitudes with regard to *anga fakatonga* (the Tongan way).

4. Kinship and Transnationalism

Cluny Macpherson and La'avasa Macpherson

Introduction

Kinship frames Samoan social organisation and Samoan transnationalism. It defines the matrix within which people, capital, ideas and technologies move between the nodes of 'transnational Samoa'. This matrix of relationships was the foundation of transnational Samoa: it provided the potential for a transnational Samoa, and the practices gave it form. Commitment to kin, expressed in visits and participation in ceremonials, gifts and exchanges, creates, maintains and reflects an active transnationalism. Without these regular and affirming exchanges there is no active transnationalism.

If kinship is, in effect, the foundation of transnational Samoa, then anything that transforms the character of kinship has the potential to reconfigure Samoan transnationalism. Anything that weakens kinship bonds between origin and overseas communities, which are the 'nodes' of transnational Samoa, has the potential to undermine it. Conversely, anything that strengthens those bonds ensures the survival of an active Samoan transnationalism. Therefore, any attempt to explain the condition of Samoan transnationalism must focus first on the conditions of kinship and the factors affecting it in any given node. This chapter argues that commitment to kinship is shifting in Samoan migrant enclaves as kin relationships are modified to meet the changing needs and circumstances of the migrants and their descendants (Macpherson and Macpherson 1999). These changes are transforming Samoan transnationalism.

This chapter outlines the role that kinship played in the establishment and maintenance of transnational Samoa, and the ways in which the transformation of kinship within migrant enclaves in New Zealand is now affecting the contours of Samoan transnationalism. First, we examine the connections between kinship and social organisation which evolved on small islands and their transformation in urban, industrial environments. Using material from a longitudinal study, we outline the form and significance of kin-based activity among new Samoan migrants in New Zealand in the 1950s. Then, we trace the expansion of kin-based activity in the 1950s and 1960s, its elaboration in the 1970s and early 1980s, and its contraction from the mid–1980s. We identify factors that have produced these shifts and conclude that the latest changes will weaken the commitment to kinship and may have profound consequences for transnational Samoa which it underpins.

Kinship in Samoan Society

Samoan society evolved largely uninterrupted in the small, isolated but well-endowed group of islands for 3,500 years until the late 18th century. The central feature of Samoan social organisation was kinship (Kramer 1994). Society consisted of clusters of localised, co-resident kin corporations or *āiga*. Rights over land and sea were vested in the various, usually related, *āiga* which lived in villages in an area (Gilson 1963). A chief, or *matai*, selected by senior members of the *āiga,* held the corporation's chiefly title and managed its resources on behalf and for the benefit of its members. Effective *matai* used the resources of their *āiga* to enhance its material and socio-political wealth; ineffective *matai* squandered *āiga* resources. At any time, the size and power of *āiga* varied according to the quality of leadership: well-led *āiga* attracted members and poorly-led ones tended to lose them (Macpherson 1997). Over time, certain *āiga* consolidated gains and came to control more land and to enjoy more permanent social prestige and political influence. This led to more or less fixed relations between *āiga* of villages and districts, and to the emergence of relatively stable local polities.[1]

Samoans had links with the *āiga* of four grandparents. Of these, the most significant were links with the *āiga* with which they resided at a given time and which became their 'strong side' or *itu malosi*. For individuals, *āiga* membership established social location and significance, conferred rights to use agricultural land and a house site, and to protection by the *āiga*. These rights were offset by a number of parallel obligations, including the requirement to serve (*tautua*) one's *matai,* to protect the land and to defend the honour of the *āiga*. The rewards for service were a degree of psychological and material security, and, for males at least, the prospect of eventual leadership and power.[2]

Kinship in Action

Extended kin groups constituted the matrix within which goods and services were continuously exchanged in more or less public transactions. The least public involved the informal day-to-day exchange among relatives of goods such as money and food, services such as labour and advice, and equipment such as canoes and tools. The more public transactions involved the mobilisation of kin and resources in larger, formalised exchanges associated with commemoration of rites of passage, and physical and sociopolitical capital creation. Those who derived a livelihood from the use of the kin group's resources were bound to participate in both forms of activity. Participation was, in each case, underpinned by two related beliefs: that kinship confers upon one the obligation to give to kin who make legitimate requests, and the right to expect that at some time in the future the goods and services given to others will be returned. Both forms of exchange reproduce and reaffirm kinship and kin-groups.

Exchanges are 'sites' where some discharge existing 'debts', and others incur new 'debts' to their kin. On a given occasion, persons A, X and Y may discharge existing debts to person B by contributing to a wedding sponsored by B. On that same occasion, B may incur new debts to contributors D, E and F who also contribute, but who are under no obligation to participate and have no pre-existing debt to settle. The exchange process generates a residual indebtedness that binds kin over time. At any time, residual indebtedness within an *āiga* bound members to one another.

In other respects, the two forms of exchange have quite different outcomes for the reproduction and reaffirmation of kinship. Informal exchanges remind individuals of their dependence on kin for essential equipment, goods and services. Larger, formal mobilisations of kin group resources reaffirm the importance of cooperation among larger groups of kin, and of the sociopolitical benefits of active membership in a larger corporate entity. On these occasions, groups publicly demonstrate their ability to cooperate, to mobilise resources, and their right to public attention and respect from those both inside and outside of the *āiga*.

The isolation in which this form of social organisation evolved ended with the arrival of Europeans (Gilson 1970). But, despite the appearance of change, when Western Samoa won independence in 1962 after 130 years of exposure to European society, fundamental elements of Samoan social organisation remained largely intact. A monotheistic religion had replaced a polytheistic one and had been co-opted by Samoan society to bolster its traditions. A national polity, based on a modified Westminster system, had been created but was based on and existed alongside traditional polities, which continued to provide local government and to enjoy considerable autonomy. The leaders of the new state[3] were chosen on the basis of traditional social status and the new parliament comprised *matai*[4] elected by *matai* suffrage. 'New' social institutions, such as women's committees, existed alongside 'traditional' women's organisations within villages and promoted new initiatives,[5] but did so with the consent and support of traditional village polities. Village mayors, *pulenu'u,* who were appointed by government to form a link between traditional polities and the national government, existed with the support of villages and remained under their control (Meleisea 1987).

Following independence, the non-monetised, subsistence economy was replaced by a monetised, mixed subsistence and cash cropping one that produced commodities for both local and international markets. However, this had occurred without significant transformation of either the land tenure system or the lineage mode of production. Most Samoans continued to live on and farm *āiga* land under the authority of *matai* and to contribute labour and part of their production as a form of rent to the *matai*, who used it on behalf of the *āiga* to enhance its socio-political status. As a consequence, kinship remained a fundamental principle of social and economic organisation in independent Samoa, albeit one changed by contact with capitalism (Macpherson and Macpherson 1999, 33). It would become the vehicle for the transnationalisation of Samoan society.

After independence, forces for rapid social change emerged both inside and outside Western Samoa.[6] The most powerful force was developing beyond Samoa. Throughout the 1950s, New Zealand governments promoted industrialisation to diversify the country's economy. Labour shortages, a consequence of low pre-war population growth rates and losses in WWII, hindered the process, so to offset these, governments promoted immigration from Europe and the Pacific (Ongley 1991; 1996). People were drawn in increasing numbers from rural, semi-subsistence, kin-based villages in Samoa, the Cook Islands, Niue and the Tokelau Islands, to wage-work in socially and ethnically heterogeneous, urban industrial centres. Kinship became both the motive and the vehicle for transnationalisation of these societies.

Foundations of Migrant Samoan Kinship

It is difficult to imagine circumstances more likely to undermine a system of extended kinship based on common ownership of resources that had evolved in a small, rural village-based society. Yet, early studies of the migrants showed that kinship remained a central feature of migrant community organisation (Macpherson 1974; Pitt and Macpherson 1974). Kinship played a central role in Samoan transnationalism: chain migration, in which early migrants opened the way for later migrants from their families, produced Samoan enclaves in New Zealand and connected the nodes of transnational Samoan society. This raises the question of why extended kinship remained significant in the new environment.

Residential and occupational concentrations in the enclaves provided the critical masses of migrants in which central elements of a Samoan world-view and life-style were more likely to survive. Samoans became concentrated in a restricted range of occupations and in low-income residential areas in and around cities where economic growth and diversification was occurring (Ongley 1991; 1996). Concentration was also fostered by racism on the part of some 'gatekeepers' in the private housing market, concentrations of government-owned rental housing and by the tendency to cluster new, owner-occupied housing in tracts around city fringes.

New Zealand's immigration policy favoured less 'expensive', better 'educated', younger, single migrants. Families in Samoa also encouraged younger, single people who had demonstrated commitment to service (*tautua*) to their kin group to migrate in the belief that they would continue to acknowledge their membership of and obligations to their *āiga*, and would remit money and goods

(Pitt and Macpherson 1974). Migrants who met the costs of sponsoring the migration of kin did so in order to bring others who would share the costs of supporting the non-migrant *āiga* and, therefore, also had good reason for identifying people committed to Samoan values and practices.

To ensure that new migrants remained committed to these, most were sent to live, at least initially, in households with relatives who had demonstrated continuing commitment to *āiga*. Many of these people were integrated into Samoan migrant communities and encouraged new migrants to associate with other Samoans (Pitt and Macpherson 1974). Pressure from household-heads and migrant peers combined to ensure that the new arrivals remained committed to *tautua* to family in the island (Macpherson 2002). The consequence was the rapid growth of socially 'traditional' Samoan populations in New Zealand cities in the 1960s (Pitt and Macpherson 1974).

Each of these elements ensured that kinship remained important and that most migrants remained connected to the villages and families from which they had migrated. This connectedness was reflected in the flow of people, ideas, money and resources between the origin and enclave communities which became transnational Samoa.

Migrant Kinship: The Early Period

In the early phase of Samoan settlement, kinship remained an important feature of migrant social organisation. Within enclaves, related individuals and households exchanged goods and services informally in the same ways as they had in Samoa. This pattern was a consequence of choice and familiarity, and of a lack of familiarity with the dominant society's organisation and institutions. Kinship remained a matrix within which goods, services and information were routinely exchanged. Daily, informal exchanges among migrant kin had much the same consequences as they had in Samoa: they reproduced dependence on kin, and a preference for dealing with relatives in a range of matters (Macpherson 1974).

In this early period, however, the second role of kin groups, the mobilisation of greater human and physical resources to commemorate life crises, or *fa'alavelave*, was more difficult to reproduce. Generally, there were too few members of *āiga* present able to fund the celebrations in ways considered appropriate. Young migrants were acutely aware of their lack of the cultural knowledge required to manage such events and of the absence of older people with the necessary competence. Lack of familiarity with air travel discouraged many older people, who were familiar with ceremonial and protocol, from travelling to New Zealand. Fine mats, or *'ie toga*, a central element of these ceremonies, were not readily available in New Zealand. Finally, the absence of appropriate Samoan-owned or controlled venues for the celebration of such events and dominant group's reluctance to hire facilities to unknown migrants, made finding places in which to celebrate life crises difficult (Macpherson 1974).

So, when migrant life crises occurred throughout the 1950s and early 1960s, celebrations were transferred to Samoa where the critical mass of most *āiga* remained and where the necessary personnel, expertise, venues and fine mats were readily available. There, they were performed by chiefs and elders of the *āiga* according to traditional protocols. Parties of kin moved between New Zealand and Samoa to ensure that members' achievements were appropriately commemorated and that the kin group demonstrated its ability to mobilise and its claim to recognition. These movements were central to the continuing connection between nodes of kin groups and to transnational Samoa.

In sum, expatriate *āiga* continued to exchange goods, services and information informally but were unable to carry out other more formal activities so important to the reproduction of commitment to kin groups: the periodic, public demonstration of a group's power and claims to recognition. The co-dependence of 'home' and 'migrant' nodes also necessitated the connections which underpinned emerging transnationalism. But this was about to change.

The Elaboration of Migrant Kinship

Between the mid–1960s and the mid–1980s, the New Zealand economy and the country's Samoan population both grew rapidly. Kinship was changing. Whereas formerly it had been primarily a matrix within which goods, information and services were exchanged informally and routinely, it was becoming the basis for the organisation of larger, more complex traditional events and for the celebration of new events. Several factors lay behind this transformation.

First, migrants who attended ceremonies in Samoa began to acquire the necessary cultural knowledge, skills and confidence to organise and manage them. Those returning from events in Samoa brought with them the fine mats given in recognition of their service to their families, which created a growing supply of a crucial element of the ceremonies.[7] Second, as a consequence of continuing migration, expatriate *āiga* were growing and the critical masses necessary to fund and manage major celebrations were developing in New Zealand. These later migrants included chiefs[8] with the necessary experience to manage life crises and migrants with the knowledge and desire to sponsor the events. Third, increasing familiarity with air travel led more older people to travel to events in New Zealand. Indeed, many older Samoans visited expatriate children and grandchildren during the summer and returned to Samoa at the onset of winter. Their presence meant more events could be held in New Zealand. Finally, Samoan church building, which began in the late 1960s and continues in the present, resulted in the creation of Samoan-owned and controlled buildings in centres of Samoan population concentration and provided venues for Samoan activities.

This combination of factors transformed the organisation of migrant kinship over the next two decades.

The same principles were used to encourage expatriate members to participate in these events as in Samoa. These included appeals to their sense of pride in and responsibility to their *āiga*, and pointing to the indirect benefits of increasing the group's sociopolitical status in both New Zealand and Samoa. The same strategies were used to plan and manage the events. Leaders of the sub-lineages established the resource requirements of gatherings. The *āiga* was, typically, divided into traditional sub-sections, which were assigned responsibility for labour and resources. Leaders of each sub-section then became responsible for mobilising its resources for the occasion.

Extended kinship provided an ideal vehicle for organising and funding events that were beyond the capacity of individual households. Participation, now effectively voluntary,[9] was underpinned by the same principles as it had been in Samoa: kinship conferred on one the obligation to give to kin who made legitimate requests and the right to expect that at some future time the goods and services given to kin would be returned. It also maintained a level of residual indebtedness within an *āiga* which bound members to one another over time.

The use of kin-based organisation to replicate these events had unanticipated social consequences. It periodically reaffirmed the significance and potential benefits of membership of extended kin groups. Participation in the events renewed bonds between *āiga* members who did not routinely meet and extended individuals' social networks. The celebration of these events, typically reserved for those with records of unstinting service to the *āiga*, reminded members of the benefits of active participation in its affairs. Effectively-managed events won kin groups sociopolitical prestige within the migrant community and in Samoa, and all benefited by association. Indeed, for the reproduction of extended kinship and kin-based social organisation, the events' latent functions were as important as their manifest ones.

In this period, these events were controlled by *matai* who followed protocols with which they were familiar and in both scale and form the events were largely replications of such events in Samoa. The complementary requirements of these events, cultural competences from the home community and labour and resources from the migrant community, underpinned transnationalism. But several factors were about to change this forever.

The Emergence of 'Ceremonial Inflation'

Continuous chain migration had made expatriate *āiga* larger and wealthier. Untitled migrants, who had by now become established, sought and claimed leadership roles within the enclave. They now had more disposable income and also had access, in many cases, to the income of their New Zealand-born children with which to back their claims. New migrants, who were generally firmly committed to a Samoan world-view and lifestyle, were also willing contributors to and participants in these events. This process was intensified because migration had transformed traditional limits on families' access to resources. Families which in Samoa had lesser titles and limited numbers of people and resources, were no longer constrained by these facts. Migrant families' resources were limited only by the numbers of wage-earners and the leaders' ability to mobilise their support. This provided both opportunity and incentive for some families to seek upward mobility by challenging larger, better-established ones in ways that would not have been possible in Samoa.

Perhaps the most significant factor, however, was the re-emergence of the competitive dynamic in migrant Samoan society. This was in large part a consequence of the growing number of *matai* whose role was to use resources to enhance a kin-group's sociopolitical status and of a growing pool of resources with which to work. As kin-groups sought to establish their claim to status and recognition in the migrant enclave through demonstrations of collective strength and ability to mobilise resources, a form of 'ceremonial inflation' occurred. This inflation manifested itself in two ways: a growth in the scale of these formal events and the creation of new ones.

The Elaboration of Traditional Ceremonies

Weddings, arguably the most frequent of the 'traditional' celebrations,[10] serve as a useful illustration of the way in which these new dynamics transformed these events. Over 20 years, typical weddings became larger and more expensive. Guest lists grew from around 50 to 500 people. Wedding photos during the period reflect the growth of bridal parties from four to around 16. Small, family-catered celebrations held in church halls became large, commercially-catered events held first in reception lounges, then medium-priced hotels and finally, in the early 1980s, in the banquet halls of the city's most expensive hotels.

When there were no more exclusive venues to 'conquer', competition focused on more expensive menus, larger bridal parties, booking the most expensive Samoan bands and the elaboration of formal Samoan exchanges that went alongside the wedding. The role of kin moved from sewing, cooking and serving to the raising of money to purchase specialist services such as bridal gown making, limousine hire and videography of the event. Alongside the wedding formalities, were another set of 'traditional' activities based on the exchanges between the bride's and groom's families which provided further scope for elaboration.

New factors increased the size and social complexity of these events. In Samoa, guests and *matai* were typically from either the bride's or the groom's families and well-known to all involved, which meant that the necessary protocols could be planned with some confidence. In New Zealand, guests included workmates, fellow church-goers and unrelated friends, and it became increasingly difficult to plan for these. The uncertainty raised the possibility of denying unexpected guests due deference, and forced sponsoring families to raise more money to cover these possibilities to avoid appearing ignorant of Samoan etiquette.

As guest lists grew, so did the number of *matai* who attended the weddings in an 'unofficial' capacity. Each of these chiefs could claim the right to speak and could reasonably expect a gift for having contributed prestige to the event. Failure to provide appropriately generous gifts for all who claimed them left a family with a reputation for meanness or, worse still, for attempting to stage something for which they lacked the knowledge and resources. Families were forced to estimate how many might attend and to provide for the upper estimate or risk public embarrassment. There were not only more *matai*, but also more complex relations between those present, as social networks extended to include the increasing numbers of non-Samoans invited to weddings. The increasing number of European (*Papalagi*) guests attending raised questions of how they were to be integrated into ceremonial sequences and their presence acknowledged. Those controlling the events needed ever more skill to ensure that all who were entitled to either social deference or gifts were identified and acknowledged publicly.

The formal exchanges of gifts, which occurred between the bride's and groom's families at the conclusion of the ceremonies, also became more complex and more expensive. As the bride's and groom's families competed to acknowledge the importance of the other by conspicuous demonstrations of their own wealth, pressure for ever-more formal and more generous gifts grew. The numbers of fine mats, or *'ie toga*, given by women's families at large weddings, grew from around 20 to over 2,000. The value of gifts of goods (*oloa*), usually food and money, given by grooms' families to brides' families also grew dramatically, as did the formality surrounding the exchanges.

Finally, gifts received by the representatives of the bride's and groom's *āiga* on these occasions had then to be redistributed among members of their *āiga* who had contributed to the wedding, as acknowledgment of their part in the proceedings. As the number of sub-lineages contributing grew, so too did the political complexity of redistribution. An un-diplomatic redistribution would mean that the family would have considerable difficulty securing support later from those whom they offended.

But despite the risks inherent in poor 'performances' on these occasions, *āiga* continued to mount larger, more complex weddings because the sociopolitical rewards of good performances were high. The same could be said of the growth of new kin-sponsored occasions which emerged in New Zealand over the period, and carried the same sociopolitical possibilities and risks.

The Creation of New Ceremonies

Graduation ceremonies, which began to occur in the 1960s and 1970s as Samoans started to graduate from New Zealand universities, illustrate this process. Graduation was of great significance and families sought to commemorate members' academic successes publicly, but because the only tertiary institutions in Samoa were theological colleges and training colleges which did not award degrees, there was no established protocol.

Early graduation ceremonies were small, informal and relatively unstructured events, held usually in homes or church halls, in which families and friends gathered, shared a meal, held a brief service of thanksgiving and made speeches in which graduates were commended for their efforts and thanked for bringing honour to the family, and younger members of the family were encouraged to emulate them. These were usually reserved for the celebration of university graduations.

But as *matai* and *āiga* sought new sites in which to demonstrate their growing human and material resources, graduations presented an opportunity to extend and formalise the ceremony.[11] Families started to invite guests whom they wanted, ostensibly,[12] to thank for contributions to graduates' success and the 'top table' came to include ministers of religion, Sunday School teachers, music teachers, university faculty, sports coaches, colleagues, members of parliament and so on. They too were increasingly invited to speak on the graduates' achievements and potential, and to congratulate the graduates and their families. In many cases, these speakers were given gifts, often fine mats and food, in recognition of their contributions both to the graduate's success and to the dignity of the celebration.

Increasing numbers of Samoan graduates from an ever-wider range of tertiary institutions and courses provided an increasing number of opportunities for the evolution and refinement of a protocol of sorts. Over time, an extended format started to emerge in which thanksgiving services were followed by formal meals, speeches by graduates and representatives from both sides of the graduate's family, dances, formal photographs and gift-giving. As with weddings, a competitive element led to pressure for larger, more elaborate and more expensive graduation ceremonies.

The Limits to Growth

By the mid–1980s, limits to expansion and elaboration were becoming apparent. The time, energy and resources required to meet the obligations of an expanding and increasingly active transnational kin group began to exceed the resources available to its overseas members. Servicing the growing demands of the kin group in different nodes was placing social and financial pressure on migrant members, on whom the burden fell most heavily. Some pressures were the consequence of expansion itself; others were the products of demographic and cultural factors, while still others were the result of a general economic contraction of the New Zealand economy. Each of these factors is treated separately here for analytical purposes.

As kin-sponsored events became larger, and the numbers of contributing relatives increased, so did the number and size of debts incurred on those occasions by those who sought to mobilise *āiga*. A new category of debts was created when friends and workmates from outside the *āiga* contributed to the events, generating still more debts which honour demanded be satisfied. Migrants encountered real problems as they attempted to repay existing social debts by contributing to more frequent and expensive ceremonies, sponsored by those to whom they were indebted. There was simply not enough time or resources to settle escalating debts within the migrant enclave, before even contemplating meeting kinship obligations in other nodes. Yet expectations, fuelled often by the mistaken impression that migrants were wealthier than they were, continued to grow. For a time, individuals borrowed from finance companies and took larger or more expensive home mortgages in order to meet short-term obligations. These practices created more serious longer-term problems by replacing existing debts, which honour demanded be repaid, with more expensive ones which the law demanded be repaid.

The situation of migrants was exacerbated by the contraction of the national economy between 1984 and the early 1990s (O'Brien and Wilkes 1993; Roper 1993). Heavy job losses occurred in industries in which Samoans had become concentrated (Statistics New Zealand 1995), as tariff protections were removed and companies were forced to close or to move offshore (Ongley 1991; 1996). This produced increases in Samoan unemployment rates from historical levels of less than one per cent in the 1960s and early 1970s to 22 per cent for men and 21 per cent for women by 1991. Significantly, long term unemployment increased from 28 per cent in 1988 to 54 per cent in 1995 (Statistics New Zealand 1997: 346). This was accompanied by a decrease in full-time and an increase in part-time employment (Krishnan, Schoeffel and Warren 1994).

The situation of migrants was made worse by the early 1990s by four factors. First, deregulation of the labour market and restructuring of labour relations led to the loss of union protection for many workers[13] and to falls in real wages (Macpherson 1992; Statistics New Zealand 1997: 356–7). Second, the reduction of welfare benefit levels, on which Samoans were becoming increasingly dependent, placed further downward pressure on incomes. (Macpherson 1992). Third, the institution of a range of 'user pays' charges, only partly offset by reductions in direct taxation, placed further pressure on Samoan families' discretionary income. Finally, the numbers of children born to early migrants who were starting to graduate, marry and have children; the numbers of migrants' parents becoming ill and dying in the islands; and the numbers of migrants leaving the work force were all increasing. Along with the increase in the actual numbers of those people came an increase in the number of postponed demands on migrant income and time.

Migrants found it increasingly difficult to meet the postponed debts from declining incomes and find the time required to meet the costs of appropriate demonstrations of solidarity. The requirement that people take and present gifts in person required considerable amounts of time and expense in travel. In a period when conditions of work were tightening and the labour market was contracting, the real costs of time off work were becoming higher.

These factors produced a situation in which the numbers of debts being incurred by mobilisation of the extended kin group were increasing rapidly just as resources available to settle these were contracting very quickly. Failure to meet due debts led to embarrassment, *ma*, and humiliation, *masiasi*, and made people increasingly reluctant to incur debts which they would be unable to repay, for, as Samoans declare somewhat starkly, *ua sili le oti i lo le masiasi*, death is preferable to humiliation. This growing pressure was to have significant impacts on both kinship and the transnationalism which it underpinned.

Kinship and Transnationalism

More migrants began reviewing the costs and benefits of various forms of *āiga* participation as their circumstances changed and they were forced to choose between meeting the respective needs of their immediate and extended families and churches in both New Zealand and Samoa.[14] They became cautious about mobilising their extended *āiga* and incurring new debts when this prevented them from meeting the steadily increasing needs of their immediate families. Some families limited the range of people whom they would support in order to avoid the costs associated with support for all who were recognised as kin. Other families set limits on the level of their support for people on the basis of their relationships in an attempt to limit outgoings of time and money on ceremonial events. Some congregations, concerned about the escalation of ceremonial costs, acted in concert to standardise contributions to various events in order to eliminate competition and control costs within the parish.[15]

More significant for Samoan transnationalism was the re-evaluation of the costs and benefits of supporting the expanding aspirations of home communities. Migrants found themselves under increasing pressure from parents and siblings to support a wave of new and often expensive building projects, rites of passage and political ambitions in the 'home' community. Some were simply unable to afford these and even those who could were not always willing to do so. Increasingly, migrants sought to manage their obligations to these projects at home. One compromise, which seems to be increasing popular, fundamentally altered the character of transnational linkages. It involved a de facto division of responsibility: migrants performed the obligations of kinship in the expatriate enclaves, while non-migrants attended to the obligations of kinship in the village. This arrangement worked well because those in each node were aware of the context and best placed to respond more quickly to demands, but it reduced the numbers of 'transactions' between expatriate and village nodes of kin groups.

Even if this crisis had not occurred, other factors might have constrained the elaboration of kin-based activity in the migrant community. Increasing levels of intermarriage, particularly with more individualistic Europeans, created limits to participation. With approximately one-in-three Samoans marrying non-Samoans, increasing numbers of people found themselves at odds with non-Samoan spouses over the value of supporting extended family. While Samoan spouses may wish to contribute to events within their extended families, European spouses, for a variety of reasons, frequently do not. This has had more serious consequences in some households than in others, notably those in which only one spouse is employed and incomes are limited. This has resulted in some cases in a total 'ban' on contributions of time and money, and in others a limit to the level of participation. Where the latter has occurred, some Samoan spouses have decided that it is better not to attend at all, than to attend and make a contribution smaller than might be considered appropriate.

The growth of support for new religious denominations such as the Seventh Day Adventist Church and the Church of Jesus Christ of Latter Day Saints within the migrant enclave may be both a cause and a consequence of the decline in ceremonial events. Adherents of these denominations are discouraged from sponsoring large-scale kin-based events and encouraged instead to focus their energy and resources on immediate family and church. Thus one finds, increasingly, apologetic riders to death notices advising readers that Samoan customs will not be observed on these occasions.[16] At the same time, this practice may be encouraging people to join these denominations because membership provides a convenient and religiously sanctioned basis for limiting engagement and liability.

More significant for Samoan transnationalism is the declining commitment to *āiga* among overseas-born Samoans. New Zealand-born Samoans, raised in very different circumstances, often view kinship obligations differently from their parents. This is not to suggest that they have withdrawn support for these kin-based events. Anae's work on New Zealand-born Samoans show that many remain actively engaged in the whole range of activities (Anae 1997; 1998; 2001), but there is evidence that a significant group are choosing a lower level of engagement than their parents (Macpherson 1984), sometimes with the encouragement of their parents (Macpherson 1991).

The inter-generational difference stems from social values stressed in formal education; higher levels of formal education and greater economic and job security; changing composition of social networks and reference groups; high levels of intermarriage; changing patterns of religious affiliation; the emergence of new forms of ethnic identity; and critical reflection on the costs and benefits of participation in the full range of extended kin-based activities in both 'enclave' and 'island' (Macpherson 2002).

While many New Zealand-born Samoans continue to participate in extended kin group activities they do so at the request of and out of a sense of responsibility to their parents (Anae 1998). Their participation is in many cases indirect, either because of lack of language competence and familiarity with ceremonial forms, or because demands of work prevent or discourage their direct involvement. Whether their participation will continue after their parents' death is a matter for conjecture. These people, however, continue to value and to exchange information and services, and to spend leisure time with family in New Zealand. However, they do this voluntarily and typically within smaller circles of kin than their parents felt compelled to recognise, and do so on the basis of personal friendship rather than a sense of obligation (Macpherson and Macpherson 1999).

While New Zealand-born Samoans typically maintain personal connections with their *āiga* in the enclave, many have had little to do with their relations in Samoa. They report lower levels of commitment to *āiga* whom, in many cases, they have not met, and to villages in which they have neither lived nor visited. Even those who report some general commitment to relatives in the island, tend to rank this behind their commitments to their *āiga* in the enclave and recognise the latter only when asked to do so by parents. Many find that increasing difficulty in communicating in Samoan and diverging experiences and aspirations create increasing social distance between them and their Samoan *āiga*. If this process continues, there will be less contact and fewer transactions between island-based and expatriate kin, which in turn will have significant effects for the character of transnational Samoa.

Conclusion

At the heart of Samoan transnationalism is kinship or *āiga* which generates the matrix of relationships that extend across national boundaries and form the conduits along which cash, goods and ideas flow. Extended kinship is alive and well in Samoa because it remains crucial to access to land and marine resources, chiefly titles and socio-political status. However, an active and ongoing transnationalism requires an active commitment on the part of kin living abroad to the practices which give transnationalism form.

In expatriate Samoan communities in New Zealand, social and economic factors have reduced the numbers, scale and complexity of occasions for which the extended family is mobilised within the enclave. This in turn has attenuated the competitive pressures that drove social inflation during the 1970s and early 1980s. As economic times got harder for the less-skilled through the late '80s and '90s, the primary role of the *āiga*—a social matrix within which informal exchanges of goods and services occurs, providing some protection from harsh realities of life on the edge of a volatile economy—again became increasingly important. In this respect the role of *āiga* among migrants can be said to have almost turned full circle in the last 35 years.

The emergence of increasingly organised Samoan communities in overseas nodes, with comprehensive ranges of social activity, may localise the focus of much kin exchange and mobilisation within these increasingly autonomous nodes. The growing influence of people born and raised in these nodes may lead to declining support for activities in 'home' communities to which their ties are increasingly attenuated. The declining density of direct relations and number of transactions between nodes may undermine the foundations of transnational Samoa. The recently increased migration flows from Samoa (Bedford, 2007) may renew transnational ties and slow the decline, but are unlikely to reverse the declining number and strength of linkages between 'overseas' and 'home' nodes over the longer term.

These shifts in *āiga* organisation in the enclave may, in turn, influence the ways in which kinship is organised in Samoa for, as noted at the outset, migrant enclaves do not constitute discrete, distant communities but rather sites in which modification and experimentation are legitimated by the necessity of finding Samoan solutions to new social, economic and political realities. Those modifications that seem to meet new needs can find their way back into Samoan 'traditional' forms, and in the social space between these two settlements a meta-culture emerges which is neither a 'migrant' nor a 'traditional' culture but a contemporary Samoan one.

References

Anae, M. 1997. Towards a New Zealand-born Samoan identity: Some reflections on 'labels'. *Pacific Health Dialog,* 4 (2): 128–37.

—. 1998. *Fofoa i vaoese: Identity journeys of New Zealand-born Samoans.* PhD Thesis, University of Auckland, NZ.

—. 2001. The new 'Vikings of the Sunrise': New Zealand-borns in the information age. In *Tangata o te Moana nui: The evolving identities of Pacific peoples in Aotearoa/New Zealand,* ed. C. Macpherson, P. Spoonley, and M. Anae, 101–21. Palmerston North: Dunmore Press.

Bedford, R. D. 2007. *Pasifika mobility: Pathways, circuits and challenges in the 21st century*. Institute of Policy Studies, Victoria University of Wellington. Wellington.

Gilson, R. P. 1963. Samoan descent groups: A structural outline. *Journal of the Polynesian Society*, 72: 372–77.

—. 1970. *Samoa 1830–1900. The politics of a multi-cultural community*. Melbourne: Oxford University Press.

Kramer, A. 1994. *The Samoa Islands*. Auckland: The Polynesian Press.

Krishnan, V., P. Schoeffel, and J. Warren. 1994. *The challenge of change: Pacific Island communities in New Zealand 1986-1993*. Wellington: NZISRD.

Macpherson, C. 1974. *Toward an explanation of the persistence of extended kinship among Samoan migrants in urban New Zealand*. PhD Thesis, University of Waikato, NZ.

—. 1984. Samoan Ethnicity. In *Tauiwi: Racism and ethnicity in Aotearoa/New Zealand*, ed. P. Spoonley, C. Macpherson, D. Pearson, and C. Sedgwick, 107–27. Palmerston North: Dunmore Press.

—. 1991. The changing contours of Samoan ethnicity. In *Nga Take. Ethnic relations and racism in Aotearoa/New Zealand*, ed. P. Spoonley, D. Pearson, and C. Macpherson, 67–86. Palmerston North: Dunmore Press.

—. 1992. Economic and political restructuring and the sustainability of migrant remittances. *The Contemporary Pacific*, 4 (1): 109-35.

—. 1997. The persistence of chiefly authority in Western Samoa. In *Chiefs today: Traditional Pacific leadership and the postcolonial state*, ed. G. M. White and L. L. Lindstrom, 19–49. Stanford: Stanford University Press.

—. 2002. From moral community to moral communities: The foundations of migrant social solidarity among Samoans in Aotearoa New Zealand. *Pacific Studies*, 25 (1 & 2): 71–93.

Macpherson, C. and L. Macpherson. 1999. The changing contours of migrant Samoan kinship. In *Small worlds global lives: Islands and migration*, ed. R. King and J. Connell, 277–91. London: Pinter.

Meleisea, M. 1987. *The making of modern Samoa*. Suva: Institute of Pacific Studies, USP.

O'Brien, M. and C. Wilkes. 1993. *The tragedy of the market: A social experiment in New Zealand*. Palmerston North: The Dunmore Press.

Ongley, P. 1991. Pacific Islands migration and the NZ Labour Market. In *Nga Take: Ethnic relations and racism in Aotearoa/New Zealand*, ed.

P. Spoonley, D. Pearson, and C. Macpherson, 17–36. Palmerston North: Dunmore Press.

—. 1996. Immigration, employment and ethnic relations. In *Nga Patai. Racism and ethnic relations in Aotearoa/New Zealand*, ed. P. Spoonley, D. Pearson, and C. Macpherson, 13–34. Palmerston North: Dunmore Press.

Pitt, D. and C. Macpherson. 1974. *Emerging pluralism: The Samoan community in New Zealand*. Auckland: Longman Paul.

Roper, B. 1993. The end of the golden weather. In *State and economy in New Zealand*, ed. B. Roper and C. Rudd. Auckland: Oxford University Press.

Statistics New Zealand. 1995. *Samoan people in New Zealand. A statistical profile*. Wellington: Statistics New Zealand.

—. 1997. *New Zealand official yearbook 1997*. Wellington: GP Publications.

ENDNOTES

[1] The relative status of all *āiga* within local polities was embodied in formal statements known as *fa'alupega* which were recited periodically and publicly.

[2] While nothing prevented women from holding power and in fact women were immensely important, in practice men held most *matai* titles.

[3] The joint Heads of State and the Council of Deputies.

[4] Two seats in the new Parliament were reserved for 'individual voters' who did not have to hold *matai* titles.

[5] The traditional organisations were the wives of chiefs and orators, *faletua ma tausi*, and the association of village women, *aualuma*, which comprised women born in the village but not in-marrying women.

[6] In 1997, the constitution was revised to change the country's name from Western Samoa to Samoa.

[7] Only a small pool was necessary because they were in constant circulation and because during this time only relatively small numbers were being exchanged at any ceremony.

[8] More chiefly titles were created after 1962 and more holders were appointed to existing titles as a result of changes in electoral legislation; new chiefs were not necessarily concerned with day-to-day *aiga* management and were able to work overseas.

[9] Because migrants' livelihoods were no longer derived directly from the use of land or sea vested in the *āiga*, they were no longer legally bound by the authority of the *matai*.

[10] 'Traditional' because, while prominent unions have always been marked with much ceremony, less prominent people's unions have not and because the form is a Samoanised version of a Christian ceremony.

[11] Some graduates who had discouraged families from spending large amounts of money and who had resisted the increasing formality and ceremony had been reminded that this was an occasion *for the family*!

[12] A number of graduates noted that these occasions gave their parents an opportunity to show friends, family and guests 'how many important people they knew'.

[13] Between 1991 and 1995, union membership fell from 514,325 to 362,200 and coverage from 35.4 per cent to 21.7 per cent (Statistics New Zealand 1997) and tended to be strongest in highly-skilled and organised sectors. Those sectors in which many migrants were engaged were reorganised and significant numbers of jobs either disappeared or were casualised and effectively de-unionised.

[14] Over time, churches founded on the Samoan organisational model have become thoroughly established in New Zealand. These mainstream Samoans denominations include the Congregational Christian Church of Samoa (*Ekalesia Fa'apotopotoga Kerisiano Samoa*), the Methodist Church (*Le Lotu Toga*) and the Roman Catholic Church have become the most popular among Samoan church-goers. These congregations meet their pastors' living costs, pay their stipends and erect church buildings. The combined effect of these commitments on time and income are great and ongoing, particularly in smaller congregations.

[15] I am indebted to Galumalemana Alfred Hunkin-Tuiletufuga, for a description of how Catholic parishes in New Zealand have formulated procedures to achieve this end.

[16] This generally appears as '*Fa'maolemole, taofi le malo*' or more bluntly, 'Please, no fine mats' or 'No fa'asamoa'. Of course these injunctions are at best only partially successful, since many people feel unable or unwilling to attend funerary rites without taking a gift, for fear of encountering others with gifts.

5. Travelling Parties: Cook Islanders' Transnational Movement

Kalissa Alexeyeff

As in many Polynesian communities Cook Islander social networks are truly transnational. In 2006 only 12,000 Cook Islanders lived within the nation-state, approximately 58,000 Cook Islanders live in New Zealand and an estimated 8,000 in Australia (*Cook Islands Statistics* 2006; *Statistics New Zealand* 2006). Familial and community relationships are maintained through frequent phone calls, emails and travel back to the home islands for important occasions such as weddings and funerals, religious celebrations and sports competitions. The mobility of Cook Islanders who reside within the nation-state is also evident in the frequent travel undertaken for business purposes. Government employees and members of non-government organisations regularly travel to regional meetings and conferences. Tourism operators take dance groups on promotion tours to Europe and North America, and business entrepreneurs travel internationally to attract investment in agricultural and tourism projects.

In this paper, the term 'transnationalism' is used to refer to the increasing mobility of people, goods, information and technologies that characterises globalisation (Appadurai 1996; Kennedy and Roudometof 2002; Werbner 1999). I focus particularly on the ways in which social networks are sustained beyond the nation-state and maintained across multiple geographical sites, in order to argue that Cook Islanders, like many other diasporic communities, have responded to these global forces in a distinctly local manner (for other Pacific examples, see King and Connell 1999; Lee 2003; Macpherson 2004; Spickard 2002; Spoonley 2001, 2003). This paper examines a local style of travel called *tere pati* (literally travelling party), which involves large groups of individuals from extended family, church, village and island organisations undertaking travel to other Cook Islands communities.[1] Prior to European contact, *tere pati* were undertaken to neighbouring islands to forge and maintain social, economic and political ties. The increasing emigration of Cook Islanders has meant that the routes *tere pati* take have expanded to include diasporic communities abroad.

Guarnizo and Smith remind us that transnational relationships and actions must be grounded in specific times and places: 'Transnational practices, while connecting collectivities located in more than one national territory, are embodied in specific social relations established between specific people, situated in unequivocal localities, at historically determined times' (Guarnizo and Smith 1998, 11).

This paper examines the specificities of Cook Islands transnationalism in a number of ways. In the first section, I provide background to the contemporary Cook Islands diaspora and the influence of missionisation, colonisation and global forces on the movements of Cook Islands people. This is followed by an overview of the structure and purpose of *tere pati*, focussing on the economic, political, affective and aesthetic components of this travel. To conclude, I analyse a particular *tere pati* that involved groups travelling from New Zealand and Melbourne to the island of Aitutaki. This case study illustrates the ways in which this *tere pati*, as transnational practice, reproduces Cook Islanders' relationships.

Throughout the paper, I examine the successful maintenance of ties across the Cook Islands diaspora, however I do not want to suggest that this represents the totality of Cook Islanders experience of transnationalism. Understanding the efforts that Cook Islanders put into preserving connections to their home islands and other communities abroad is important to an understanding of transnationalism. Yet accompanying these practices of conservation are experiences of displacement and alienation that shape the lives of migrant groups in foreign countries. Additionally, Cook Islanders who remain at home keenly experience the results of emigration as loss—mainly of young, vital members of the islands—and as lack of opportunities and of income-generating possibilities for those that remain.

The Cook Islands and Migration

Over half of the Cook Islands residential population, around 9,000, live on the island of Rarotonga, the administrative capital of the group. The remainder of the population, approximately 3,000 people, are scattered across the 11 inhabited 'outer islands'. From the late 19th century, there has been a steady movement from these outer islands to Rarotonga and onwards. The movement was primarily economically motivated, spurred by the introduction of foreign trade and commerce during British and New Zealand colonial rule (1888–1965). After World War II, Cook Islanders, along with other Pacific Island migrants, provided labour for New Zealand's urban manufacturing sector (Appleyard and Stahl 1995; Connell 2002; Spoonley, Bedford and Macpherson 2003) and the flow of migrants to New Zealand and beyond has increased steadily since the Cook Islands achieved independence in 'free-association' with New Zealand in 1965. This relationship means—among other things—that Cook Islanders have dual citizenship, enabling automatic entry into New Zealand.

Cook Islanders now migrate for a variety of reasons; higher incomes, education and training opportunities are the principal motivations (see Wright-Koteka 2006 for an in-depth overview). Since the late 1990s, when the Cook Islands government introduced a neoliberal economic reform program, many have had little choice but to migrate. The economic restructuring involved halving public service employment and the removal of government subsidies for basic goods and services. While some retrenched public servants relocated into tourism, the Cook Islands main industry, approximately six to eight thousand Cook Islanders have left in search of employment (Secretariat of the Pacific Community 2005).

Like many small Pacific nations, the Cook Islands have been described as a MIRAB economy (Migration, Remittances, Aid, Bureaucracy) (Bertram 1999; Denoon, Mein-Smith and Wyndham 2000, 402; Poirine 1998). Certainly, migration figures attest to this characterisation, as do remittance figures. An NZODA (New Zealand Overseas Development Agency) report stated that money sent home from New Zealand totalled NZ $2.5 million in 1986 (1997, 19).[2] This figure only includes money sent home (via money transfer services); it does not include money taken home as gifts. Nor does it include money spent by overseas Cook Islanders on airfares for kin, reverse charge phone calls from kin, or the cost of transporting items requested from home. Inclusion of these expenses would make remittance figures significantly higher (Loomis 1990a, 1990b).

While the assessment of MIRAB economies as inefficient welfare systems dominates aid policy research, there is a developing body of research that seeks to challenge this assumption through an examination of the worldviews of Pacific Islanders and their understandings of economic and social security (Hau'ofa 1994; Poirine 1998). Poirine (1998), for instance, suggests that the MIRAB system is actually a rational, stable and sustainable system (far more sustainable than the agricultural export and tourist industries), involving a complex system of loans across transnational family groups. As the introduction of economic reforms in the Cook Islands resulted in a decline in aid and the privatisation of government bureaucracies, remittances and migration have played increasingly central roles assisting those who reside within the nation-state.[3]

As I demonstrate below, a central aspect of *tere pati* is the exchange of money and goods between travelling and hosting parties, and as such can be viewed as an integral aspect of Cook Islands remittances. But while economic transactions play an important role, transactions that take place during *tere pati* cannot be reduced simply to economics. Helen Lee (2004, 138; this volume) makes the important point that the concept of transnationalism has been utilised in the Pacific primarily to understand economic relationships of diasporic communities and further, that this focus ignores other aspects of social relations. Following her insight, I argue that transnational relationships operate in multiple registers; they have economic, aesthetic, political and affective dimensions, and in order to grasp their significance one needs to explore these enmeshed components.

Tere Pati

Cook Islanders love to travel in groups. Group travel is undertaken primarily to visit friends and family residing abroad and is considered to be the most enjoyable and economical way to travel. The movements of solitary Western tourists are often used as a point of comparison, as a tour operator suggested:

> A lot of *papa'a* (Westerners) travel to 'get away from it all'. We don't do that, what is there to get away from? We want to see our family and friends! Anyway, we would be too lonely. Us Cook Islanders, we like company.

Aside from the fact that most Cook Islanders do not have incomes that allow them to partake in tourist-style holidays, travel is primarily viewed as a directed, purposeful activity. Western tourists are sometimes referred to, somewhat derogatorily, as *utu panu*, a phrase used to describe a type of aimless wandering: 'someone with no family, a drifter, like the seeds from the *utu* tree [*Barringtonia asiatica*] floating out to sea' a young woman explained to me. She went on to tell me that she once called her irresponsible father an *utu panu* during a heated argument: 'it is the worst thing you can say to a Cook Islander; it means they don't care for their family'.

Tere pati is the most formalised type of group travel. *Tere pati* usually consist of between 20 and 100 participants and are undertaken for a range of purposes. Family groups organise *tere pati* for family reunions many of which occur every four years. They are alternately 'hosted' by families in different countries. Church groups travel abroad to participate in celebrations for religious anniversaries or to raise money for church projects such as the construction of a new hall. Similarly, sports, dance and community organisations (such as the Boy's Brigade and Girl Guides) travel to fundraise, to participate in regional and international competitions and for educational purposes.

Cook Islanders today view *tere pati* as the reinstatement of a practice that was banned during the missionary and colonial periods. Pre-missionary contact between the islands that now make up the Cooks group is evident both in oral histories and archaeological records (Bellwood 1979). Trade links with the Society Islands and Samoa were also maintained. These economic affiliations were accompanied by a history of artistic exchange (Moulin 1996). Under missionary rule, one of the first laws to be instituted by the London Missionary Society (LMS) was the prohibition of inter-island travel in attempts to control island populations. Throughout the colonial archive there are records of correspondence between colonial administrators and islanders requesting passports and permits to travel. For these administrators, the fact that islanders wanted to travel in large groups was disconcerting and potentially disruptive to their governance.

Many *tere pati* travel in matching uniforms; island-print dresses and shirts or t-shirts with specially designed logos declaring the purpose of the trip (see figure 5–1). For instance, a family will have a T-shirt made up displaying their family name, date and location of a family reunion. These T-shirts are sold to members of the *tere pati* as part of their fundraising.

Groups leaving from the Cook Islands, be they church, village, or family groups, will often prepare 'items' to perform for their hosts. Gifts are presented to hosts along with live music and dance. If the groups are from the Cook Islands they will present *tivaevae* (appliquéd quilts and cushion covers) and pandanus mats. These groups may also travel with large amounts of island food such as taro, which is distributed to hosts. In turn, individuals in the group receive presents (usually money and manchester items) from relatives and close friends who reside in the places the *tere pati* visit.[4]

Economics and Travel

Cook Islanders say that travelling in groups is the best and most economical way to see the world. As an example, a woman in the Golden Oldies netball team said she could not have afforded to travel unless it was as part of a group. 'It is a good system' she said, 'you go to places as a guest, they put on *kaika*i (feast) for you, organise your accommodation, your transport, you don't have to worry about anything. Then they come here and you look after them'.

Before a group embarks on a trip overseas, they often fundraise at home to pay for airfares and to cover other travel expenses. These funds are put into a joint bank account, usually in the name of the group leader or the person nominated as the group's accountant. The types of fundraising activities engaged in are raffles, sausage sizzles, selling plates of food and tending people's plantations. What is particularly significant about fundraising for *tere pati* is that individuals are not expected to contribute their own money but they are expected to contribute to raising funds for the group as a whole. On trips overseas, people may bring 'pocket money' for themselves but otherwise the group funds pay for accommodation and travel. Food and additional costs are generally covered by the host communities.

Many *tere pati* travel with the aim of making money for a particular community project, usually for materials to construct a church, village or island public building, such as halls, churches and schools. The primary way that *tere pati* make money is by putting on series of dance performances at nightclubs or village halls. Money is made from ticket sales and donations during the performance. A contribution bowl is placed in front of the performers, audience members get up and dance towards the performers waving money above their heads. They will place money in the bowl or tuck notes in the waist of a performer's costume. The figures I have been quoted for amounts earned through performances are sizeable. A family group that travelled to New Zealand had their children learn a series of 'items' to perform. They estimated that they made around NZ$1,000 each time they performed. A priest from a Catholic *tere pati* said that his group raised NZ$60,000 on their Australia trip and a group from the island of Mangaia raised NZ$100,000 for a new community building.

In 1997, I recorded three *tere pati* travelling to Australia and New Zealand from Rarotonga. These were the Rarotongan Golden Oldies netball team, the village of Tupapa-Maraerenga's dance group, and Arorangi village Boys Brigade. In addition, two groups from the islands of Tongareva and Mangaia passed through Rarotonga, performing at local bars to raise money, on the way to New Zealand. In terms of *tere pati* travelling to the Cook Islands, at least six community or family groups arrive in Rarotonga each year. At Christmas time, at least one or two overseas groups travel to the outer islands. The main difference between groups travelling from the Cook Islands and those originating from abroad is that the latter do not undertake fundraising activities but rather bring large amounts of gifts to the home islands. This reflects the fact that diasporic communities are usually wealthier than those at home. Nevertheless, many outer islands councils have limited the number of *tere pati* to two per year as they feel the groups put too much strain on the limited island resources, especially food and accommodation.

While fundraising is a central component of *tere pati*, other incentives are also important. The family group mentioned above formed to visit family abroad but also to teach their children 'old' stories, songs and dances. Before leaving Rarotonga, they rehearsed twice a week for four months before they travelled overseas. In this instance, *tere pati* are as much about maintaining cultural capital as about economic capital. Similarly, diasporic communities view *tere pati* back to the homeland as extremely important for children born overseas. They are considered to be a vehicle through which children can learn the Cook Islands Maori language and culturally valued skills such as husking coconuts, fishing and planting. Older members of the community spend evenings recalling their childhoods and instructing young ones on 'the ways things should be done'. Cultural and moral education, emotional connection, community service and fulfilment of economic obligations are all important to understanding the multiple ways in which Cook Islanders sustain relationships during *tere pati*.

Koni Raoni: Dance, Money and Movement

Many Cook Islanders who live abroad return home for a month or longer at Christmas time. Important events such as twenty-first birthday celebrations and weddings are often postponed until this visiting period so that as many extended family members as possible can attend. It is also the time when most *tere pati* are undertaken. In the following, I describe one such occasion that occurred on the island of Aitutaki in 1996.

Two *tere pati*, one from Melbourne and the other from Auckland, travelled to Aitutaki in mid-December. The Melbourne *tere pati* had 80 participants who slept in the Amuri village hall (the village from which most of the *tere pati* members originated). At the hall, a roster was drawn up for cleaning and food preparation duties for all members of the group. Community groups and family groups linked in various ways to the *tere pati* brought fresh fruit and vegetables to the hall on a daily basis. Many hosted large feasts at surrounding church and village meeting houses. The *tere pati* sent four shipping crates of household and farming materials by sea to coincide with their arrival. The items shipped included packets of toilet paper, cartons of tinned food and frozen chicken pieces, a tractor, and 80 mattresses which the *tere pati* used to sleep on and then donated to the village of Amuri when they left.

The family I was stayed with during this Christmas period had one brother return with his wife and three children with the Auckland *tere pati*. In addition to contributing to this group's donations, he also brought goods for his immediate family living on Aitutaki. Their shipped crate included containers of food such as large quantities of frozen steak, minced meat and New Zealand oysters and mussels. It also contained a new washing machine for the family home, a grass cutter, an outboard motor, a plastic outdoor table and matching chairs, and two pushbikes for the male nephews. They told me that it cost NZ$5,000 to ship the crate. In addition, both members of the *tere pati* and members of this particular family also gave sums of money to family members and to village organisations.

Tere pati are obliged to undertake community projects during their stay. The male members of the Melbourne *tere pati* rebuilt the hall's roof with funds raised back in New Zealand and Australia. During other years, *tere pati* have been involved in community projects such as fixing a sea wall and replastering a church. One member of the *tere pati* said 'we need to do these kinds of work to say thank you to the Aitutakians that stay here and look after our land and our village'. Similarly, at the family level, overseas members pay, with cash and goods, family at home to maintain their family homes and to clear and plant their land. Neglected land is considered a matter of shame and can also lead to challenges to ownership by other family members.

As well as these economic and political agendas, *tere pati* provide occasions for intensely pleasurable proximity between long-distance family and friends (see Alexeyeff 2009). Feasts, informal get-togethers and bar-hopping involve a great deal of drinking, eating, dancing and singing. Stories, laughter, tears, new dance moves and songs are exchanged throughout the trip. One important occasion that is held during the Christmas period on Aitutaki is the *koni raoni*: a day-long event held each December 26 and New Year's Day.[5] *Koni raoni* means 'dance round' and refers to the event's structure, which involves one of the villages travelling around the island singing and performing choreographed dance numbers. The other villages reciprocate with gifts of money, food and by joining in the dancing and singing. Like many forms of group entertainment, the aim of the *koni raoni* is to raise funds for the performing village. In 1996, the travelling village made special stops at the halls where the *tere pati* were staying 'to pay tribute' a performer told me, 'but also to get some money off those rich ones!'. At the Amuri hall, the Melbourne *tere pati* waited for the performing village. The sound of drums, trucks and motorbikes announced their arrival. After a series of speeches, prayers and listing of donations of money, the performers began to dance. On certain occasions, members of the *tere pati* dance with the performers and leave coin donations in the contribution bowl when they are finished. These interactions were accompanied by raucous laughter and screams of delight as dancers on both sides aim to variously show off their dancing skills or dance in humorous or deliberately provocative styles. After about an hour the performers are provided with food and drink before they move on to the next village.

For the *koni raoni* the Melbourne *tere pati* donned matching green t-shirts. On the front, a circular emblem featured the words 'Teupokoenua – Melbourne' (Teupokoenua is one of the Cook Islands Maori names for Aitutaki) and an emblem featuring a kangaroo and a palm tree. On the back was a map of Australia with Melbourne marked by a coconut tree. The map was surrounded by the words 'Melbourne-Aitutaki Tour 96-97'.

Figure 5–1: A *tere pati* T-shirt

These t-shirts make an important statement about the nature of Cook Islands diasporic communities and about transnationalism more generally. Both the emblem and the map visually represent the way these Melbourne Cook Islanders view their group's identity and place as dual: they are Aitutakian but also Melbournians. This twin state of belonging is a key aspect of transnational identities and Cook Islanders, like other Pacific Islander diasporic communities, have a complex range of investments in more than one country (Guarnizo and Smith 1998, 13; Lee 2003, 2004, 135: Spoonley, Bedford and McPherson 2003).

The sheer joy and excitement experienced during *koni raoni* epitomises the general mood of *tere pati* undertaken during the 1996–97 holiday period. It contrasts starkly with the emotional tenor when the *tere pati* return home. The tropical food stuffs, island brooms, coconut oil and mats given to those leaving are exchanged quietly, with no formal ceremony. At the airport, long silent hugs between family members seem to amplify the distance that will soon separate them.

Conclusion

I end with that sombre image as a reminder that the process of maintaining and reconstituting transnational communities is also accompanied by loss and dislocation. While there is much to celebrate about the tenacious way that Cook Islanders preserve their community and familial connections across geographical distance, to complete the picture of these transnational relationships we must acknowledge that globalisation also makes these relationships potentially fragile.

Guarnizo and Smith (1998, 13) use the term 'translocality' to describe the local-to-local connections that migrants forge to their locality of origin and the place to which they migrate. Many Cook Islanders view migration as a temporary strategy in order to earn higher incomes that will enable them one day to return home and live comfortably. The reality is that many end up settling permanently overseas because of job opportunities, welfare benefits or simply because they become accustomed to life abroad. At the same time, many migrants retain an emotional attachment to their homeland. It is this attachment that older, first generation migrants aim to instil in members of the second and third generations through visits to the homeland. *Tere pati* are the primary way these trips are undertaken and this practice suggests that transnational communities will continue to flourish in the future.

The 'translocality' of Cook Islanders refers not only to their multiple locations of residence but also to the 'locality' of the travel they undertake. *Tere pati* is a culturally specific style of travel. While global economic forces have largely determined that many Cook Islanders cannot afford to reside at home, they have applied distinctly local strategies in their attempts to stave off the deleterious effects of globalisation on their kin and various community affiliations. This travel is not simply about economic sustenance but also the upkeep of the agendas, obligations and emotions that constitute Cook Islanders' social relationships.

References

Alexeyeff, K. 2004. Love food: Exchange and sustenance in the Cook Islands diaspora. In *Taste this! An anthropological examination of food. The Australian Journal of Anthropology* Special Issue 15 (1): 68–79, ed. K. Alexeyeff, R. James and M. Thomas.

—. 2009. *Dancing from the heart: Movement, gender and Cook Islands globalization.* Honolulu: University of Hawai'i Press.

Appadurai, A. 1996. *Modernity at large.* Minneapolis: University of Minnesota Press.

Appleyard, R.T. and C.W. Stahl. 1995. *South Pacific migration: New Zealand experience and implications for Australia.* Canberra: Australian Agency for International Development.

Bellwood, P. 1979. *Man's conquest of the Pacific: The prehistory of Southeast Asia and Oceania.* New York: Oxford University Press.

Bertram, G. 1999. The MIRAB model twelve years on. *The Contemporary Pacific.* 11 (1): 105–38.

Connell, J. 2002. Paradise left? Pacific Island voyages in the modern world. In *Pacific diaspora: Island peoples in the United States and across the Pacific,* ed. P. Spickard, J. L. Rondilla, and D. H. Wright, 69–86. Honolulu: University of Hawai'i Press.

Connell, J. and R. P. C. Brown. 2005. *Remittances in the Pacific: An overview.* Philippines: Asian Development Bank.

Cook Islands Statistics. 2006. Rarotonga, Cook Islands. http://www.stats.gov.ck/ (accessed 19 July 2007).

Denoon, D., P. Mein-Smith with M. Wyndham. 2000. *A History of Australia, New Zealand and the Pacific.* Oxford: Blackwell Publishers Ltd.

Hau'ofa, E. 1994. Our sea of islands. *The Contemporary Pacific* 6 (1): 147–61.

Guarnizo, L. and M. Smith. 1998. The locations of transnationalism. In *Transnationalism from below,* ed. M. Smith and L. Guarnizo, 3–31. Transaction Publishers, New Brunswick.

Kennedy, P. and V. Roudometof. 2002. Transnationalism in a global age. In *Communities across borders: New immigrants and transnational cultures,* ed. P. Kennedy and V. Roudometof, 1–26. London: Routledge.

King, R. and J. Connell (eds). 1999. *Small worlds, global lives: Islands and migration.* London: Pinter.

Lee, H. 2003. *Tongans overseas: Between two shores.* Honolulu: University of Hawai'i Press.

—. 2004. All Tongans are connected: Tongan transnationalism. In *Globalization and cultural change in the Pacific Islands,* ed. V. Lockwood, 133-48. Upper Saddle River, NJ; Pearson Prentice Hall.

Loomis, T. 1990a. *Pacific migrant labour, class and racism in New Zealand: Fresh off the Boat.* Aldershot, England: Avebury

Loomis, T. 1990b. Cook Islands remittances: Volumes, determinants and uses. In *Migration and development in the South Pacific*, ed. J. Connell, 61-81. Pacific Research Monograph 24. Canberra: The Australian National University.

Macpherson, C. 2004. Transnationalism and transformation in Samoan society. In *Globalization and cultural change in the Pacific Islands*, ed. V. Lockwood, 165-81. Upper Saddle River, NJ; Pearson Prentice Hall.

Marsters, E., N. Lewis and W. Friesen. 2006. Pacific flows: The fluidity of remittances in the Cook Islands. *Asia Pacific Viewpoint* 47 (1): 31-44.

Moulin, J. 1996. What's mine is yours? Cultural borrowing in a Pacific context. *The Contemporary Pacific* 8 (1): 128–53.

New Zealand Overseas Development Agency (NZODA). 1997. *Cook Islands economic reforms to April 1997.* Rarotonga, Cook Islands.

Newnham, R. 1989. Pearls and politics: The impact of the development of the cultured-pearl industry on Manihiki. MA Thesis. University of Canterbury, Christchurch.

Poirine, B. 1998. Should we hate or love MIRAB? *The Contemporary Pacific* 10 (1): 65–105.

Secretariat of the Pacific Community. 2005. Demographic Profile of Cook Islands: 1996–2002. http://www.spc.int/prism/country/ck/stats/NewsEvents/CIDemogProf.htm (accessed 19 July 2007).

Spickard, P. 2002. Introduction: Pacific diaspora. In *Pacific diaspora: Island peoples in the United States and across the Pacific*, ed. P. Spickard, J. L. Rondilla, and D. H. Wright, 1–27. Honolulu: University of Hawai'i Press.

Spoonley, P. 2001. Transnational Pacific communities: Transforming the politics of place and identity. In *Tangata O te Moana nui: The evolving identities of Pacific peoples in Aotearoa/New Zealand*, ed. C. Macpherson, P. Spoonley, and M. Anae, 81–96. Palmerston North: Dunmore Press.

—. 2003. Reinventing Polynesia: The cultural politics of transnational Pacific communities, transnational communities. Working Paper, Transnational Communities Programme. Institute of Social & Cultural Anthropology, University of Oxford.

Spoonley, P, R. Bedford, and C. Macpherson 2003. Divided loyalties and fractured sovereignty: Transnationalism and the nation-state in Aotearoa/New Zealand. *Journal of Ethnic and Migration Studies.* 29 (1): 27–46.

Statistics New Zealand. 2006. QuickStats about culture and identity: 2006 Census. http://www.stats.govt.nz (accessed 15 July 2007).

Werbner, P. 1999. Global pathways: Working class cosmopolitans and the creation of transnational worlds. *Social Anthropology* 7 (1): 17–35.

Wright-Koteka, Elizabeth. 2006. *Te uu no te akau roa*: Migration and the Cook Islands, MA Thesis. Massey University http://stagingv.massey.ac.nz/ shadomx/apps/fms/fmsdownload.cfm?file_uuid= 58BA33E9-96BF-57F6-8956-3F21B33308C1&siteName=massey (accessed 21 January 2008).

ENDNOTES

[1] The usual spelling of the phrase is *tere party*. I once saw a shipping crate on Aitutaki with the words 'Aitutaki *tere pati*' written in red paint; *pati* is a Maorification of the word party. I also adopt this spelling. The Samoan equivalent is called *malaga* and the Tongan version *malanga*.

[2] More recent figures are not, to my knowledge, available at the time of writing.

[3] The movement of money is not always from the nation-state to communities abroad. The island of Manihiki had a prosperous pearl industry during the 1990s and money was regularly remitted from this island to relatives living overseas (see Marsters, Lewis and Friesen 2006; Newnham 1989). For an important overview of remittances in the Pacific see Connell and Brown (2005).

[4] I discuss the significance of food exchange within the Cook Islands diaspora in Alexeyeff (2004).

[5] The term *koni raoni* is specific to Aitutaki. Other islands in the Cooks (but not Rarotonga) also have Christmas celebrations that involve dancing, singing and fundraising between villages.

6. Food and Transnationalism: Reassertions of Pacific Identity

Nancy Pollock

Food reinforces ties between Pacific peoples and their island homes, while linking them to a wider world. Food globalises while it localises, thereby crossing national boundaries. It links families through exchanges and shared ideologies and diversifies over time and space. Increased options of foods from the land or from the supermarket are part of that diversity. Brands such as McDonalds and Coca-Cola are 'not the tip of some globalizing iceberg, but rather the markers of a particular superordinate level of identity on a par with saving the rainforest' (Miller 1997, 80). Food is an identity marker that both links families overseas to their island home and distinguishes the two communities.

This paper aims to demonstrate that mobile communities have carried their gastronomies with them across space and time, modifying them according to social and environmental dictates. The cultural values embodied in these gastronomies have been subject to a number of influences that can be captured in three 'foodscapes'. Foodscapes, I argue, are additional to Appadurai's *ethnoscapes*, which he sees as 'the landscape of persons who constitute the shifting world in which we live: tourists, immigrants, refugees, exiles, guest workers and other moving groups and individuals who constitute an essential feature of the world...' (1996, 33). Mediascapes, technoscapes, financescapes and ideoscapes, plus foodscapes, indicate 'irregular shapes, imagined in their complexity, and the product of deeply perspectival constructs' (ibid, 33). Perspectives on foodscapes allow us to depict the mobilisation of cultural differences 'in the service of a larger national or transnational politics' (ibid., 15). They have a place in the construction of insights into this 'shifting world' of modernity and identity (ibid, 33).

Throughout history people have been transferring their foodways as they move across land and sea, linking with the past as well as considering novel food choices. 'A historical overview is just as useful when looking at food and food systems as it is when considering globalisation as a whole...It is analytically useful to link up what is happening now to what has already happened' (Mintz 2006, 4). Transnationalism offers an alternative approach to globalisation as it provides a focus on cultural distinctions. As populations spread, foods gain significance as much for their novelty as for their ties to the past. Foodscapes depict those historical and spatial links.

Here, I contrast Pacific foodscapes that link Asian influences with modern influences emanating from a Euro/American background (often referred to as westernisation). The first oriental foodscape depicts the gastronomies of early voyagers as they established new communities with foodstuffs they carried with them. A more recent foodscape, largely post World War II, captures Asian gastronomic influences that recent Chinese communities have brought with them. The third set of influences, that stem from occidental ideologies, have led to a proliferation of western foods imported to the islands, as well as the options in supermarkets. All three foodscapes are blended to offer a range of options, whether in the form of taro chips or hamburger buns, each depicting interpretations of cultural identity.

Foodscapes represent different forms that gastronomies can take as a result of past and present influences. Brillat-Savarin introduced the term gastronomy through his focus on the many features of 'taste' as the key element of gastronomy: 'It examines the effect of food on man's character, his imagination, his wit, his judgement, his courage, and his perceptions...It is gastronomy which determines the point of esculence of every foodstuff, for they are not all palatable in identical circumstances' (1970, 53). While he depicts individual tastes, he provides a broader framework than just the material aspects of food. Modern gastronomy includes six key features that contribute to the depiction of a foodscape:

- foodstuffs in material form, their origins and diversity;
- food ideology that is manifest in how foods are used in eating situations and the values on which food use is based;
- specific food-associated events, such as preparation, cooking, preservation, eating, and feasts;
- social relationships in which food events are embedded;
- myths and legends associated with particular foods and food event (Pollock 2008).

A gastronomic framework is dynamic as it is challenged by new options that may be accepted, rejected, or adapted in some way, as exemplified by the Pacific custom of serving taro with fish, linking land and sea, or rice topped with instant noodles as a quick meal.

A transnational approach to gastronomies celebrates food as a means of cultural expression. It contrasts with a globalisation approach which stresses economic over other cultural concerns; Stiglitz has highlighted the need for alternatives to the homogenising capitalist approach to globalisation in which 'economic interests take precedence over other values, particularly cultural identity (2006, 129). He suggests that global approaches should support those discontented with the corporate interests that dominate trade and violate basic values such as heritage, language and a sense of cultural identity (ibid, 131). Foodscapes underline that respect for food in the enhancement of cultural identity.

An anthropological approach supports a transnational approach and is counter-intuitive to globalisation arguments. Significant differences between eastern and western gastronomies can be found in urban, rural and overseas communities. Resistance to innovations such as McDonalds and responses to body size as linked to 'over-eating' are two examples. As Miller's anthropological view of capitalism suggests 'anthropologists might argue that global institutions tend to look superficially similar wherever one finds them but if [they] are able to examine the evidence carefully they will find that underneath this façade of similarity may be discerned authentic differences' (1997, 14). Furthermore, he points out that 'institutions that generate new differences are just as important as new forms of homogeneity or old forms of separation' (ibid, 15). Tracing transnational influences through foodscapes enables us to highlight the cultural continuities and innovations, choices that communities make to enhance their identity.

Oriental Influences—Earliest Settlements

The earliest foodscape for the Pacific depicts many Asian and Chinese influences (Pollock 2008). Many starch plants entered the Pacific from Southeast Asia, thereby establishing strong gastronomic links with the island nations. Travellers shared a common Austronesian language (Bellwood 1997; Irwin 2006; Kirch 2000). Agricultural expansion began some 6,000 years ago, but accelerated 3,000 years ago as Lapita peoples spread across Oceania, according to Bellwood's (2005) farming/language dispersal hypothesis. This early oriental foodscape provides us with a significant time period against which to understand Pacific gastronomic patterns today.

The earliest settlers who moved out of southeast Asia across the Wallace Trench brought taro roots, coconuts and other foodstuffs, some to eat on the voyage, while saving the taro tops for planting at their new landfall (Allaby 2007; Pollock 1992; Walter and Lebot 2007). Other species of taro, yams, bananas and breadfruit were introduced by subsequent waves of settlers. This increased the diversity of local foods still in use today to ten starch foods, seven of which have a homeland in Taiwan and island Southeast Asia (Allaby 2007; Pollock 1992).

A major feature of oriental influences on gastronomy is the emphasis on the starch food as the dominant component of daily food intake, accompanied by a small portion of sauce or fish. The starch element was considered 'real food', termed *kakana dina* in Fijian and *karan unun*, in Hanunoo, Philippines (Conklin 1957; Pollock 1986). The combination of slices of taro or yam and a small amount of fish or piece of coconut as accompaniment we term a 'meal' in English, but that is a late European concept, as discussed below.

These food plants depended on human agency for their dispersal and propagation, as they reproduce only by vegetal propagation. Subsequent waves of migrants brought new species, new varieties and new ideas, as revealed by botanists' reconstructions from DNA, along with archaeologists' findings of materials associated with plant production and historical linguists' study of early linguistic forms (Bellwood 2005; Blench 2005; Kirch 2000). The result has been the continuing diversification of gastronomies.

All these starch staples have to be cooked today, so we assume that earlier varieties also had to be cooked to make them edible. The earth oven was the means used to cook quantities of starch foods to last several days, and became men's work. Some foods such as breadfruit could be roasted in the coals of a fire in a shallow pit on the ground. Southeast Asian peoples have cooked their foods over such fires, as writers from Europe and America have shown (Yo 1995). Boiling necessitated pots, used in high status Chinese households to cook rice, but in the Pacific, Lapita pottery did not become available until about 1500 BC; whether those pots were used for cooking has not been definitely established (Green, personal communication, 2007). They may have been used only for high status family members and visitors. Such gastronomic reconstructions are tentative as they are inevitably based on contemporary values, both sociocultural and biological.

Sharing the starch and its accompaniment once a day between extended family households enabled one earth oven to feed 10–15 people. Ancestors were also offered food and drink (see Firth 1967) a practice considered vital to ensuring continuity of a food supply for the whole community. 'First fruits' ceremonies marked a community's acknowledgment of the importance of those ancestors in establishing a good food supply. Myths of the origins of food plants have perpetuated accounts of the movement of ancestral populations and the foods they brought with them.

This early foodscape depicts a strong gastronomic base that includes not only the foods themselves, but also modes of cooking and serving, and the ideology of food as the centre of sociality. These features mark a continuity with the southeast Asian homeland cultures (Bellwood 1997; Howe 2007). Subsequent introductions have been adapted and changed, but key features are still recognisable.

Modern Oriental Influences

Gastronomic links with Southeast Asia have been further strengthened with the settlement of Chinese and other Asian communities in the Pacific over the last 150 years. While national boundaries have become more distinct and barriers to food transfers have been erected in the form of import and agricultural regulations, rice and other oriental food habits have established a pervasive presence in Pacific households, whether in rural Samoa, an outlying island of Yap or metropolitan communities. Rice has been added to the food inventory as the centrepiece of many household foodscapes; rice is the hallmark of a transnational food.

Rice gained popularity in the Pacific after World War II as a cheap food, particularly for low-income urban communities. It can be served like the earlier starches, i.e. with a small accompanying dish such as grated coconut. It can be bought in bulk, stores readily, cooks reasonably quickly, fills and satisfies hungry adults and children, and thus is an ideal food for households on a small income.

Rice has its own gastronomic associations. It must be boiled and thus requires a special kind of fire, and a pot that will hold enough to feed large households. Boiling is women's work. Cooking it requires experience that female children learn early. Rice with warm sweet tea is the weaning food on outer islands of the Marshall Islands. Rice has not been acceptable as a feast food, except in Guam. It is an important aid food during environmental disasters as well as financial downturns. Rice has become important to island food security in the face of food shortages for both household and national economies (Pollock 2002).

Rice comprises a major proportion in both volume and cost of Pacific food imports, whether from the Philippines, Australia or the US (e.g. Tonga Trade statistics 2004). Attempts to reduce this dependency on imported rice have largely failed in the face of strong demand. Most urban centres in the Pacific have at least one Chinese takeaway shop that has contributed to a gastronomic profile based on rice. Chinese restaurants and takeaway food outlets, established in island urban centres, along with Indian curry houses, and Thai and other Asian-style eating places, offer different tastes in food. Some dishes, such as Samoan chop suey may be served at home, or during feasts, with recipes adapted to local tastebuds. Market gardens established by Chinese families in Tahiti and elsewhere have contributed fresh vegetables not formerly used in Pacific cuisine. Chinese food use is not necessarily associated with any particular aspect of oriental ideology; the foods have been adapted to blend with a Pacific foodscape.

While takeaway foods have become a global phenomenon, the small Asian restaurants provide a marked contrast to American corporate fast-food enterprises such as KFC and McDonalds. Asian restaurants reflect a change in attitudes to Asian immigrants and rely largely on their own family labour (for US examples, see Mintz 2006, 18). In 1993, Chinese migrant families moved to Nauru to establish 83 small businesses attached to Nauruan houses to cater for the fast-food needs of the media and other followers of the South Pacific Forum meetings held that year on Nauru. Many had to return to China after the Forum, but a few stayed to join the Chinese community on Nauru to sell cooked rice to Nauruans. Chinese takeaway restaurants offer similar/familiar dishes and tend to be cheaper than McDonalds, fried chicken and other fast foods that derive from a western influence. Both forms of fast foods have gained appeal among Pacific communities, whether in Suva or Auckland.

Japanese and Indian influences on gastronomy have not been as pervasive across the Pacific, despite their strong presence in the region. Nauruans recall being paid a match box of rice per day during the 1943–45 Japanese occupation of the island. Few Japanese or Indian restaurants have been established in urban centres, with the exceptions of Honolulu and Suva. Soy sauce and curry powder are two ubiquitous links to Asian gastronomies.

Oriental influences on Pacific gastronomies have been enduring as well as expanding. They extend beyond foodstuffs to the prevalence of the starch component, simple cooking styles, an emphasis on sharing with relatives and the community, respect for food, and its importance in spiritual rather than material wellbeing. A monetary economy supports Asian-style takeaway foods and restaurants, as well as supermarket offerings, and Chinese gardeners' produce. All reinforce Asian influences on today's Pacific gastronomies.

Occidental Influences

European and American influences on food habits and gastronomies reached the Pacific much later, i.e., only in the last 200 years. Traders, whalers, administrators and missionaries arrived with strong ideas about food and gastronomic practices. The earliest of these visitors such as Captain Cook exposed Pacific peoples to new foods and new gastronomies when they hosted chiefs on board their ships. They left plants and animals that they hoped would become established to supply victuals for future ships. Missionaries had a more pervasive influence as they lived alongside communities which they expected would adopt the new western gastronomic ways, as part of the civilising process (Pollock 1989). But Pacific communities were not so eager to replace their long-established eating and cooking habits with things that cost hard-earned money.

Only since World War II have many western gastronomic approaches proliferated. Western foodstuffs and ideologies spread as a result of aggressive marketing activity, rather than migrants' influences. An alternative use of 'transnationalism' to refer to the operations of large-scale multinational corporations is epitomised by reference to global food giants such as Nestle, Coca-Cola and McDonalds (see Miller 1997 with specific reference to Trinidad). Such companies vigorously sought to establish their products across the Pacific. Hot bread shops and fried chicken outlets represent these marketing principles, as do tuna processing and local beer and soft drink manufactures. These multinationals provided business models for creating new jobs as well as gastronomic opportunities.

Commercial food outlets have proliferated, from small family-owned food stores to supermarkets, as Hau'ofa (1979) demonstrates for Tonga. Supermarkets located near the market place and bus depots became a social hub linking rural communities with their urban relatives (Pollock 1995). New gastronomic trends were passed on, including new recipes, new technology and new values of time and tastes associated with food. The desirability of the latest imports, recommended by visiting family members from New Zealand or Australia, has continued the process of widening gastronomic horizons.

Family responsibilities had to be rearranged as new gastronomic principles became accepted. Serving three meals a day, as missionaries recommended, interrupted work patterns, and cooking on a kerosene or electric stove became women's work. With men and young people away all day, others had to help with picking crops, cooking, feeding young children and washing clothes. Food parcels that travel both ways between Rarotonga and Auckland continue to express the love and affection that sustain family ties (Alexeyeff 2004). In urban centres, office workers buy their midday food at takeaway stores catering for these new needs.

Income has become a major determinant of what a household can put on the table. Cheap imports such as rice and canned fish were the limit for many households in the 1960s. Corned beef has become an icon of this new transnational trade in foodstuffs, as Michel Tuffery (2007) illustrates with his life-size cow sculptures made entirely from corned beef cans. He specifically links his art forms to his views as a New Zealand-born Samoan of the history of food exchanges that express Samoan identity across transnational boundaries (for an image see the Te Papa museum website).

New western ideas of gastronomy have introduced conflicting messages about the link between food and wellbeing. Missionaries advised housewives to feed their men meat, but this was not readily available in the islands until refrigerated transport was developed in the 1880s, and then the taste had to be acquired. Meat has always been more expensive than fish. A Pacific meal of taro eaten with fish remained the epitome of Pacific gastronomy because the components were readily available, filling, did not cost money and fulfilled long-established gastronomic ideals.

A repertoire of 'good foods', whether local or imported, has raised many questions, both for government officials and women's groups (see e.g., Schoeffel 1985). These new foods, promoted by the media, medical advisors and nutritionists were based entirely on western ideology and bio-medical reasoning. At first, they derogated Pacific gastronomic habits but these gained positive value for their high fibre, low salt and low sugar content, in contrast with western gastronomic habits that contributed to increased rates of cardiovascular problems and diabetes (Coyne, Badcock and Taylor 1984). Brenda Sio produced a Samoan food pyramid for World Food Day in Samoa 1996 which included Pacific foods alongside western foods differentiating the good labelled *Ioe* (yes) versus *Leai* (no) (Sio 1996); this proved a more effective nutrition education message than previous, monocultural ones. Obesity has emerged in the new millennium as a major health concern linked to poor food choices both in the islands and in overseas communities, as was demonstrated by a front cover story of *Islands Business* in March 2007.

Western gastronomic influences introduced a drastically new set of ideals and practices that became major commercial intrusions. But we must distinguish their introduction from their adoption. The new gastronomic principles could not override the identity that had become established between Pacific communities and their foodways inherited from their ancestors and established by migrants over several thousand years.

Blendings

Blending of old and new, island and metropolitan foods, messages from family and the media, advice about good food and image management all bombard present day consumers. Any search to maintain a Pacific identity through food choices becomes complex. Households choose foods according to a number of criteria that include previous influences and new opportunities. A study of decisions about food access for low income households around Wellington revealed a large gap between desires and realities, and greater problems for large Maori and Pacific island families. With only $100 per week to spend on food, four factors dominated their choices: taste, time, health and cost. Foods had to suit family tastes, be quick to put on the table, be as healthy as possible and come within the budget. Fruit and vegetables and better cuts of meat were often too expensive. Sometimes McDonalds was the easy solution, though it took up a major part of the weekly food budget (Pollock, Dixon and Leota 1996). This survey alerts us to limitations to gastronomic options.

The gastronomic package reveals some of the alternative ways that blending is occurring. The foodstuffs, combinations, meals and eating situations, special food events and recognition of social relationships all form part of the messages and practices embedded in the presentation of identity through food.

Foodstuffs available in the Pacific today represent a long heritage of choosing varieties that suit tastes, seasonal availability and other local criteria. The concept of 'good food' is changing today, as it also did in the past. Taro is very expensive for everyday use in metropolitan households, as is fish when feeding a large group. Ice cream, cakes and desserts have intruded more into public eating occasions than ordinary daily meals. Coca-Cola and fried chicken have been heavily promoted by outside commercial agents and sweet biscuits are a grandmother's solution to soothing a little one—the label 'good' or 'bad' is not a consideration then. Agencies such as Fiji Food and Nutrition Committee and Pacific Islands Nutrition and Dietitians Association, together with the Food and Agriculture Organization, all offer guidance on best choices among foods available. But ultimately households use foods that fit their own gastronomic ideals.

Meals and eating situations are more diverse for urban communities, whether in Apia or Auckland. Meal times for family units compete with other activities. The 'ideal' combination of taro and fish may remain for older family members, while for younger members the fast foods, fruits and vegetables may suit their fitness image. Nutritionists' ideal meal of meat, vegetables and dessert may be too expensive or outside their identification. Distinctions between snack and meal foods depend on local interpretations, i.e. pizza might be either. Cooking styles may represent a blending, as when taro or fish is cooked in tinfoil in the electric oven; fried food, particularly chicken, has become highly favoured though nutritionally problematic, yet a highly acceptable gift when a family flies a 'chilly bin' full of KFC from Auckland to Rarotonga. A balanced meal has many dimensions in today's world. Feasts remain an opportunity, or challenge, for families to lay out their identity through their contributions of taro, raw fish, chicken and cakes.

Social relationships are strengthened and challenged by the blendings of old and new gastronomic principles, and by exchanges of food that express what Cook Island people call *aro'a* (Alexeyeff 2004, 76). Feasts are important times for socialising around food, with much thought and planning as to which families contribute particular foods. Fish and beef (including canned corned beef, *pisupo* in Samoan) are all expensive in metropolitan settings, as are taro and the other imported iconic foods. However, the social mores of giving override any economic considerations, so that a family may take out a loan to buy their food contributions. Individual food choices are a major departure from the sociality of sharing an *umu*, as in rural island communities, or sending food across the seas. Those individuals with money to buy their lunch develop personal food preferences that may differ markedly from family food preferences. But when they exercise those preferences, they distance themselves from their family and its cultural gastronomic values. Expectations of what a family should or can offer to a funeral feast undergo public scrutiny and comment. Upholding social obligations through food is a key feature of reconstituting communities, particularly in overseas settings.

Food messages, whether as myths from the past, or recipes and routes of access to favoured island foods, are replacing the canoe and oral traditions. The telephone, texting and art all provide media both for motivating the oral and visual and other gastronomic senses, and for educating a wider public. All these options further enhance the diversity that has marked gastronomic transfers across time and space.

Blending has resulted in Pacific societies developing their own identifying foods together with a distinctive gastronomy. Over time, new foods and new ways of using those foods have been added to the gastronomy, *not substituted*. Good food is symbolised for Tongans and Pohnpeians by yams while for Fijians it is taro/dalo, and in the Marshall Islands it is breadfruit. When these groups come together in a metropolitan setting such as Honolulu or Wellington, each participating group ensures that its particular food is represented. Pacifica meetings in Wellington became noted for the Cook Island 'mayonnaise' that their people contributed to a Pacific event. Each Pacific community has selected its distinctive gastronomic features to distinguish its specific identity.

Conclusions

Food habits and gastronomies have followed three major transits into the Pacific, two from the orient and one from the occident (Euro/American). Three foodscapes depict the links between Pacific gastronomies today and those of the past. The Asian influence is of long duration and deeply embedded in gastronomic principles such as the starch/accompaniment principle, as when taro should be served with fish, while modern influences such as canned foods from both west and east have added to the diversity of foods and their uses. Adaptations of principles, for example the foods appropriate and available to give at feasts, have been elaborated and have added to the diversity of choices available to households today. The commercial spread of so-called global foodstuffs, such as McDonald's, increases the diverse options available to individuals and households, but they are not a full substitute for island foods. Whether in Nuku'alofa or Sydney, constraints on food choices due to family ties, tastes and available cash challenge expressions of identity through food.

References

Allaby, R. 2007. Origins of plant exploitation in Near Oceania. A review. In *Population genetics, linguistics and culture history in the south west Pacific*, ed. J. S. Friedlaender, 181–98. Oxford: Oxford University Press.

Alexeyeff, K. 2004. Love food—exchanges and sustainability in the Cook Islands. *Australian Journal of Anthropology* 15: 65–80.

Appadurai, A. 1996. *Modernity at large. Cultural dimensions of globalization*. Minneapolis: University of Minnesota Press.

Bellwood, P. 1997. *Prehistory of the Indo-Malaysian archipelago*. Honolulu: University of Hawai'i Press.

—. 2005   The farming/language hypothesis in the East Asian context. In *The peopling of East Asia*, ed. L. Sagart, R.Blench and A. Sanchez-Mazas, 1-25. London: Routledge Curzon Press.

Blench, R. 2005. From the mountains to the valleys: Understanding ethnolinguistics. In *The peopling of East Asia*, ed. L. Sagart, R. Blench, and A. Sanchez-Mazas, 31-50. London: Routledge Curzon Press.

Brillat-Savarin, J.-A. 1970 [1821] *The Philosopher in the kitchen*. Harmondsworth: Penguin.

Conklin, H. 1957. Hanunoo Agriculture. FAO Forestry Development Paper #12, Rome.

Coyne, N, J. Badcock and R. Taylor. 1984. The effect of urbanisation and western diet on the health of Pacific island populations. SPC Technical Paper 186. Noumea.

Firth, R. 1967. *The work of the gods in Tikopia*. London: George Allen and Unwin.

Hau'ofa, E. 1979. Corned beef and tapioca. Development Studies Monograph 19. Canberra: The Australian National University.

Howe, K. (ed.) 2007. *Vaka Moana*. Auckland: David Bateman Press and Auckland War Memorial Museum.

Irwin, G. 2006. Voyaging and settlement. In *Vaka Moana*, ed. K. Howe, 59-74. Auckland: David Bateman Press and Auckland War Memoriam Museum.

Kirch, P. 2000. *On the road of the winds*. Berkeley: University of California Press.

Miller, D. 1997. Capitalism, an ethnographic approach. Oxford: Berg.

Mintz, S. W. 2006. Food, history and globalization. *Journal of Chinese Dietary Culture* 2 (1): 1–22.

Pollock, N. J. 1986. Food classification in Fiji, Hawaii and Tahiti. *Ethnology* 25 (2): 197–118.

—. 1989. The early development of housekeeping and imports in Fiji. *Pacific Studies* 12 (2): 53–82.

—. 1992. *These roots remain*. Hawaii: The Institute for Polynesian Studies and University of Hawaii Press.

—. 1995. Introduction. In *The power of kava*, ed. N. Pollock. Special issue of *Canberra Anthropology* 18 (1 & 2): 1-19.

—. 2002. Vegeculture as food security for Pacific communities. In *Vegeculture in eastern Asia and Oceania*, ed. S. Yoshida and P. Matthews, 277-92. Osaka: Japan Center for Area Studies.

—. 2008. Chinese dietary influences in the Pacific. In *Proceedings of the 10th symposium of Chinese dietary culture*, ed. J. Chou. Taiwan: Foundation of Chinese Dietary Culture.

Pollock, N. J. and D. Dixon, and J. Leota. 1996. Food decisions in Wellington low income households. Report to the Department of Social Welfare, Wellington.

Schoeffel, P. 1985. Dilemmas of modernisation in primary health care in Western Samoa. *Social Science and Medicine* 19 (3): 209–16.

Sio, B. 1996. Taumafa Samoa mo le Lumanai 'Samoan Food for the Future'. Poster for World Food Day, Samoa, sponsored by FAO, Rome.

Stiglitz, J. 2006. *Making globalization work*. New York WW Norton.

Tuffery, Michel. 2007. First Contact. Art exhibition, cur. Helen Kedgley. Porirua: Pataka.

Walter, Annie and Vincent Lebot. 2007. *Gardens of Oceania*. Canberra: Australian Centre for International Agricultural Research.

Yo, A. Y. 1995. *At the South-east Asian table*. Oxford: Oxford University Press.

7. Attitudinal Divergence and the Tongan Transnational System

Mike Evans, Paul Harms and Colin Reid

Although Tonga is small and its impact on the global geo-political stage is limited, the way in which the country fits into the contemporary global system has attracted its share of attention. Since Marcus' early and cogent observations on the fact of Tongan transnationalism (1981), a great deal of ethnography has been done both in Tonga and with Tongan communities overseas. In just the last 10 years there have been significant full length ethnographies of contemporary Tongan political economy. Evans (2001) and van der Grijp (1993, 2004), for example, have written extensively on the way that the current Tongan economy is shaped by the world economic system. While van der Grijp is interested in processes of globalisation, Evans' work extends to transnationalism—but more to the manifestations on transnational practice in Tonga than a considered assessment of the Tongan transnational system as a whole (see Lee 2006). More detailed work on remittance practices has also been done (Brown 1994, 1995; Brown and Connell 1993). Others, including Besnier (2004), have written eloquently on the ways in which Tongan economic and linguistic practices have embraced a cosmopolitan view of both themselves and the world, and subtly on shifting engagements with tradition and exchange (Addo and Besnier, 2008).

A second trend in recent ethnographic work has been a focus on the Tongan migrant communities; work by Lee (2003) and Small (1997) has focused on the lives, practices and prospects of Tongan migrants. Most recently, we have seen work by Tongan ethnographers, like that of Ka'ili (2005), which focuses on the continuities in Tongan cultural practices in overseas communities.

Much contemporary work derives from concern about just how robust transnational ties are, especially over generations (see Lee 2003, 2004, 2006). Questions about the stability of migration streams, the potential for capital accumulation via migration and remittances, the stability of remittances from migrating and second-generation Tongans are key for Tongan individuals and families, and indeed, for the greater Tongan polity and economy. Whether and how remittances streams continue over time is, arguably, the core element to the stability of many Pacific Island economies, and certainly this is true of Tonga. In her 2004 article '"Second generation" Tongan transnationalism: Hope for the future', Lee develops an argument in support of the 'remittance decay hypothesis' (from Brown and Foster 1995), based primarily on her discussions with second generation and younger migrants who indicated that they have no intention of remitting to people in Tonga in the future, in part because they had no one left in Tonga to whom to remit.

Remittances play a fundamental role not only in the Tongan economy, but also in the maintenance of the Tongan gift exchange system. Evans (1999, 2001) shows in detail how remittances of both cash and kind play an on-going role in the creation and maintenance of relationships between both individuals and groups in multiple locations within the transnational system. While it is true that the notion of 'transnational corporations of kin' developed by Bertram and Watters (1985; see also Marcus 1981), is problematic (see James 1993 and Munro 1990), the notion that remittances are then to be understood in terms of the actions of individuals (James 1991, 1993; Lee 2004) is also debatable (Evans 1999: 143-144). Gift exchange, of which remittances are a type, are inherently relationship producing. Some of the greatest threats to the continuity of resource streams into Tonga are probably those based on the attenuation of gift exchange relationships which include people in Tonga, because of potential loss of the capacity to use lands to produce materials (Evans 1999). One of the problems with all these assessments of trajectory of the Tongan transnational system however, is that there is not yet a demonstrable decay in the flows of material through what we are calling the Tongan Transnational System (TTS). This is not to assert that the resource flows that energise the TTS need remain stable, but rather to make the claim that in spite of some very obvious transformations in the social, political, and economic landscape in the TTS, a decline is still not demonstrable—this in the face of claims that the end is nigh that go all the way back to Christine Ward Gailey's work on commodification in the 1980s (Gailey 1987).

While a good deal of attention has been paid to Tongan transnationalism, a contemporary anthropology of Tonga and the TTS is problematic because the system is geographically large, and the people operating within the system so diverse (Lee 2004, 2007a, 2007b; Small 1997). The anthropological conceit of a unified singular 'culture' that can be investigated and described has been under pressure for quite some time. This pressure came first from political economists who demanded that the embeddedness of economies and cultures within the world system be recognised (Asad 1973; Wolf 1982; Worsley 1984), and more recently from post-modernist authors suggesting, not unreasonably, that the experience of human social life is positioned by such things as age, gender, class and sexuality, and thus totalitarian images and representations of a culture were just that: totalitarian (see for example Haraway 1988). It is this later sensibility that shapes much recent work. After the little girl Dorothy in the Wizard of Oz, we might observe that no one, not even people actually living in Kansas, is in Kansas anymore.

In this paper we argue, by way of demonstration, that there is some untapped and certainly under-used potential in quantitative methods for assessing and describing contemporary transnational systems. Currently most quantitative analyses regarding Tonga are devoted to economic data—remittances and the like—but in other areas of the social sciences quantitative methods are used over a much wider range of phenomena. For several reasons, statistical analysis of sociological data is virtually non-existent in contemporary anthropology. While we recognise that there are real and immediate limitations and constraints to quantitative questionnaire style research, in this paper we discuss the results of just such a quantitative survey undertaken in Tonga and in the Tongan community in New Zealand. We offer this as a small contribution to conceptualising and describing the Tongan Transnational system—one of the striking elements of this way of describing the TTS is that fragmentation of attitudes and commitments, and therefore behaviour, seems less pervasive than some ethnographic accounts might suggest.

Developing a prognosis for Tongan migration and remittance behaviour on the basis of attitudinal assessments is not uncommon (James 1991, Lee 2004, Small 1997). Indeed we might make a cautious claim that in the absence of economic data demonstrating the expected decay in remittance behaviour, attitudinal assessments are the meat of the argument. But one key limitation to our current understanding of how people throughout the TTS think about the values and practices that underpin the system, is a lack of systematic assessment or reporting. That is, because qualitative methods are generally employed, it is difficult to determine the relative intensity or distribution of attitudes within the TTS. Though it has become quite uncommon to use quantitative surveys in anthropology, one of the advantages of such techniques is that analysis of attitudes, and most importantly the differences in attitudes within a sample, can be conducted. It is important to note here that difference within a sample is important in terms of how it is positioned—that is, for example, in terms of how gender, age, and location (i.e. subject position!) are related to variations in attitude. Neither the critique above, nor the analysis offered below, are intended to suggest that ethnographic representation is somehow flawed; no quantitative analysis can replace the impact of nuanced ethnographic practice. Nonetheless quantitative analyses do have something to offer, and this something has been all but lost to anthropology over the last couple of decades.

Towards a Quantitative Assessment of Attitudes in the Tongan Transnational System[1]

To develop such a quantitative description of the TTS, a questionnaire-style survey assessing the attitudes of people regarding key elements of Tongan identity was conducted in Tongatapu and Auckland in 2005. Participants were

Tongan adults (n=691) aged 16 years and older living in Tonga (n=504) and in the Tongan community in Auckland (n=187).[2]

The survey used was a questionnaire developed collaboratively and administered to each of the respondents.[3] It was comprised of four sections relating to: 1) demographics; 2) elements of Tongan identity; 3) rank order of important characteristics of a Tongan; and 4) characteristics of a good woman and a good man. This paper makes use of the first two sections: demographics and elements of Tongan identity.

In the 'demographic' section of the survey, people were asked basic questions such as gender, place of birth, place of residence, year of birth, time spent away from Tonga, level of education, occupation and church denomination membership. The 'elements of Tongan identity' section consisted of a series of items in which people were asked to assess their responses to particular statements along a seven-point Likert scale.[4] For example:

Over the course of a lifetime, these things are the responsibilities of all Tongans:

Teaching daughters to weave and make ngatu (i.e. barkcloth)

1	2	3	4	5	6	7
strongly disagree	disagree	no difference		agree		strongly agree

Seven dependent variables (or factors) were derived from the 64 items in the 'elements of Tongan identity' section of the questionnaire using a factor analysis.[5] This technique is one that groups statistically related individual items into larger and more robust meta-items (i.e. factors) that can then be used for subsequent analysis. In lay terms the technique establishes which items relate to the same underlying attitudes and groups them together. That is, the items in a factor are grouped together because they follow the same patterns of variation (are statistically similar to one another). Only those factors that include a minimum number of items (in this case, three) and meet certain statistical tests for reliability and robustness are used. The items included within each factor were then assessed in order to identify the common theme unifying the items. The items that form the factors are interesting in and of themselves as they are indicative of a collective view of the inter-relation between societal values.[6]

Factors Identified [7]

The first factor was identified as value placed on common goals and projects over individual ones. Items include:

In order to be a real Tongan, one must...

- Contribute to the funerals of relatives, church members, and friends
- Participate in a Tongan church, not some other church
- Regularly give generously to church.

One cannot be truly Tongan if one does not…

- Support schools one attended in the past
- Support projects in villages one grew up in
- Support collective Tongan projects in the place one is living
- *Faka'apa'apa* (show respect) to the nobility
- *Faka'apa'apa* to the king
- Share like a Tongan, e.g, share cigarettes at a *faikava*, or school supplies in the classroom
- Have *koloa faka-Tonga* (traditional Tongan wealth items)
- Give *koloa faka-Tonga* appropriately.

The issues bundled into this factor concern cooperation, mutual aid, and sharing; all the items are concerned with the common good and orderly society as people know it to have been in the past and mostly still want it to be today. Giving to church, to family events and rituals such as funerals—including having and bringing *koloa faka-Tonga* appropriately, donating to schools and village projects both in one's village of origin and in the place one presently resides—are all ways in which one shows oneself to be a part of a greater collective, hence having certain obligations. Similarly, attending a Tongan church, as opposed to a *pālangi* one, is to acknowledge responsibility to the social circle in which one grew up. The idea that a person must share like a Tongan to be identifiably Tongan encompasses this factor. The broad statement here is that Tongans take responsibility for their part within the social groups in which they participate. To show *faka'apa'apa* to the King, and the *hou'eiki* (high ranking people, i.e. nobles) also shows that one knows one's place in society. The King and the *hou'eiki*, among other things, are symbols of social order and centres for expressing social loyalty, and to be part of the group led by them is to have responsibilities within that group. To say it is important to *faka'apa'apa* to the *hou'eiki* is not so different from saying that it is important to contribute to one's village or to funerals in one's extended family—contributing appropriately to one's place within social order.

The second factor identified represents value placed on maintaining family relationships and cultural continuity. Items include:

Over the course of a lifetime, these things are the responsibilities of all Tongans…

- Travelling overseas to visit relatives there
- Hosting relatives visiting Tonga from overseas
- Participating in church
- Being known to participate in church
- Teaching daughters to weave and make *ngatu* (bark cloth)
- Teaching boys to be capable farmers
- Teaching children to be good at *faiva faka-Tonga* (Tongan dance)

- Teaching children about their ancestors and family history
- Seeing that children learn about Tongan art and history.

These items are about a kind of cultural continuity, including continuity in family structure and gender roles. The answers describe the socio-cultural environment that is comfortable for people. The importance of visiting family and hosting family when they visit, shows that family relations are not broken by international borders or distances. That people gave similar answers to the desirability of boys learning to farm, and girls learning to weave and make *ngatu* suggest that cultural change, especially that affecting gendered work and continuity with the past, is unattractive to most people. That young people should learn to be good dancers fits in with that—'traditional' Tongan skills are still valued. The importance of knowing about family and Tongan history also fit neatly into this category of important ways to maintain continuity with the past. Likewise, attending church is an important way to reproduce cultural values and to ensure a degree of conformity with the past.

The third factor meeting the criteria represents appropriate *faka'apa'apa* in everyday face-to-face relationships. Items include:

These are important parts of being Tongan...

- Showing *faka'apa'apa* to one's sister/brother
- Showing *faka'apa'apa* and deferring to one's parents
- Using language appropriate to one's social circumstances
- Respecting church leaders.

This is about *faka'apa'apa* on a more personal scale. It is about knowing one's place in one's own family and immediate social circumstances, and enacting that knowledge appropriately through one's relations with those others.

The fourth factor represents *obvious aspects of Tongan identity*. Items are:

In order to be a real Tongan, one must...

- Eat Tongan food a few times a week
- Be fluent in Tongan
- Speak Tongan on an everyday basis
- Be skilled at *faiva faka-Tonga*
- Have lived in Tonga for a significant period of time
- Have Tongan ancestors.

These are the most obvious, maybe most emotional, outward aspects of identity. Whether or not you can know if someone feels like a Tongan in their heart, you can always judge them by what goes into their mouths and what comes out. Living in Tonga is also one of those obvious signs of identity. Dancing is a fun, public mark of Tongan identity, especially overseas. Dancing is emotionally compelling and because the Tongan version is so difficult to do, competence or excellence at it definitely says something about a person.

The fifth factor represents *comparing quality and character of life in Tonga and overseas*. Items are:

- Tongans in Tonga have a better life than Tongans overseas
- Tongans in Tonga are more *fiemālie* (happy and content) than Tongans overseas
- Tongans in Tonga are more Tongan than those living elsewhere.

Each of these items asks people to compare life in Tongan with life overseas: where people have a better life, where people are more content and whether island Tongans are 'more Tongan' than overseas Tongans.

The sixth factor identified represents *attitudes about the hou'eiki as a people*. Items are:

- The *hou'eiki* are role models for Tongans today
- The *hou'eiki* are models of religious faith in Tonga today
- The *hou'eiki* are models of effective government work for Tongans today.

All these items speak about people's perceptions of *hou'eiki* in terms of how they behave in the contemporary TTS. This is distinct from more diffusely held ideas about *faka'apa'apa* more generally as a concept or ideal.

The seventh factor represents *iconic aspects of Tongan identity*.

Tongans are Tongans because they...

- Will always return to Tonga
- Value their families' interests over their personal interests
- Share generously in intelligent ways.

The items dealing with Tongans returning to Tonga, putting family before self and being thoughtfully generous are all three characteristics of *anga faka-Tonga* (the 'Tongan way') that both Tongans and almost any outside analyst who has ever been to Tonga would readily recognise as primary identifying characteristics of *anga faka-Tonga*. This makes them characteristically different from the obvious ethnic markers in Factor Four, which are also readily understood as characteristically Tongan, but are more superficial aspects of Tongan identity and daily life than these foundations of identity and social organisation and interaction.

Figure 7–1: Mean of Responses for each of Seven Factors

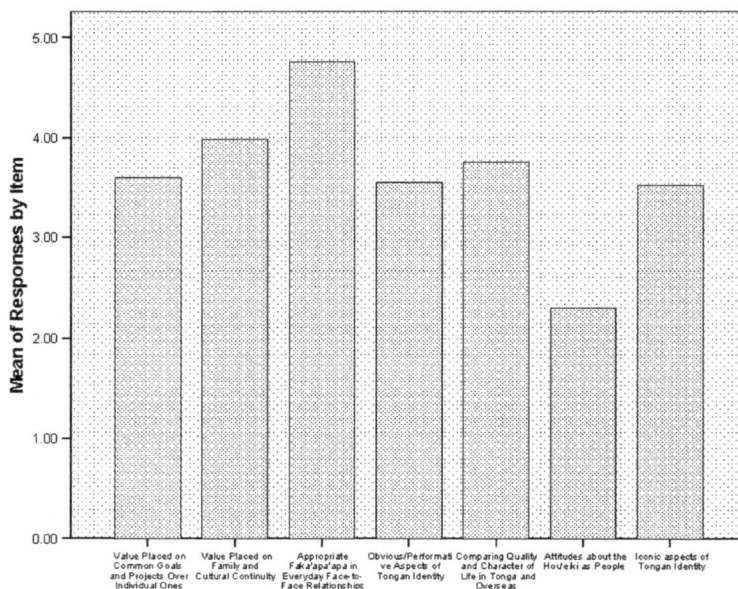

In Figure 7-1 we see the relative weighting of evaluation for each factor by the entire sample. Though this graph does not control for any independent variable, it is interesting if not definitive. In this graph '5' indicates a strong commitment to the underlying elements contained within the factor, '3' is an indication of neutrality, while anything under '3' indicates a negative evaluation. It is worth noting here that the most esteemed factor is that of *appropriate faka'apa'apa in everyday face-to-face relationships*, while the least is *attitudes about the hou'eiki as a people*. The next step in our analysis was to use the factors identified here to examine variation within the total sample. To do this a number of key characteristics of the respondents were chosen for examination. These 'independent variables' were used to investigate whether there were any statistically significant effects of gender, age, education, church membership, or residence patterns as described below.

Axes of Variation (independent variables)

Seven independent variables were assessed:

1) & 2) An independent variable of primary interest was *current place of residence*. The 10 initial categories (Ha'avakatolo, Sopu, Fo'ui. Nuku'alofa, Ha'apai, Vava'u, Tongatapu, New Zealand, United States and Australia) were reduced to three. These categories are: Nuku'alofa (Sopu, Nuku'alofa), the rest of Tonga (Ha'apai, Vava'u, Ha'avakatolo, Fo'ui) and overseas (New Zealand, US, Australia). Thirty one per cent of respondents (n=214) resided in Nuku'alofa, 26.5 per cent resided

overseas (n=187) and 42.5 per cent (n=290) resided in Tonga, but outside Nuku'alofa. In order to assess these data via the technique of a multiple regression equation, two dummy variables were computed.[8] One new variable, labelled *Current Residence 1*, compares those living in Nuku'alofa to all others (Nuku'alofa=1, others=0). The second new variable, *Current Residence 2*, compares those living overseas with all others (overseas=1, others=0).

3) *Church membership* was dichotomised based on whether a denomination was Tonganised or not.[9] The initial variable was comprised of seven categories, specifically, Free Weslyan, Free Church of Tonga, Latter Day Saints, Church of Tonga, Roman Catholic, Tokaikolo and other. The majority (83.7 per cent) of respondents identified themselves as belonging to Tonganised churches (all categories shown above except Latter Day Saints) and 16.3 per cent indicated that they belonged to a non-Tonganised church (Latter Day Saints).

4) *Time spent away from Tonga* was measured on a four-point ordinal scale. About one quarter of respondents (26.5 per cent) had not left Tonga, slightly more had been overseas for less than 12 months, about one quarter had been overseas for between one and 10 years, and one fifth (19.8 per cent) had spent at least 10 years away from Tonga.

5) *Gender* split was almost 50–50, with 50.8 per cent being males.

6) Mean *age* was 34.4 years (sd=14.3 years).

7) *Education* was measured on a four-point ordinal scale, asking respondents for the highest level of schooling obtained. Slightly less than half of respondents had not completed high school (47.5 per cent), one-in-four had finished high school (26.3 per cent), 17.8 per cent finished a tertiary degree or diploma, and 6.5 per cent had finished a university degree

Analysis

Multiple regression allows for simultaneous statistical control of multiple covariates and is robust in dealing with various levels of measurement and moderate degrees of measurement error (Tabachnick & Fidell, 2001); it is thus an appropriate technique for this situation. The seven independent variables described above were regressed on each of the dependent variables (i.e. the factors) in turn, for a total of seven regressions. That is, in the first regression, the independent variables—current residence 1, current residence 2, church membership, time spent away from Tonga, gender, age and highest level of schooling—were regressed on the dependent variable *value placed on common goals and projects over individual ones*. The following six regressions include the same seven covariates each time, with only the dependent variable being replaced each time.

Each of the seven equations was found to be statistically significant. The results of the analysis are presented here first in narrative form and then in a summary table:

Value placed on common goals and projects over individual ones: Six explanatory variables influence responses to this scale. Those living overseas tend to score lower on this scale than those living in Tonga outside Nuku'alofa, controlling for the effect of all other variables in the equation (a condition that applies to the remaining results reported). Longer duration of overseas living also results in lower scores, as does membership in the Latter Day Saints church compared to those belonging to other churches. Older age is associated with higher scale scores. Of all variables in this model, level of schooling is most strongly associated with this scale, as Tongans with higher levels of schooling tend to score lower on this scale. (Level of schooling is either the most important or second most important explanatory variable for all seven scales, and is always negatively related, i.e. more education is related to lower scale scores.) The relative ranking of the remaining five explanatory variables, in descending order, is age, overseas current residence, time spent overseas, and church membership. (Gender has no effect on any of the seven dependent variables and is not included in the remaining results reported.)

Value placed on maintaining family relationships and cultural continuity: Responses to this scale are uninfluenced by current residence, or church membership. Age is related, again positively (older Tongans score higher than do younger Tongans in general), as is time spent overseas in the same manner as with the previous scale (negatively). Church membership is unrelated. In order of importance, in descending order, we have level of schooling, age and time spent overseas.

Appropriate faka'apa'apa in everyday, face-to-face relationships: Age, level of schooling, and time spent overseas are related to scores on this scale. As with the previous two dependent variables, level of schooling is negatively related and age is positively related. Current residence, and church membership are unrelated. Of the statistically significant covariates, time spent overseas is ranked as most important, followed by levels of schooling and age, respectively.

Obvious/performative aspects of Tongan identity: Level of schooling is negatively related with this scale, as is time spent overseas. Age is positively related. Current residence is unrelated, as is church membership. Level of schooling is in relative terms most influential, followed in order by age and time spent overseas.

Comparing quality and character of life in Tonga and overseas: While level of schooling and time spent overseas remain significant explanatory variables and in the same direction as in all regression equations discussed above, age drops out and current residence emerges as the dominant covariate. That is, Tongans living overseas are more likely than Tongans resident in Tonga but outside Nuku'alofa to score low on this scale. Likewise, but not to the same extent, those resident in Nuku'alofa tend to score lower than Tongans resident in Tonga but outside Nuku'alofa. Relative rankings of the explanatory variables are current residence overseas, level of schooling, time spent overseas and current residence in Nuku'alofa. There were significant differences between the ideas of people living overseas and people living in Tonga at the time they filled out the forms.

Attitudes about the hou'eiki as a people: Two variables are related to this scale: level of schooling (negatively) and church membership, also negatively. The order of importance is schooling followed by church membership. The effect sizes are relatively small, which is reflected in the low R-squared (.03) and F statistic and its associated significance level (f= 2.62; p < .05).

Iconic aspects of Tongan identity: Responses to this scale are influenced in this model by two variables: level of schooling (negatively) and current residence. Tongans resident overseas tend to score lower than Tongans in Tonga (outside Nuku'alofa). For the second time, current residence emerges as the most important influence in the model on the dependent variable.

Additional observations: Overall, current residence does not exert significant effects on four of the seven scales, i.e., it appears that place of residence—whether overseas, in Nuku'alofa, or elsewhere in Tonga—does not influence the value that Tongans place on maintaining family relationships and cultural continuity, their view of the appropriateness of *faka'apa'apa* in everyday face-to-face relationships, their views of the obvious aspects of Tongan identity, or attitudes about the *hou'eiki* as a people. Current residence is weakly related to value placed on common goals and projects over individual ones. The two exceptions are for the dependent variables *comparing quality and character of life in Tonga and overseas*, and *iconic aspects of Tongan identity*. Of the remaining variables, level of schooling is most important overall. Age exerts a significant influence on four dependent variables and time spent overseas is a significant influence on five dependent variables. Church membership has an effect in two equations, while (again) gender has no effect in any equation. These data are summarized, with appropriate statistical detail in Table 7-1, as shown.

Table 7–1: Multiple Regression Results for the Seven Models: Unstandardised Correlation Coefficients and Model Fit (R-squared)

Independent variable	Factor 1	Factor 2	Factor 3	Factor 4	Factor 5	Factor 6	Factor 7
School	-.25***	-.18***	-.06**	-.17***	-.19***	-.12**	-.17***
Current residence 1	-.02	-.09	-.03	-.01	-.20*	-.03	-.08
Current residence 2	-.26*	-.04	-.05	-.08	-.49***	-.17	-.43**
Gender	-.10	.01	.03	.02	-.08	-.04	-.04
Age	.01**	.01***	.01**	.01***	-.00	-.00	.00
Church	-.21*	-.14	.04	-.08	.08	-.27*	-.07
Overseas	-.08*	-.06*	-.04*	-.09*	-.10*	-.01	-.02
F-statistic	14.35***	10.36***	5.70***	9.38***	14.02***	2.62*	6.82***
R-squared	.16	.12	.07	.11	.15	.03	.08

* $p \leq .05$; ** $p \leq .01$; *** $p \leq .001$

The data in Table 7–1 are presented as unstandardised correlation coefficients in order to help the reader to see the effect of variation in the independent variables (level of education, etc.) on the dependent variables. For example, we can see that for each difference in the level of education (1–4), there is a marked effect on factor 1, *value placed on common goals and projects over individual ones*, and with each increase in level of education (School) comes a corresponding decrease of -0.25 on a five-point scale; in other words, we can read the effect in the actual measure of the original data. It is important to recall here that this figure is for the effect of education within the *multiple regression analysis*, i.e., it is the effect of level of education when considered in the context of all the other independent variables at the same time.

The limitation of the presentation of the analysis using the unstandardised correlation coefficient is that we cannot assess the relative effect of the independent variables within a factor, because the scale of the effect varies. For example, we might think that there is a radically different effect from age than from level of schooling on factor one, but, because there are only four different values for level of education, and as many values for age as there are ages in the sample, the two are not comparable in relative terms. For this reason, the standardised correlation coefficient (called the *beta*) is usually calculated; the *beta*, however, measures relative effect across the independent variables (i.e. it is a standardised measure) but the values calculated are not directly comprehensible in terms of the original scale and are difficult to assess in terms of direct impact. In the interests of brevity, we present analysis of the *beta* in Table 7-2 showing the rank order of the independent variables on each factor.

It is this last table that shows most simply the effects of the independent variables. We have drawn out the detail in our narrative description, but a quick glance at the general pattern expressed in Table 7-2 indicates that 'level of schooling' and 'age' have the strongest and broadest relative effect in the analysis.

We do not speculate or offer further opinion on the root causes of the patterns that have emerged here, but rather leave it to the careful reader to contemplate the analysis in terms of their own specific interests.

Table 7–2: Relative Importance of Statistically Significant Independent Variables within each Model, Based on the Standardised Correlation Coefficient

Independent variable	Factor 1	Factor 2	Factor 3	Factor 4	Factor 5	Factor 6	Factor 7
School	1	1	2	1	2	1	2
Current residence 1	-	-	-	-	4	-	-
Current residence 2	3	-	-	-	1	-	1
Gender	-	-	-	-	-	-	-
Age	2	2	3	2	-	-	-
Church	5	-	-	-	-	2	-
Overseas	4	3	1	3	3	-	-

Conclusion

There is broad agreement among contemporary analysts of the Tongan Transnational System that change is afoot and that shifting attitudes brought on by increasing engagement with the world system, migration and globalisation are root causes of whatever change might come. There is less certainty about the degree and nature of change within the TTS, and the relative uniformity of patterns of change within the system. In the above analysis, we used quantitative data to establish the patterns of variation emerging within and between Tongans living in Tonga, and those living in Auckland. These variations are more complex than location alone can account for and contradict overly simple Tonga/Overseas Tongan community distinctions. We suggest that providing a quantifiable context with which to compare existing qualitative and narrative analyses of the degree and direction of transformations and distinctions within contemporary Tongan identity, while by no means definitive or without methodological caveats, is a valuable, and currently neglected, area of research. We would further suggest that employing techniques like these can add to discussions of the present and emerging nature of transnationalism more generally. Carefully and appropriately done, such analyses allow us to quantify divergence within transnational systems. We are not suggesting that such a turn should or could replace qualitative analyses, but rather that statistical assessments can provide a valuable context in which qualitative materials can be read and understood.

References

Addo, P-A. and N. Besnier. (2008). When gifts become commodities: Pawnshops, valuables and shame in Tonga and the Tongan diaspora. *Journal of the Royal Anthropological Institute* vol 14 (1): 39-59.

Asad, T. (ed.). 1973. *Anthropology and the colonial encounter*. Highlands, N.J.: Humanities Press

Bertram, G. and R. Watters. 1985. The MIRAB economy in South Pacific microstates. *Pacific Viewpoint* 26: 497–519.

Besnier, N. 2004. Consumption and cosmopolitanism: Practicing modernity at the second-hand marketplace in Nuku'alofa, Tonga. *Anthropological Quarterly* 77: 7–45.

Brown, R. 1994. Migrants' remittances, savings and investment in the South Pacific. *International Labour Review* 133 (3): 347–67.

—. 1995. Hidden foreign exchange flows: Estimating unofficial remittances to Tonga and Western Samoa. *Asian and Pacific Migration Journal* 4 (1): 35–54.

Brown, R. and J. Connell. 1993. The global flea market: Migration, remittances and the informal economy in Tonga. *Development and Change* 24: 611–47.

Brown, R. and J. Foster. 1995. Some common fallacies about migrants' remittances in the South Pacific: Lessons from Tongan and Western research, *Pacific Viewpoint* 36(1): 29–45.

Evans, M. 1999. Is Tonga's MIRAB economy sustainable? A view from the village, and a view without it. *Pacific Studies* 22 (3/4): 137–56.

—. 2001. *Persistence of the gift: Tongan tradition in transnational context*. Waterloo: Wilfred Laurier Press.

Gailey, C. W. 1987. *Kinship to kingship: Gender hierarchy and state formation in the Tongan Islands*. Austin: University of Texas Press.

Haraway, D. 1988. Situated knowledges: The science question in feminism and the privilege of partial perspective, *Feminist Studies* 14: 575–99.

James, K. 1991. Migration and remittances: A Tongan village perspective. *Pacific Viewpoint* 32 (1): 1–23.

—. 1993. Cutting the ground from under them? Commercialization, cultivation, and conservation in Tonga. *The Contemporary Pacific* 5 (2): 215–42.

Ka'ili, T. 2005. *Tauhi vā*: Nurturing Tongan sociospatial ties in Maui and beyond. *The Contemporary Pacific* 17 (1): 83–114.

Lee, H. 2003. *Tongans overseas: Between two shores*. Honolulu: University of Hawai'i Press.

——. 2004. 'Second generation' Tongan transnationalism: Hope for the future? *Asia Pacific Viewpoint* 45 (2): 235–54.

——. 2006. 'Tonga only wants our money': the children of Tongan migrants. In *Globalisation, governance and the Pacific Islands*, ed. S. Firth, 121-35. Canberra: Pandanus Press.

——. 2007a. Generational change: The children of Tongan migrants and their ties to the homeland. In *Tonga and the Tongans: Heritage and identity*, ed. E. Wood-Ellem, 203–17. Melbourne: Tonga Research Association.

——. 2007b. Transforming transnationalism: Second generation Tongans overseas. *Asian and Pacific Migration Journal* 16 (2): 157–78.

Marcus, G. 1981. Power on the extreme periphery: The perspective of Tongan elites in the modern world system. *Pacific Viewpoint* 22 (1): 48–64.

Munro, D. 1990. Transnational corporations of kin and the MIRAB system: The case of Tuvalu. *Pacific Viewpoint* 31 (1): 63–6.

Pett, M. A., N. R. Lackey and J. J. Sullivan. 2003. *Making sense of factor analysis: The use of factor analysis for instrument development in health care research*. Thousand Oaks, California: Sage Publications.

Small, C. 1997. *Voyages: From Tongan villages to American suburbs*. Ithaca: Cornell University Press.

Tabachnick, B. G. & L. S. Fidell. 2001. *Using multivariate statistics* (fourth ed.) Needham Heights, MA: Allyn & Bacon.

van der Grijp, P. 1993. *Islanders of the south: Production, kinship, and ideology in the Polynesian Kingdom of Tonga*. Leiden: KITLV Press.

——. 2004. *Identity and development: Tongan culture, agriculture, and the perenniality of the gift*. Leiden: KITLV Press.

Wolf, E. 1982. *Europe and the people without History*. Berkeley: University of California Press.

Worsley P. 1984. *The three worlds*. London: Weidenfeld & Nicolson.

ENDNOTES

[1] At the request of the editors we present this analysis in a colloquial style. We do so out of a desire to make the paper accessible to the anticipated readership of this volume and in the knowledge that this may disconcert those more familiar with the conventions of quantitative sociological work. Such is the current schism between qualitative and quantitative traditions in the contemporary social sciences that positioning this paper is somewhat problematic—we have done our best to balance the sensibilities of both broad traditions here.

[2] The sample was selected by Paul Harms; this sample was serendipitous. Most of the data was collected within church congregations, church choirs, and other institutional contexts both in Tonga and New Zealand; these were places where Harms was more and less known to the people involved. The best return rate on forms handed out was in contexts where he was most familiar with the greatest number of people and they were about as familiar with him (see Evans 2001, 10–11 on the significance of social relationship and survey response in Tonga). The church minister, the choir director, or the school principal was asked to introduce the researcher (Harms) and then the research was explained. The endorsement from a trusted leader was significant; survey forms were only handed out in places where such a leader was known to the researcher. In Auckland, in various congregations of the *Siasi 'o Tonga* (Church of Tonga) a church official introduced Harms. Initial contact happened at a regular Monday night *faikava* (kava drinking party) which involved young men in the *Siasi 'o Tonga* from all over Auckland and often also their church ministers. In some places, people filled in the forms immediately, but usually people would take them home and return them later. Some forms were also completed by Tongan students at the University of Auckland. Those were mostly filled in on the spot, although some were returned later. Similarly, a small number of forms were given to friends who handed them out to friends and colleagues; these were returned filled in. Though this sample was not random, we have every reason to believe it representative; further, the techniques for analysis have been selected to control for variation in gender, age, location, and level of education.

[3] The survey was developed by Paul Harms in both English and Tongan (of which he is a fairly fluent speaker). Half of the questions were written in each language, and then translated to the other. The questions and their organisation were based on a combination of ideas about the key issues in Tongan identity. This first draft was revised (and reduced in size) by Evans and then the questions were revised again in Tongan by Harms. Harms' questions were then evaluated by a number of Tongan first language speakers, including Siaosi Kavapalu, Seini Laungā, Suli Liava'a, and Fatai Vave, who all made important comments and suggestions. Tongan demographer Viliami Liava'a's input was especially helpful. There was a final revision of the content and wording of the Tongan form further according to these comments, and then a final revision to the English version to match it. Distribution of the survey in Tonga was assisted by Siaosi Kavapalu and Sione Koloamātangi.

[4] Because of concern over the impact of having a seven–point scale but only five written cues, the seven–point scale was reduced to a five–point scale by collapsing the values for 2 & 3 and 5 & 6.

[5] A factor analysis using principal components analysis and varimax orthogonal rotation was used for scale construction. The distribution for each item was examined to identify any non-discriminating items (those for which 90 per cent or more chose the same response) for deletion. The criteria for retention of a factor for the purpose of scale construction were: 1) at least three items retained per factor; 2) eigenvalue of at least 1.0; 3) interpretability of the factor. Individual items were retained for each factor analysis derived scale when associated factor loadings were 0.40 or higher (Pett, Lackey and Sullivan, 2003). Pett et al. (2003) also suggest 10 to 15 subjects per item for factor analyses, a standard met in this study. The retained items identified in each factor were assessed for internal reliability, based on a Cronbach's alpha of at least 0.65, and then summed to create each respective scale. Among the 17 factors having eigenvalues of 1.0 or greater, seven met the criteria for inclusion laid out above. Further statistical detail is beyond the scope of this paper.

[6] Herein lies one of the key problems with quantitative techniques—this statement is true only insofar as the questions asked reflect societal values in reasonable ways. In other words, asking sensible questions is a pre-requisite for getting sensible answers! In this study, the creation of good questions was achieved via the process outlined in footnote #3.

[7] Many of the observations that follow were contributed by Paul Harms.

[8] The new variables, technically referred to as 'dummy' variables, were computed to satisfy the statistical requirements of multiple regressions. Specifically, all the variables in a multiple regression are assumed to be measured at the interval level. The technique is robust enough to handle this conversion.

[9] This division of churches is somewhat problematic, as it effectively analyses the LDS as distinct from all others in the sample. Further, it could be argued that significant elements of LDS practice are in fact

Tonganised. We recognise these issues and make only a weak claim here that the Tonganised/non-Tonganised distinction captures a meaningful axis of variation.

8. Griffith's Transnational Fijians: Between the Devil, the Deep Blue Sea...and their Pastors

Mark Schubert

This chapter is about Fijians and their movements to and from an isolated rural area in Australia (Schubert 2008).[1] Pacific Islanders go to some of the most unlikely, isolated places and form communities and ways of communicating with other like-communities as survival tactics. This occurs in the face of pressures both in their homelands and their 'receiving' countries. Pacific Islanders endure adverse economic and political conditions at home. Although migration is an apparent solution to this 'squeeze' (Peutz 2006, 230), Islanders arriving in the United States, Australia and New Zealand find themselves being squeezed by an unforgiving labour market in which they must find a role to survive and often, in the early stages of migration, an absence of supportive kin networks. Quite aside from these post-entry issues, there is the initial problem of obtaining migrant entry.

In response to such pressures, a few hundred Pacific Islanders, specifically Tongans, Cook Islanders, Samoans, Vanuatuans, Solomon Islanders, Papua New Guineans, along with more than a hundred Fijians and fifty Fiji Indians have moved to Griffith, in south-west New South Wales, Australia. The majority of the Fijians and Fiji Indians of Griffith have emigrated in reaction to movements in societal structures of two different types on which they were dependent. The first were political and economic structures closely tied to each other, and also to structures outside Fiji. Fiji's major post-colonial political organisation was and is based on a division between Fiji Indians and Fijians. This division has its basis in a constitution underwritten by a schema that Fijians, as Fiji's foundation people, have pre-eminence over Fiji Indians. However, this unwritten understanding and articulated constitutional point has been continually contradicted by events, specifically in 1987, when a Fiji Labour Government won an election and although led by a Fijian, was perceived by many Fijians as an 'Indian' Government. Its election victory was enabled by Fiji's voting system, itself a child of the same Constitution.

The Fiji Army's suspension of Fiji's Constitution after a military coup that same year displeased the neighbouring governments of Australia, New Zealand, the United States, and also Fiji's pre-independence colonial power, Britain. Their unions boycotted transportation of goods to Fiji, which affected everyone; tourists stayed away; and aid, a source of so much public sector funding, was suspended. There were multiplier effects to Fiji's banking and credit system. These events directly affected some of Griffith's Fijians and Fiji Indians.

The political instability of 1987 had further long-term effects. It left some Fiji Indians feeling insecure about their futures, a feeling Pangerl (2007) identified as persisting almost two decades later among Fiji Indians. It stimulated changes in attitudes to land leasing, which affected the parents of some of Griffith's Fiji Indians. It also enabled, in subsequent years, a government policy of affirmative action for Fijians.

The second type of structures in which movements pushed Griffith's Fijians and Fiji Indians into emigration — cultural ones — were not experienced as a result of one epishift in a set of linked macro-structures on which so many depended. They were instead the effect of shifts in household relationships about which beliefs as to their differential roles, responsibilities and inheritance rules were fairly commonly held and reproduced from household-to-household across Fijian and Fiji Indian societies; for example, household relationships between husband and wife, interrupted by divorce, death or abandonment, or between parent and child because of emigration. Other of Griffith's Fiji Indians and Fijians either did not have to face such personal events or were unaffected by the more general ones, which enabled them the room to choose what they wanted and how they would achieve it.

Griffith is not a place in which one would expect to find Fijians, Fiji Indians and other Pacific Islanders. Although it is the largest population centre in the Murrumbidgee Irrigation Area and has a regional population of about 23,000, of which 14,000 people live in the 25 square kilometers of the town, its ecology and climate bear little resemblance to the wet, mountainous greenery by the sea, from which Fijians and Fiji Indians originate, and has been described by one of its natives, Hollywood-based film director Philip Noyce, as 'a small town…surrounded by a desert' (Petzke 2004, 4). It is dry, flat and windy, its flatness and red earth punctuated only by the green leafy tops of orange trees and monotonous, unending rows of grape vines. In summer, Griffith's temperatures can climb to 45°C and in winter drop to minus 4°C.

How do we account for the creation and maintenance of communities such as these Fijians and Fiji Indians on the edge of Australia's desert? Contrary to the manner in which Griffith's Fijians organise themselves, Griffith's Fiji Indians are largely isolated from each other due to their having had very few pre-migration relations; having arrived in Australia and Griffith at different times; and having different types and levels of incorporation into Australian society (the majority of them have arrived in Australia as documented migrants). Their mutual isolation is also a residual outcome of the process of indenture from India to Fiji that left their forebears with the experience of lack of kin and absence of adequate numbers of members of their own and other castes to re-establish a caste system in Fiji (Jayawardena 1971; Grieco 1998). Their mutual isolation is, however, complemented by some limited links, but mainly between those of the same religion, Indian region-of-origin and family type.

The focus of this paper is Griffith's Fijian population. The step-migration of Fijians to this unlikely location on the edge of the Australian desert is the result of two factors. Firstly, Australian migration entry rules over the last two decades have increasingly favoured migrants with skills and capital, and such requirements have meant that Fijians (and others) have found it increasingly difficult to obtain permanent entry to Australia. Secondly, with political instability in Fiji causing uncertainty, especially for urban Fijians and those predominantly dependent on cash for their livelihoods, Fijians have had to deploy entry tactics to Australia such as marriage to an Australian citizen for visa sponsorship, and overstaying after entering on a tourist visa, as a means of delaying or avoiding return to Fiji.

While I was conducting fieldwork in 2003 and 2004, 49 of the 79 Fijians (67 per cent) in Griffith were either undocumented or had been so at some time in the previous two decades. Twenty of them had been sponsored in some form and only five had arrived in Australia as authorised, permanent, migrants.

The tactic of overstaying has been no guarantee of avoiding harassment or removal from Australia by immigration authorities. In fact, it was and is a sure way to invite it. But settlement in Griffith, about four hours drive from the nearest Department of Immigration office in Canberra, has been a tactic used by Fijians to minimise detection by immigration authorities in the cities and in the hope that, at some future point, immigration entry rules may change or some other means of being documented, such as spousal sponsorship, will be found. While undocumented Fijians wait for this day, their settled relatives and friends, both documented and undocumented, can provide plentiful low or unskilled work for them, including orange, grape and vegetable picking. Griffith's economic base is agricultural output of four types: fruit, vegetables, rice, and meat stock such as cattle and poultry (Griffith City Council 2003).

Many of these agricultural products provide the basis for a range of secondary industries. With about 25 per cent of Australia's wine grapes grown in the area, there is an extensive wine-making industry. Sixteen of Australia's largest wineries have plants in the area which accounts for 80 per cent of all wine produced in New South Wales (Griffith City Council 2003). Other fruit and vegetable produce is processed by two large processing plants and poultry is processed by Australia's second largest processor of poultry meat (Griffith City Council 2003).

The abundance of Griffith's agricultural and secondary agricultural output means a low unemployment rate. Australia's 2001 Census showed that Griffith's unemployment rate was 4.9 per cent, significantly lower than either the New South Wales rate of 7.2 per cent or the national rate of 7.4 per cent (Australian

Bureau of Statistics 2001). Affluence is evident in the abundance of expensive cars driven along Griffith's main street, Banna Avenue, a thoroughfare lined with chic restaurants, bistros and bars, the likes of which one would normally expect to find in Melbourne's Brunswick or Lygon Streets, Brisbane's West End or Sydney's Balmain.

While undocumented Fijians generally work in different locations from their documented kin and friends, in the evenings and on weekends they retreat to their own 'Fijian spaces' to recreate and choreograph Fiji, whether with the daily ritual of *yaqona* (kava) drinking, or the less frequent rites of passage (*vakabogiva*) that follow usually four nights after births, deaths and the onset of puberty. These take place in domestic spaces, as well as in their churches and community meetings.

With a relatively permanent, core Fijian group with permanent residence or citizenship, there is a continual flow of Fijians through Griffith; for example, visiting relatives and friends who arrive to earn as much cash as they can, while they can, before deciding whether 'going on the run' from immigration authorities will pay off financially. In some cases, Fijians are on their way to Iraq as 'security specialists', or to East Timor as police officers. Others are simply relatives and friends from New Zealand with that country's citizenship.

There is also frequent movement from Griffith to Fiji for short holidays, funerals, weddings and births. Other temporary destinations are New Zealand and, in one case, frequent visits by a Griffith resident (Australian citizen) husband to his Fijian wife working in California without authorisation, but whose work in California paid for rent of his flat in Griffith.

The Fijians in Griffith are also connected to Fiji through a range of means including email, mainly from the local library and the town's two internet cafes, and telephone. Apart from the favourite topic of conversation in Griffith, which is 'who has been caught by...who is on the run from...who is waiting to get their papers from...Immigration', a frequent topic of conversation is the relative benefits of the many available phone cards that can be purchased from any of Griffith's corner milk bars to provide the cheapest possible overseas phone calls. The most popular card Fijians used for phoning overseas when I was conducting fieldwork was *Good Morning Pakistan*.

Strolls with Fijian friends along Griffith's main thoroughfare on summer evenings were frequently interrupted as one or another headed to a nearby phone booth and, with a spare phone card in his pocket, phoned a friend in Fiji to discuss a debt, an approaching wedding in Fiji, or a proposal to bring a relative to Australia on a tourist visa. In one household, I frequently observed the husband making a phone call to his wife's aunt, who was staying without documents in the US; then calling his mother in Sigatoka; then, on two occasions, calling a recruitment agent in Dubai to enquire about a job vacancy in the United Arab Emirates that he had seen on the internet.

In another case, apart from the local phone calls into and out of the household over one day, I observed a phone call to Lautoka in western Fiji to arrange for the safe transportation of the family's youngest child from his boarding school in central Fiji to Nadi Airport; then a call to the child's sister in Sydney to ensure he would be picked up from the airport to catch the right shuttle flight to Griffith. Later that night, when the child had arrived home in Griffith, the father, using the same card, phoned his brother, a *talatala* (pastor) in Seattle, and spoke and joked for two hours.

The flow of Fijians into and out of Griffith is determined by more than just an autonomous desire to stay to live and work or find greener fields elsewhere. The pressure from Australian immigration authorities on one side, and authority figures from Fiji on the other, makes it difficult for many in the Griffith community to move on and, for others, difficult to stay. The Immigration Department's increasingly frequent visits to Griffith have forced undocumented Fijians to decide between taking their chances in Griffith, where they are familiar with the physical layout and live in a set of trusted Fijian relationships; or move to another town and risk detection in an unfamiliar location and relatively untested social network. There is some risk in being undocumented among one's documented kin and friends as some Fijians' disagreements and altercations can result in being 'dobbed in' to the immigration authorities.

Fijians refer to the Immigration Department as *tevoro* (devil), a concept that locates departmental officials on the antagonistic, profane side of a migration cosmology that, in making sense of and justifying their migrations and undocumentedness, Fijian settlers construct out of a constellation of discourses and narratives that can draw on pre-Christian mythology, the post-migration power of Fijian Christian worship practices, and appeals to Biblical discourses of Israel, oppression, famine, flight and a Promised Land. In the first case of pre-Christian mythology, for example, some of Griffith's Fijians from Fiji's southern island of Kadavu tell the story of an octopus, the totem for some Kadavus, which caught a shark and would not let it go. Pleading to be released, the shark agreed to the octopus' deal that Kadavus should, from that time on, never be harmed by *any* sharks, *anywhere*. This story is then usually quickly followed up by the relating of an incident in which a young boy from Kadavu stowed away on a ship to Sydney. When he arrived in Sydney Harbour, the story goes, he jumped ship and was never seen again. 'The Harbour authorities kept on saying that the sharks in the Harbour must have eaten him. But *we knew!…we knew that he was safe! The sharks never hurt people from Kadavu!'* said my Kadavu informant, an elder in the Seventh Day Adventist Church.

There was also a frequently related story of a Fijian congregation in Sydney that, through the construction of the story's characters, pits undocumented but righteous and clever Fijians against secular, white, plodding immigration officers. The story goes that in a church, the benediction was about to be delivered by the *talatala*. But just as he closed his eyes to deliver it for the large number of Fijians present, he was told by one of the deacons that the *tevoro* (immigration authorities) were outside the church waiting to detain him for having overstayed his visa. As the rest of the congregation closed their eyes, he began to *masu* (pray) but, as he so did, he moved close to a window at the back of the church through which he climbed and took flight down the road, leaving his congregation with their eyes closed, while putting as much distance as he could between himself and the *tevoro*. Some versions of this story have an addendum to the effect that half of the congregation followed the *talatala* in flight from the *tevoro* for the very same reason.

Hybridised Biblical discourses are used in conversation, not to show the powers on which Fijians can ultimately draw when faced with white, secular immigration officers, but to justify their own undocumented migrations to Australia and subsequent step-migrations to Griffith. For example, undocumented Milly, who along with her husband Michael had been given shelter and food by her distant relative Meri,[2] combined the quite distinct Old Testament stories of Abram and Sarai (Genesis 12) with Joseph's brothers (Genesis 42), as she explained: 'All we wanted to do was to come to Australia to eat, to drink, to survive … we couldn't in the village in Fiji … we were just like Abram and Sarai who went into Egypt because of famine in Canaan.'

The use of such a hybridised Biblical rationale fits within a far wider, grander Biblically-based discourse that some Fijians use to frame the coups in Fiji in 1987 and 2000. According to Daniel,[3] from western Fiji, who was one of George Speight's gunmen in the 2000 coup attempt, and who was visiting relatives in Griffith:

> It is not the Indians who are our problem. The Indians are our brothers and sisters. It is the Lauans and the others without land who are the problem. We people from the interior of Viti Levu…we have land…we are the true rulers of Viti, not these Islanders, who use Fiji and its wealth for themselves. God gave *us* the land. These others play around with it, abuse it. They have led us away from God. So God uses the Indians to win power in Fiji to punish we Fijians when we stray from Him, like God did to the Israelites by allowing the Philistines to invade and punish them.

On the other side of the *tevoro* in this equation are the *talatalas* who pass through Griffith from Fiji. The messages they deliver can be summarised in the admonition 'do not stray from *vakavanua* (Fijian way), from the protocol of the village'. Like their migrant congregations, they frequently draw sermons from the Old Testament that frame Fijians as the Israelites and Australia, with its money and secularism, as Babylon. 'Return home' is the underlying message, but also, 'if you must be in Australia, *be* Fijian'.

Talatalas complain that when Fijians return to Fiji with a life and assets in Australia, or with money earned from casual labour during a holiday, they expect to be listened to in the village and the church, an expectation that stands regardless of the position they held in the village prior to emigrating. 'They have learned about *human rights* in Australia', a Seventh Day Adventist *talatala* from Suva on a three-week evangelistic campaign in Griffith complained to me, 'but they don't know how to be Fijian'.

In spite of a generic respect for their *talatalas*, Griffith's Fijians pay lip-service to their admonitions. The logic of this lip-service is simple: if one does not have permanent residence or citizenship, returning to Fiji means being unable to go back to Australia without being barred for a significant period from applying for a visa for a return trip, an exclusion period of up to five years. So, for the undocumented, staying unlawfully in Griffith is the most economically rational choice.

For Fijian permanent residents and citizens of Australia, the logic of their lip-service is also very simple. First, a permanent return to Fiji is financially unattractive. Second, to be Fijian, to be all-inclusive and have open pockets would be disastrous in a ruthless market economy like Australia's. Griffith does provide some relief from the expectation that its settled Fijians will provide an economic buffer to the newly arrived and undocumented. Living costs, especially for food, can be significantly reduced by creating relationships with farmers by providing them with a ready Fijian labour force at harvest time, as many of the long-settled Fijians have done. The farmers are often happy to provide, in return, the best agricultural produce that is surplus to their own or their markets' requirements, at no cost to the Fijians and other Pacific Islanders.

The buffer that the long-settled Fijians and those who have accumulated sufficient assets to carry the costs for those who have not yet achieved such a level does, however, have a limit. After a formal interview with a couple who continually had Fijian kin and friends lodging with them (including me for six months), they asked me if I could help a couple, who had been living with and depending on them for about four years, to obtain a visa of some kind to reduce the financial burden on them, the hosts. The unmanageable cost to them had not been the household utility costs or food, but the cost of medicines and medical specialist treatment, which they claimed had accumulated to AUD$30,000.

So, how do we account for the creation and maintenance of this Fijian community on the edge of Australia's desert? It has emerged out of attraction to work as a means of survival and its distance from government surveillance. But Griffith's attractiveness to Fijians is more than that. Along with the continued availability of work and the ability Fijians have to communicate with other Fijians in Australia, Fiji and elsewhere, even in its relative isolation Griffith is still close enough to the major transport portal of Sydney to enable quick and cheap movement to and from Fiji. Sydney can be reached from Griffith in one hour by air and about six hours by car, bus and train; and a few hours after arriving in Sydney, a Griffith Fijian can be in Fiji sitting doing *tanoa* (drinking kava) in his or her home village or out looking for cousins in their town market place. Thus Griffith not only allows its Fijians to physically survive and, if needed, avoid the Immigration Department, but it also allows a few Fijians to be truly *transnational* (with more relationships in Australia with non-Fijians), but most to be truly *transmigrant* (with more relationships with Fijians in Australia and Fiji) (Scott 2003) through living in a place that enables the Fijian part of Griffith to be one section of a larger, single Fijian community that extends across three (or more) nation-states.[4] While Australia and Fiji have no common borders, Griffith, located inland, plays for its Fijians the role that the US-Mexican border does 'for many Mexicans who travel between…Aguililla (Michoacin) and Redwood City (California), between which such separate places become effectively a single community' (Clifford 1994, 304). To paraphrase Rouse (1991, 14) this occurs through the continuous circulation of money, information, cultural affirmations and people.

Thus for Fijians moving between such communities, nation-states and their borders are simply in their way. At one time, Fijians, like other Pacific Islanders migrated, traded, colonised and waged war across their deep blue sea in sea-going vessels. In the 21st century, Fijians still move across that deep blue sea, although now mainly through the air above it and then across deserts to places like Griffith. While such journeys and settlements take place against a backdrop of unpredictable secular, white Australians who can put a stop to Fijians' migration projects, Griffith's Fijians' moral self-constructions and justifications, based on identification with Biblical characters and their divinely inspired quests, give them a feeling of moral power greater than anything to which an Australian immigration officer has access.

References

Australian Bureau of Statistics. 2001. Census of Population and Housing. http://www.abs.gov.au (accessed 10 February 2006).

Clifford, J. 1994. Diasporas. *Cultural Anthropology* 9 (3): 302–38.

Grieco, E. M. 1998. The effects of migration on the establishment of networks: Caste disintegration and reformation among the Indians of Fiji. *International Migration Review*, 32 (3): 704-736.

Griffith City Council. http://www.griffith.nsw.gov.au (accessed June 2003).

Jayawardena, C 1971. The disintegration of caste in Fiji Indian rural society. In *Anthropology in Oceania: Essays presented to Ian Hogbin, ed.* L. R. Hiatt and C. Jayawardena, 89-119. Sydney: Angus and Robertson.

Pangerl, M. 2007. Notions of insecurity among contemporary Indo-Fijian communities. *The Asia Pacific Journal of Anthropology* 8 (3): 251-264.

Petzke, I. 2004. *Backroads to Hollywood—Phillip Noyce.* Pan Macmillan: Sydney.

Peutz, N. 2006. Embarking on an anthropology of removal. *Current Anthropology* 47 (2): 217–41.

Rouse, R. 1991. Mexican migration and the social space of postmodernism. *Diaspora* 1 (1): 8–23.

Schubert, M. E 2008. *'When I get my paper': Migration, survival and relationships of Fiji Indians and Fijians in Griffith, New South Wales.* Unpublished PhD thesis, University of Queensland.

Scott, G. 2003. Situating Fijian transmigrants: Towards racialised transnational social spaces of the undocumented. *International Journal of Population Geography* 9: 181-198.

ENDNOTES

[1] Based on unpublished PhD thesis *'When I get my paper': Migration, Survival and Relationships of Fiji Indians and Fijians in Griffith, New South Wales*, University of Queensland 2008. My eternal thanks to my late wife Judi Watts-Schubert (24/8/1955—19/1/2007) for her reading of the original conference paper and putting up with this project during our tragically short marriage (16/10/2004—19/1/2007). Jodi, I miss you, love you…and always will.

[2] These are pseudonyms.

[3] A pseudonym.

[4] Fiji, Australia and New Zealand (we might even include the west coast of the USA).

9. Transnationalism of Merchant Seafarers and their Communities in Kiribati and Tuvalu

Maria Borovnik

Introduction

Seafarers cannot be immediately recognised as contributing to the transnationalism of their home countries. Criss-crossing internationalised, de-nationalised and national waters during their employment on merchant vessels and living with multi-national crews, seafarers could rather be seen in many ways as pioneers of global citizenship.[1] Despite the dynamic of their employment and the transversal and circulating movement between home and shipboard communities, seafarers from Kiribati and Tuvalu still maintain strong links to their families and cultures at home. These family and cultural connections include regular remittances, money sent back home, but also in exchange the reception of culturally meaningful material from families, and the maintenance of activities and memories while working on ships, connects seafarers to their homes. This chapter adopts a framework that considers transnationalism as a dynamic, multi-dimensional and multi-inhabited space.

Recruitment of Pacific seafarers working for international merchant vessels had for a long time a rather informal touch. The British owned *China Navigation* company (now *Swires,* UK, based in Hong Kong*)*, for example, recruited men from the Gilbert and Ellice Island colony since 1959 (Connell 1983, 33), originally for their transport ships between Nauru, Tarawa and Funafuti, and then by manning their international merchant ships with men from the same region. This informal and on-the-job trained recruitment changed, however, significantly in 1966 when the German Hamburg Süd Dampfschiffahrtsgesellschaft (HSDG or Hamburg Süd) discovered employment opportunities on the shores of Tarawa (Sieg 1999).

The discovery of recruiting opportunities in the central Pacific was followed by the construction of marine training facilities on Betio, Tarawa (Marine Training Centre or MTC),[2] and after a number of successful deployments onboard German and British vessels, the HSDG decided to establish a recruitment agency in 1969, consisting of a conglomeration of German and British shipping companies, that would make the international employment of young I-Kiribati[3] and Tuvaluan men possible. It was only about ten years after the establishment of SPMS that first Tuvalu in 1978 and then Kiribati in 1979 became independent from the former British Protectorate. Already in early years, the British based shipping company had left SPMS, and the agency consisted from then on of German shipping companies only.[4] SPMS facilitated signing up of men to their vessels under exceptional national German agreements.[5]

After independence, Tuvalu opened its own marine school, which is now the Tuvalu Maritime Training Institute (TMTI) on Amatuki Island of Funafuti atoll; and a Funafuti based recruitment office, which is now the Tuvalu Marine Service (TMS). Only a few years later, independently from SPMS/TMS, a German company decided to recruit Tuvaluans only through the Alpha Pacific Navigation Limited (APNL) agency. Kiribati's options for employment of seafarers also extended, when a conglomerate of Japanese tuna companies decided in 1989 to invest in training and recruitment of men on fishing vessels. Since 2002 employment on Norwegian cruise liners has become possible for men and, since 2003, for women working aboard in catering services. The SPMS has recently taken a leap of faith when under relatively strict pre-conditions and safety measures, the first I-Kiribati women seafarers have been trained in 2005 as cooks and stewards and recruited onboard merchant vessels.

The development in training and recruitment facilities in Kiribati and Tuvalu, can be seen as a reflection of the entry of the shipping industry into globalisation in the late 1960s and beginning 1970s. These early initiations were followed by a rapid development of merchant shipping as a multinational and international industry, characterised by a progression into 'internationalising' crews, management and ship nationality. It is true today that merchant multinational crews are under multinational management, registered under special 'de-nationalised'[6] agreements on ships with international flags, traversing through international and de-national maritime space (Borovnik 2004, Lane 1999; Sampson 2003). It can be argued that within this complex and highly competitive global system it is the maintenance of strong cultural identities and values, together with the acceptance of mobility as a means of network activities of family or community members, and the responsibility of sending remittances to their home countries, that have led to the successful and ongoing participation of I-Kiribati and Tuvaluan seafarers for almost forty years.

The recruitment history, however, also reflects on the division of the two world-systems that Germany and Kiribati/Tuvalu symbolise, and also the economic aspects of such relationships that accompanied the globalisation process of the shipping industry. There were, and still are, significant levels of unemployment and low economic resources in Kiribati and Tuvalu, which made it possible for old and well established European companies to offer employment contracts that would be attractive for Tuvalu and Kiribati and lucrative for their own management. In doing so, managers of HSDG emphasised both their economic interest and their concern in helping to develop small countries in the

Pacific. Hence, the establishment of marine training facilities first on Tarawa, and then later on Funafuti ensured a high standard of employment for I-Kiribati and Tuvaluan seafarers. The provision of good training, nowadays based on international Standards of Training Certification and Watchkeeping (STCW), has resulted from what Lane (1999, 24) describes as 'values of pride in craft'. Long established shipping companies desired links between strong nation based values of employment standards with 'mundane rituals and symbols' of 'organically linked' shipboard societies, and hence sustained 'an occupational culture' even though members of these societies had become multinational (Lane 1999, 23f). This aspect of 'pride in craft' can still be found in the attitudes of some of the older or retired I-Kiribati and Tuvaluan seafarers today, especially those that are now working onshore, in marine training institutions, or for recruitment agencies.[7]

As a result of deregulation processes and structural changes in the shipping industry, 'there are at any one time approximately one million seafarers aboard ships, operating in international ports and waters, who live and work in communities which are multinational and which exist *beyond* national boundaries' (Sampson 2003, 260, emphasis in original). Elsewhere I have discussed the combination of sharing a work environment that involves travelling through waters of different national or de-national regulations, and in such a confined space as a vessel, as a reality on the 'edges' of transnationality (Borovnik, 2003, 2004; and see Sampson, 2003; Yeoh et al, 2003). The long established rituals and links between shipboard communities, employers and merchant seafarers create transnational communities in a wider sense, when we adopt a framework that includes dynamic circulating spaces and when we include the regular maintenance of strong links and activities between international seafarers and their home countries.

This paper is based mainly on extended information gathered on Kiribati through six months fieldwork in 1999, where a total of 136 individual interviews and six focus groups were conducted on Tarawa and two outer islands with seafarers, their wives, parents and family members, village elders, both men and women, government officials, managers and employees of recruitment agencies, union leaders, women's groups, church leaders, medical personnel, and others. Some of these interviews were interpreted by local field assistants. Some of this qualitative information, and remittances data, was then updated by two subsequent short visits to Kiribati in 2004 and 2006, and a few days in Tuvalu in 2006.

I will, in the following section, provide brief background information on Kiribati and Tuvalu and then place this chapter into the framework of transnationalism, by linking it with seafarers and with mobility in the Pacific. Transnational frameworks discuss the nation state as significant, but in the context of Pacific seafarers a more dynamic concept must become the key unit of analysis, linking directly to the concept of family. This argument will then be illustrated by relating it to seafarers from Kiribati.

Kiribati and Tuvalu

Kiribati and Tuvalu, both low lying atoll island states, have relatively small land surfaces with 810.5 square km for Kiribati and 24.4 square km for Tuvalu. Due to their Exclusive Economic Zones they have vast maritime space, 3.5 million square km for Kiribati and 750,000 square km for Tuvalu (Asian Development Bank 2002a, 2002b; Connell 2003, 92). Population sizes are small: an estimated 97,000 for Kiribati, and just 10,000 people in Tuvalu. Problematic, however, is the high percentage of young population[8] and rapid urban growth[9] which leads to density and environmental problems in both capital islands, Tarawa and Funafuti. As small island economies these countries face challenges such as small market size, distance from markets or main centres, higher transportation costs, and because of their remote location, both sea freight charges and costs to passengers are high.

Distances and high transport costs are a disadvantage for island economies, as it makes tourism difficult and circular labour migration costly (World Bank 2006). Both countries' economic growth is concentrated on their public sectors (Asian Development Bank 2002a,b) with consequentially small private sectors; the Tuvalu private sector contributes approximately 30 per cent to GDP, with only 15 per cent business participation (Conway 2006); private sector employment in Kiribati accounts for 25 per cent in total (Asian Development Bank 2002a). Added to the economic challenges are environmental challenges, such as low rainfall, lack of natural resources, the occurrence of cyclones in Tuvalu, and the threat of sea level rise.

Existing migration schemes for Kiribati and Tuvalu are small. In contrast to many other Pacific nations, Kiribati and Tuvalu do not have the privilege of free access to one of the Pacific Rim countries. Under the Pacific Access Quota, however, both countries are granted entry for 75 people each to New Zealand. This access has a number of strict conditions, such as applicants having to hold a job offer at the time of application (New Zealand Immigration 2007). Since 2006 New Zealand has offered a 'seasonal working scheme', allowing some Pacific Islands, including Tuvalu and Kiribati to apply for contract work in vineyards and orchards.

In view of the relatively vulnerable economic circumstances and the restriction of free movement, it can be said that the seafarer scheme has turned out to be very successful for both countries, making a significant contribution to the Kiribati and Tuvaluan economies. Remittances make an estimated contribution of 15 to 20 per cent to Kiribati's and 50 per cent to Tuvaluan's national income.

Kiribati currently receives remittances of AUD$12-13 million dollars (Borovnik 2006); Tuvalu AUD$3-4 million (Boland and Dollery 2005).

Placing Seafarers in the Concept of Transnationalism

Considering the dynamics of current international types of contract labour migration it is the recognition of multiple and constant interconnections and networks across international borders that has made the framework of transnationalism popular and suitable for the inclusion of labour circulation and movements that are more than just uni or bi-directional (Glick Schiller, Basch, Szanton Blanc 1995; Pries 1998,). These include the shift from the consideration that contract labour across national borders would have only been sought out in order to achieve economic advancement (Portes 1997), to the inclusion of social and cultural aspects, for example that migrants as well as circulating contract workers lead dual lives with regular contact between migrant and home community (Portes Guarnizo, Landoldt 1999). The new concept also includes multiple circular movements that can lead to frequent and strong links between countries, common identities, and to the development of transnational spaces, mobile livelihoods and transnational communities (Duany 2002; Portes 2003; Vertovec 2001, 2003; Wimmer and Glick Schiller 2003). Of particular interest for the circumstances of seafarers is the aspect of negotiation of common identities that had been recognised by Vertovec (2001), and that social practices between migrants and their communities at home could be regarded as articulations of transnationality (Lee 2007; Levitt, DeWind and Vertovec 2003).

These notions on transnational space and mobility have led to geographical space becoming an increasingly fluid concept. Crang, Dwyer and Jackson (2003:445) argue that it is not the boundaries of the nation states but the processes that matter: 'the nation state continues to play a key role in defining the terms in which transnational processes are played out'. These authors, however, feel that transnational space should also include 'fluid maritime space' and this could be expressed by Leontis' (1997:181) concept of *emporion*, which is based on an old Greek meaning of circulations of 'traffic in merchandise, especially by ship'. Other authors, for example Gilroy (1993), Young (1998), and Steinberg (1999) have in different geographical contexts also referred to movements, especially by ship, and involving international communities, as connecting and continuing relationships, including social-cultural and economic ones, that have been made in the different spaces of home, across and abroad (Borovnik 2005:136).

Expanding on such discussion, Crang, Dwyer and Jackson (2004) continue by emphasising processes and connecting spaces, by defining transnationalism as a dynamic, complex, multi-dimensional and multi-inhabited encompassing field. It is because of this definition that we can now conclude that international seafarers and their families are no longer on the 'edges' of transnationalism, but are fully fledged members of transnational practice. It may be easily recognised that seafarers are encompassed in a field that occupies a dynamic and complex mobile livelihood onboard ship, under agreements and regulations of different national context, needed in order to make international employment possible. This dynamic space is multi-dimensional both in a geographic and socio-cultural sense; and it is multi-inhabited by the varying nationalities of ship-owners, managers, officers and multinational crews, and the fact that ships are registered under so called 'foreign' or international flags.

Movements and Networks of Pacific People

Social and organisationally informal networks in combination with transnational movements and the exchange of practices and information have been increasingly recognised as highly functional. These networks are also regarded as contributing effectively to development because of the aspects of fluidity and reciprocity that are involved (Bebbington 2002; Gibson-Graham 2005; Henry, Mohan and Yancopulos 2004). In this theoretical context, two recent publications have acknowledged and referred to the long history of cultural and family connections and networking over time and space in context of migration and mobility in the Pacific. The first one, a working paper by Barcham, Scheyvens and Overton (2007) suggests a 'New Polynesian Triangle', extending from historical Polynesia, and relatively restricted movements during colonial times, to an extended and more complex Polynesia that participates and is affected by the dynamics and neoliberal politics of globalisation and has perhaps, despite such politics, extended to include places and transnational communities in Australia, New Zealand and the USA.

Movements within such a new Polynesian transnational space must include the multi-dimensional nature of migration and the ties that bind people to their homeland, resulting in movements of people and their expressions of identity that are multidirectional (Barcham, Scheyvens and Overton 2007). The authors refer in particular to Polynesian families living in nations with strong political links to the Pacific Rim, including Samoa, Tonga, Cook Islands, Niue and Hawai'i. They refer to the expanding concepts of transnationalism but emphasise the important aspect of culture and family as key unit of analysis, and advocate a clearer understanding of the complexities of transnational flows, such as remittances, that can be both multi-directional and embrace symbolic and cultural meanings, which may be seen as equally significant to economic importance (see also Borovnik 2005; Koteka-Wright 2006; Marsters, Lewis and Friesen 2006 in this context).

Basing their arguments on Hau'ofa (1993:6), Barcham, Scheyvens and Overton (2007:8) explain that 'in an increasingly unfavourable geo-political climate, Polynesians have moved even further afield – yet this expansion of movement has, for too long, been disregarded', and people expand their movements by crisscrossing the boundless ocean as always. These arguments are based on the frequent flows between Oceania and the Pacific Rim, and reject discourses on migration that only focus on aspects of permanence and assimilation in new places, by showing that in the context of Polynesians we cannot conclude as such. Although this paper did not include Micronesia, it can clearly be linked to the transnational practices and experiences of seafarers in the Pacific, and hence, these arguments can be regarded as suitable for Tuvaluan as well as I-Kiribati families.

The second publication concerned with 'The Pacific Islanders and the Rim: Linked by Migration' is a special issue in the *Asia Pacific Migration Journal* edited by Carmen Voigt-Graf (2007a) which addresses the larger region of Oceania. Again, the 'extraordinarily large migration flows' in the region are being observed (Voigt-Graf 2007b, 143), and the large Polynesian component at least in New Zealand and Australia has been recognised. This issue also addresses the MIRAB debate and strong views on remittance dependence in 1995 (Brown and Connell 1995). The contributors expand on these debates by including aspects on social networks, identities and cultural changes in more detail, addressing shifts in migration discourses including now second generations and a more positive view on remittances. This issue, however, also addresses the multiple directions and symbolic of transnational flows and the need for more research on the social aspects of the affects of migration and labour circulation (see Connell 2007; Lee 2007).

In conclusion, discourses on transnationalism, especially in the context of Pacific seafarers have now included different scales of geographies as well as social, cultural and economic components of networks resulting from the multiplicity of movement articulations especially within the Pacific context under the influence of globalisation.

Seafarers and their Homeland: Examples from Kiribati

The previous discussions make it possible to argue that there are certain occupational aspects linked to networking, multidirectional flows and exchange that can be observed in the I-Kiribati seafaring experiences. Firstly, the long absence from home, which has in the last couple of decades been up to two years at a time, interspersed with often short time periods at home, from a few weeks to several months. Strong cultural connections to Kiribati are, secondly, responsible for networking across dynamic space and over long space and time distances. These include the preservation of cultural knowledge, practices, and remittances flows as part of seafarers' family and community obligations. Lastly, the exchange of old and new experiences combined with the 'adventure' of moving between and observing unfamiliar places, the strict working conditions, and the new multicultural experiences onboard, that merge with old values and the homeland experiences of seafarers.[10]

In order to place such aspects within content, I will look at some different examples. Seafarers usually experience a mixture of fear and excitement at going onboard merchant vessels for the first time, especially when they are single and this is their first time away from home. The excitement may then wear off, and feelings of longing for their homelands become prevalent. These feelings may deepen as men begin to cope with the monotony of work on vessels and the confined spaces that allow them little personal distance from their colleagues.[11] One 34 year old man had been working for a period of 16 years for SPMS at the time of interview. His first trip was on a general cargo vessel for a period of two years which he started when he was 18 years old. He talks about the excitement of this first experience in 1983: 'I thought it was [as though] I started an adventure. ... I was still single. I met my wife in 1988 and we got married in 1992'. He then goes on to explain how he boarded his first ship in Durban, a place he had never been to before, where it was freezing cold from his point of view, and how he journeyed from there to Brazil. The following quote expresses his feelings:

> It was a new country and so a new thing for me. That's what it [was] like when I was stepping on [land in Brazil]. When I first got off the ship and I was walking around down there, I thought, it's a different world! I have never been in this part of world before ... When I first went out I wasn't actually very homesick, because the ship kept on going to different places all the time. And you sort, you know, it's a good place, you can see, you know, you look forward to see new places. And then, on the second ship, yeah, I sort of started feeling lonely and started feeling very homesick.

> *MB: Why was that?*

> Well, you get to spend a lot of time on the ship and you are there about six months already and you are thinking, ah, I've been here too long really, you know, it's time to go home. And you miss your friends, and your lifestyle and what you were used to do at home. Like me, if I would get work in Kiribati, there is no way I would like to stay in another country. I'd come back to my country again.

> *MB: Why is that?*

> I just love my country <laughter>

When I asked more specifically, what exactly he loved so much about 'his' country, this seaman explains that the main reason was 'the family', and then generalising his experience with other I-Kiribati, who also always will return home for this same reason, says, 'you know [Kiribati is] very easy especially for living and all that kind of thing; especially, the activities that we are doing all the time; we can't do that on the ship'. This example shows the close relationships that the I-Kiribati seamen keep with their home country as a place they belong to because their family lives there and because this is the place of their upbringing, where family land is based and also where they know how to get around.

Remittances as a means for networking and keeping in contact have been discussed in detail among scholars working in the Pacific (for example by Connell and Conway 2000; Koteka-Wright 2006; Lee 2007; Marsters, Lewis and Friesen 2006). A more detailed discussion on remittances flows between seafarers and their families can be found in Borovnik (2006). A key point of this chapter is that as previously mentioned, overall remittances sent back to Kiribati (and Tuvalu) have increased. Remittances are often sent both to individual family members and to seafarers' personal bank accounts. In some cases seafarers have arranged joint bank accounts with their wives. Remittances from seafarers are of particular interest because they are usually arranged upon boarding vessels, and these arrangements guarantee, usually, a relatively steady flow of income for dependents, interrupted only when a seafarer is in between contracts. In the Kiribati context, however, it has been demonstrated that not only is there a direct benefit for individual families from remittances, but that remittances will reach a larger group of extended family members through firstly, the system of *bubuti,* or non-refusable request, that allows extended family members to request money, goods or favours when in need; and secondly through family and community obligations, such as providing school fees for nieces and nephews and sending money directly to churches or communities; and thirdly through obligations that family members receiving remittances have to follow up (Borovnik 2006).

This system is well illustrated by the following example: at the time of this interview the interviewee was a retired seafarer of unknown age. He had participated, as he explains, in one of the first intakes into MTC in the 1960s, although he had stopped working in 1986 as he needed to come home to support his mother who had become very ill at that time. This man now lives with his wife and extended family on one of the outer islands of Kiribati, and remembers that he used to send back fifty (Australian) dollars to his wife and thirty dollars to his parents in his early years of deployment. Then after a while, he sent more money. He explains:

> [When I was on] my seventh ship I sent to my wife only fifty, yeah, fifty; and to my parents fifty also. Ah, and [on] my tenth ship it is more. I sent more money; to my wife one hundred, and to my father one hundred also. Two hundred I sent. I sent all the rest of my money to my bank. Save it. I have [keep] twenty dollars, yeah? I sent all my [other] money to my bank. But [sometimes] I have fifty dollars, and the rest I send to the bank.

The money he kept monthly while working on board could vary from twenty to fifty dollars, and this was spent on drinks, clothes and smaller items needed. The amount of money this man had sent to his own bank account lasted him and his family for five years after he retired. However, while still employed, his family enjoyed the use of a stereo, a motorcycle, a radio, a kerosene stove and a suitcase.[12] He also used to bring back perfumes, necklaces and a ring for his wife. His earnings allowed him to regularly contribute to the Catholic Church, sometimes three hundred dollars, sometimes one hundred, depending on what he decided at each time. After his mother died, he would have liked to go back to work, but his wife wanted him to stay at home, so he did. Instead he helps out now with some casual jobs in his own community.

In order to make time on board more bearable some family members and wives send items to their men, such as pillow cases, *Te Uekerae,* the local newspaper, video tapes filmed by a local company with traditional I-Kiribati features, photos and even audio tapes with greetings. A 37 year old woman married to a seafarer, working as cook, explains:

> Because he said that he is lonely every day, every night, when he finishes work and he always drinks and what? Watches the video after work, then he sleeps to six o'clock in the morning, or five, to wake up and prepare all the breakfast for, them, the crews and the officers. That's what he said to me. … Then, I make the pillow cases [with labels that say] 'Don't forget to say a prayer before you wake up'. Hm! And then 'Merry Christmas and Happy New Year', because Christmas is his birthday. So, [I put] one in the pack like this. I send it to the ship and his fish and the parcel is full to the top! Hm! You know what? With a birthday card, the *lavalava,*[13] that I make it with cotton. The pillow cases… <then whispers> He's a nice guy. Do you want to see his photo?

With the help of these few illustrations it is possible to explain some of the characteristics of exchange and regularity that accompany the very particular circumstances that seafarers and their families have to abide with. The combination of a strong sense of family and cultural connections and obligations with activities that help following up such connectedness have established a well working multi-directional and multi-dimensional network of transnationality between seafarers and their families. Aspects that explore newly learned ship-board community values and understandings have not been included in this chapter, although these form part of the articulations of seafarers' transnationalism. What we can see, with help of the above illustrations, is that through direct flows between individuals the wider extended family networks and community are also included. Even the conservation of seafarers' identity with their home countries are a consequence of such flows.

Conclusions

It is not the boundaries of the nation-state but the processes, symbols and meanings within it that are the defining terms in which transnational processes are played out. Indeed that theme was one of the key arguments made by Crang, Dwyer and Jackson (2003:445) in combination with Barcham, Scheyvens, and Overton (2007). The illustrations chosen for this chapter help to confirm these defining elements. The strong connections between family members and the high standard of personal obligation to cultural practices draw I-Kiribati seafarers to live in or to return to their home country. It is these complex networks of communication and remittance flows that enable and sustain interactions between shipboard and home communities and even though initiated by individuals that ultimately connect seafarers with their home countries.

This chapter has discussed the importance of shifting away from strictly confined geographical space and national borders to a new concept of transnationalism embracing liminal space that includes different dimensions, such as the maritime and mobile space of shipboard communities, and focuses on families and communities as key units of analysis. Nation states remain still significant in terms of a mutual idea of homeland, as the example of Kiribati could show, but the emphasis lies on connections to families and places, and the complexities and multi-dimensions of how these connections are lived. A new concept of analysis also must still include the geographical and political history of Oceania, and the history of employer/employee relationships that are increasingly affected by global forces. This concept will then include clearly the history of Kiribati and Tuvalu that have been linked by seafaring for half a century. The shipping industry, both serving as an end and as a means for transport of goods and people, is truly a global force. We may conclude that processes within the Tuvaluan and I-Kiribati culture, and a long history of family obligations have built the well functioning networks between seafarers and their home countries that have led to increasing opportunities to participate in such a global system, yet retain the crucial values of home and keep these intact over time.

References

Asian Development Bank. 2002a. Kiribati. Monetization in an atoll society. Managing economic and social change. Asian Development Bank report in consultation with the Government of Kiribati and with support from AusAID.

—. 2002b. Tuvalu. 2002 Economic and public sector review. Asian Development Bank report in consultation with the Government of Tuvalu and with support from AusAID.

Barcham, M., R. Scheyvens, and J. Overton. 2007. Rethinking Polynesian mobility: A new Polynesian triangle? *Centre for Indigenous Development*

Working Paper Series No.3
http://cigad.massey.ac.nz/documents/wps_Barcham%20et%20al%20wp%203_2007.pdf
(accessed 28 April 2008).

Bebbington, A. 2002. Global networks and local developments: Agendas for development geography. *Tijdschrift voor Economische en Sociale Geografie* 94 (3): 297–309.

Boland, S. and B. Dollery. 2005. The economic significance of migration and remittances in Tuvalu. Working Paper Series in Economics number 2005–10, University of New England, School of Economics.

Borovnik, M. 2007. Labor circulation and changes among seafarers' families and communities in Kiribati. *Asian and Pacific Migration Journal* 16 (2): 225–50.

——. 2006 Working overseas: Seafarers' remittances and their distribution in Kiribati. *Asia Pacific Viewpoint* 47 (1): 151–61.

——. 2005. Seafarers' "maritime culture" and the "I-Kiribati way of life": The formation of flexible identities. *Singapore Journal of Tropical Geography* 26 (2): 132–50.

——. 2004 Are seafarers migrants? Situating seafarers in the framework of mobility and transnationalism. *New Zealand Geographer* 60 (1): 14–21.

——. 2003. *Seafarers in Kiribati. Consequences of International Labour Circulation.* PhD diss., University of Canterbury, Christchurch.

Brown, R. and J. Connell (eds). 1995. Special Issue on 'Migration and Remittances in the South Pacific'. *Asia Pacific Migration Journal* 4 (1).

Connell, J. 1983. *Migration, employment and development in the South Pacific: Kiribati.* Noumea, New Caledonia: ILO.

——. 2003. Losing ground? Tuvalu, the greenhouse effect and the garbage can. *Asia Pacific Viewpoint* 44 (2): 89–107.

——. 2007. At the end of the world: Holding on to health workers in Niue. *Asian and Pacific Migration Journal* 16 (2): 179–98.

Connell, J. and R. Brown. 2005. Remittances in the Pacific: An overview. Manila: Asian Development Bank.

Connell, J. and D. Conway. 2000. Migration and remittances in island microstates: A comparative perspective on the South Pacific and the Caribbean. *International Journal of Urban and Regional Research* 24: 52–78.

Conway, J. 2006. Tuvalu 2006 economic report: From plan to action (final draft) prepared for Ministry of Finance, Economic Planning and Industries and the Asian Development Bank.

Crang, P., C. Dwyer, and P. Jackson. 2003. Transnationalism and the spaces of commodity culture. *Progress in Human Geography* 27 (4): 438–56.

Duany, J. 2002. Mobile livelihoods: The sociocultural practices of circular migrants between Puerto Rico and the United States. *International Migration Review* 36 (2): 355–88.

Gibson-Graham, J. K. 2005. Surplus possibilities: Postdevelopment and community economies. *Singapore Journal of Tropical Geography,* 26 (1): 4–26.

Gilroy, P. 1993. *The Black Atlantic—Modernity and Double Consciousness.* Cambridge, Massachusetts: Harvard University Press.

Glick Schiller, N., L. Basch, and C. Szanton Blanc. 1995. From immigrant to transmigrant: Theorizing transnational migration. *Anthropology Quarterly* 68 (1): 121–40.

Hau'ofa, E. 1993. Our sea of islands. In *A new Oceania: Rediscovering our sea of islands,* ed. E. Waddell, V. Naidu and E. Hau'ofa, 2–16. Suva: University of the South Pacific.

Henry, L., G. Mohan and H. Yancopulos. 2004. Networks as transnational agents of development. *Third World Quarterly* 25 (5): 839–55.

Jackson, P., P. Crang, and C. Dwyer. 2004. Introduction: The spaces of transnationality. In *Transnational Spaces,* ed. P. Jackson, P. Crang, and C. Dwyer, 1-13. Routledge: London, New York.

Koteka-Wright, E. 2006. *Te uu no te akau roa': Migration and the Cook Islands.* MA thesis, Massey University, NZ.

Lane, A. D. 1999. Flags of convenience: Is it time to redress the balance? *Maritime Review* 31-5.

Lee, H. 2007. Transforming transnationalism: Second generation Tongans overseas. *Asian and Pacific Migration Journal* 16 (2): 157–78.

Leontis, A. 1997. Mediterranean topographies before balkanization: On Greek diaspora, *emporion,* and revolution. *Diaspora* 6 (2): 179–94.

Levitt, P., J. DeWind, and S. Vertovec. 2003. International perspectives on transnational migration: An introduction. *The International Migration Review* 37 (3): 565–75.

Marsters, E., N. Lewis, and W. Friesen. 2006. Pacific flows: The fluidity of remittances in the Cook Islands. *Asia Pacific Viewpoint* 47 (1): 31–44.

New Zealand Immigration 2007. Pacific Access Category. http://www.immigration.govt.nz/migrant/stream/live/pacificaccess/ (accessed 19 November 2007).

Portes, A. 2003. Conclusion: Theoretical convergences and empirical evidence in the study of immigrant transnationalism. *The International Migration Review* 37 (3): 874–92.

Portes, A., L. E. Guarnizo, and P. Landolt. 1999. The study of transnationalism: Pitfalls and promise of an emergent research field. *Ethnic and Racial Studies* 22 (2): 217–37.

Pries, L. 1998. "Transmigranten" als ein Typ von Arbeitswanderern in pluri-lokalen sozialen Räumen. *Soziale Welt* 49: 135–50.

Sampson, H. 2003. Transnational drifters or hyperspace dwellers: An explorative of the lives of Filipino seafarers aboard and ashore. *Ethnic and Racial Studies* 26 (2): 253–77.

Steinberg, Ph. E. 1999. The maritime mystique: sustainable development, capital mobility, and nostalgia in the world ocean. *Environment and Planning D: Society and Space* 17: 403–26.

Vertovec, S. 2001. Transnationalism and identity. *Journal of Ethnic and Migration Studies* 27 (4): 573–82.

—. 2003. Migration and other modes of transnationalism: Towards conceptual cross-fertilization. *The International Migration Review* 37 (3): 641–65.

Voigt-Graf, C. 2007a. Special Issue on 'The Pacific Islanders and the Rim: Linked by Migration'. *Asia Pacific Migration Journal* 16 (2).

—. 2007b. Pacific Islanders and the Rim: Linked by migration. *Asian and Pacific Migration Journal* 16 (2): 143–56.

Wimmer, A. and N. Glick Schiller. 2003. Methodological nationalism, the social sciences, and the study of migration: An essay in historical epistemology. *The International Migration Review* 37 (3): 576–610.

World Bank. 2006. Expanding job opportunities for Pacific Islanders through labour mobility at home and away. The World Bank: East Asia and Pacific Region, Poverty and Economic Policy Unit.

Wu, B. 2002. Seafarers: The first global villagers? *The Sea* 157: 4.

Yeoh, B., K. D. Willis, and S. M. A. Khader Fakhri. 2003. Transnational edges—introduction: Transnationalism and its edges. *Ethnic and Racial Studies* 26 (2): 207–17.

Young, R. G. 1998. *Pathways as metaphors of movement: A study of place, mobility and embodiment in Fiji*. PhD thesis, Victoria University, NZ.

ENDNOTES

[1] Some team members of the Seafarers International Research Centre (SIRC; for more information see http://www.sirc.cf.ac.uk/) in Cardiff have suggested that seafarers are pioneers of global citizens or can be regarded as global villagers (eg. Lane 1999, Wu 2002);

[2] This was originally the Marine Training School (MTS)

[3] Note that I-Kiribati means coming from or belonging to Kiribati

[4] The SPMS office explained in 2006, that currently six companies are involved.

[5] It was only in the 1980s that Germany introduced its official foreign ship register

[6] The term de-national refers to 'deterritorialised' spaces and/or actions; in other words those that operate 'beyond' national boundaries (see also Sampson 2003: 260).

[7] Training facilities for both domestic and international merchant seafarers are available throughout the Pacific. Fiji and PNG offer excellent quality training for international ratings and officers, Vanuatu, Samoa, Tonga, and the Solomon Islands also are involved in training especially for international ratings and domestic officers. The largest numbers, however are being provided by Kiribati, followed by Tuvalu and Fiji.

[8] In Kiribati, 40 per cent of the population in 2000 was under 14 years old (Asian Development Bank 2002a:139).

[9] Currently 44 per cent of the Tuvaluan population lives on Funafuti (Asian Development Bank 2002b:2).

[10] This last aspect has been described in detail in Borovnik 2005.

[11] Agencies try to have smaller or larger groups of I-Kiribati on one vessel, and the same applies to Tuvaluans, in order to help with emotional hardship that men experience. This is, however, not always possible.

[12] This is the order in which this man mentioned those items.

[13] Traditional men's clothes

10. 'I Never Wanted to Come Home': Skilled Health Workers in the South Pacific

John Connell

> I know I can't live away from Samoa for too long. I need a sense of roots, of home—a place where you live and you die. I would die as a writer without roots; but when I go home I am reminded that I'm an outsider, palagified (Albert Wendt, in Beston and Beston 1977).

Little has been written on return migration to the island states of the Pacific. More generally and despite its significance in many countries, there is a limited global literature on return migration, and even less that focuses on the return migration of skilled workers. This chapter traces the return migration of skilled health workers, in three Pacific island states (Fiji, Tonga, Samoa) and evaluates the rationale for and consequences of return and their contribution to development. As the short title—the words of a returned health worker—and the opening quotation from the distinguished Samoan author, Albert Wendt, indicate, there is both contradiction and ambivalence in the structure, nature and impact of return. Ambivalence and uncertainty are complicated within a more transnational world, through the flexibility and fluidity of more instantaneous physical and electronic communications and contacts.

The global rise in the migration of skilled workers has been perceived as a response to the accelerated globalisation of the service sector. Such professional services as health care are very much part of the new internationalisation of labour, as demand for skilled health workers in developed countries has remained high, seemingly paradoxically because of relatively low wages and poor working conditions in these destination countries (Connell 2008b). In the Pacific, as elsewhere, the migration of health workers is no new phenomenon. At least as early as 1989 a medical degree from the Fiji School of Medicine was regarded by some as a 'passport to prosperity'. However there have been few studies of any facet of this migration and those that have been done have until quite recently been largely qualitative (Naidu 1997; Rotem and Bailey 1999), while just as few studies in the Pacific region have examined other forms of skilled migration (cf. Liki 2001; Voigt-Graf 2003; Voigt-Graf, Iredale and Khoo 2007). In short, there is remarkably little information on the migration of skilled workers, let alone their return migration, in the Pacific region. This chapter seeks to help to fill this gap by addressing the significance of return migration of one small group of skilled workers in three island states.

Especially for small states, the migration of skilled workers has been seen largely as a one-way process, a critical component of the brain drain, and thus a major problem. Migration (and attrition) represent a costly loss of scarce and expensively–trained human capital. Loss of significant numbers of key health workers affects core national strategies for health sector development, creating problems for health care, and for human resource planning and development. Conversely, return migration in the Pacific is often seen as a migration movement dominated by retirees and those who have failed elsewhere: return has even been seen as an admission of failure (Maron and Connell 2008). Those who remained overseas were the success stories and though many of these publicly expressed intentions of return, in private they had moved towards permanence (Macpherson 1985). In other words, the returnees were apparently those least likely to make a significant positive contribution to their home countries. However, in the absence of detailed examination of return migration, such conclusions were largely drawn from anecdotes rather than ethnographic or survey data.

More recent studies, especially in the Caribbean, have gradually begun to recognise the diversity of return migration, alongside the diversity of reasons for return (Conway et al 2005; Gmelch 1992; Thomas-Hope 1999). Similarly for many Cook Islands migrants, the acquisition of new skills overseas was a contributing factor in the decision to return, particularly with the accompanying elevation of social status and income, hence there was a significant return movement of those who had succeeded elsewhere (Hooker and Varcoe 1999; Rallu 1997; see also Marcus 1981:60). Likewise in Tonga, returnees represented a cross-section in terms of age and employment, unskilled and skilled, including health workers, poorly educated and those with second degrees (Maron and Connell 2008). Yet in both these two national contexts there were relatively few such skilled migrant returns compared with the number of those who had left, and information on health workers is minimal.

At a global level, the situation is similar. The return migration of skilled health workers is assumed to be relatively limited in most places, though data are scarce, hence benefits from enhanced overseas skills—a compensatory brain gain—are considered to be few. Fragmented evidence from many parts of the world suggests that return migration of skilled health workers fails to occur largely for the same reason that migration previously occurred. Indeed, migrants are less likely to be tempted back by a system that they left, probably at least in part because of its perceived shortcomings. The extent of overall return migration of skilled health workers has been perceived to be so slight that Kingma (2005) has referred to the 'myth of return'.

Fiji, Samoa and Tonga

Samoa, Tonga and Fiji are all small island states. Fiji with a population of about 825,000 people is the largest in the region, Samoa has about 170,000 people, and Tonga 102,000. Both Tonga and Samoa have about as many ethnic islanders overseas as at home. By contrast, about 10 per cent of Fiji islanders live overseas. Limited land resources, few natural resources, isolation and fragmentation, weak infrastructure and governance all pose problems for administration and development, and economic growth has been weak in recent years. Most countries experience some problems of hardship and poverty of opportunity, and none have significant economic growth. Migration has consequently increased, mainly to the metropolitan states of Australia, New Zealand and the United States.

Metropolitan countries have also traditionally been the destinations for tertiary studies, but both doctors and nurses are educated in the region: doctors (and most other specialised positions) from each of the countries are trained in Fiji and nurses in the home countries. Fiji has the largest health care system in the region, but it has been the most affected by migration since 1987, when ethnic tensions and military coups prompted a series of resignations and departures, and relatively few returns. The health systems of each of the countries have also been significantly affected by migration, particularly of doctors and more specialised occupations such as lab technicians and dentists, for whom human resource planning is more difficult. In all three states the migration of doctors is considered to be more significant than that of nurses in terms of proportions who had migrated, their impact on the health care system and the cost of replacement (Brown and Connell 2004). Since the 1990s, recruitment of Fijian nurses by New Zealand, the UAE, Palau and the Marshall Islands has further emphasised the evolving migration structure and external orientation of health workers.

While the scale of international migration is affected by the vicissitudes of the international economy, migration is primarily affected by uneven development, income levels and the desire for access to education and health services. Each of the countries has experienced significant recent migration both generally and of skilled workers particularly. Skilled workers, and especially skilled health workers, are a significant proportion of immigrants from Pacific island states to metropolitan states. Many developed countries, including Australia, the USA and New Zealand, have a particular shortage of health workers, especially in remote areas.

For each of these countries, but less so for Fiji, where there are distinct, local alternative economic opportunities, there is to a significant extent a 'culture of migration' in which migration is pervasive, based on historical precedent, and part of everyday experience; perceived as legitimate, not as either rupture or discontinuity in personal and household experience, but as an integral part of life (Connell 2008a). Migration is normal and mobility, intermittent return visits and return migration are part of that. Moreover it is embedded in strategies for extended household development rather than simply the outcome of decisions taken by a small number of individuals. International migration has long had a critical and virtually uncontested role in island societies and economies. The migration and return migration of skilled workers is embedded in this broad context of continuity.

Migration of Health Workers

The present study was part of a detailed study of almost 550 health workers in nine Pacific island states and, to a lesser extent, in two key destinations: Sydney and Auckland. This chapter focuses on the three largest island states that are key countries of origin (Tonga, Samoa and Fiji), and on the small sample of the health workers who were return migrants. Overall, 64 of the sample were return migrants (see Table 10–1). More than two-thirds of the sample were nurses, about 95 per cent of the nurses were women, and about two-thirds of the doctors were men, all a reflection of the structure of Pacific health sectors.

Early migration of skilled health workers from the Pacific was primarily related to quality of life issues related to the employment context (poor working conditions, inadequate facilities, limited opportunities for research or career development); income (particular professional salary structures, costs of living) and a variety of social factors (educational opportunities for children, morale). In this century, wages and salaries were ubiquitously seen as inadequate. Two-thirds of all nurses and almost half (46 per cent) of all doctors are primarily motivated to migrate for income reasons, a conclusion that is common across countries and across migrant groups (Connell 2004). The specific significance of income is a function of income differentials between Pacific island states and metropolitan states; thus, Tongans were more likely to migrate than Fijians or Samoans because of greater wage differentials between home and international destinations (Brown and Connell 2004). Doctors are almost twice as likely to migrate as nurses, partly because wage differentials are greater but also because men tend to be the decision makers and most nurses are women. Migration occurs in an extended family context.

Economic and political problems in parts of the region have contributed to emigration, exacerbated by economic restructuring, reductions in the size of the public service and deterioration in local working conditions. Work can be difficult and challenging. As one Fijian doctor said:

> people need to be compensated for their hard work and after hours duty. At present, work can be very stressful for those who are trying hard to improve the standards of health care. Why would one put in extra hours

of work especially when they are underpaid? The 'good Samaritan' and 'Nightingale' days are over.[1]

Table 10-1: Returned Health Workers in Fiji, Samoa and Tonga

		Nurses		Doctors		Total	
Number of respondents		No.	%	No.	%	No.	%
	Fiji	10	31	8	26	18	28
	Samoa	12	36	8	26	20	31
	Tonga	11	33	15	48	26	41
	Total	33	100	31	100	64	100
Female respondents		No.	% of total respondents	No.	% of total respondents	No.	% of total respondents
	Fiji	10	100	3	9.7	13	20.3
	Samoa	12	100	5	16	17	26.6
	Tonga	11	100	4	13	15	23.4
	Total	33	100	12	38.7	45	70.3
Age (years)		Mean	Standard deviation	Mean	Standard deviation	Mean	Standard deviation
	Fiji	47.3	10	37.9	5.3	43.1	9.4
	Samoa	38.8	11.1	35.1	7.3	37.4	9.7
	Tonga	46.0	10.9	40.7	10.5	43.0	10.8
Number of years away	Fiji	2.9	2.0	3.3	2.8	3.1	2.3
	Samoa	5.3	4.5	6.8	3.3	5.8	4.1
	Tonga	4.0	3.7	8.9	1.7	6.9	3.6

Difficult conditions were also a key factor in influencing migration. Some health workers resented long hours of overtime, double shifts, working on the 'graveyard' shift or on weekends, for which income is not always properly supplemented. This was particularly so in remote places where few staff are available, hence overtime hours can be long. Like the patients, health workers disliked overcrowding, long queues, lack of supplies and inadequate facilities, and the fact they could not do their job effectively, and repeatedly pointed to problems with inadequate technology, favouritism, over-long working hours, lack of support and respect. In most workplaces, it is normal for some expectations not to be met, especially where workplaces are small (so that chances of promotion are relatively few), but there was abundant evidence of lack of 'good housekeeping' and management that supports skilled workers in inevitably challenging situations.

Some of the strongest influences on migration, however, have little to do with employment, or specifically the structure of employment in the country of origin, but much to do with attempts to improve the long term welfare and status of families. In each of the countries many people entered the health professions less out of altruism, or a particular interest in medicine, than through recognition that this might be a means to maximise or at least improve family incomes and welfare. Parents have encouraged their children to enter the profession for the same reason and increasingly so as familiarity with overseas circumstances increases. Employment in the health system thus enables migration as much as being an instigator of it.

Skilled migrants make a substantial contribution to the economic wellbeing of those who remain at home, even compared with those unskilled migrants who profess the certainty of return migration. Remittances, notably in the case of Polynesian nurses, were sustained at high levels, and thus contributed substantially to the welfare of kin in the home country (Connell and Brown 2004). The creation of that income informs many family migration decisions and the use of the money within the home communities to benefit the extended family means that there is always some possibility of return migration.

Return

A significant number of health workers have returned to the Pacific island states, but not all of them return to work in the health sector. Indeed the majority probably do not (but because the survey data come from workers currently in the health sector, we cannot define this proportion). About one-third of the existing health workforce were returnees, though most of these had been overseas to train and were bonded to return, rather than having come back, usually later in life, for different reasons. In terms of reasons for return (see Tables 10–2 and 10–3), the substantial numbers listed as 'other' represent those who were bonded to return and thus had no real choice in the matter, while 'home country' in some cases was simply a more elegant way of indicating this bonding. More than half of the doctors and at least one-third of the nurses who had returned were bonded, and usually did so before significant overseas work experience. Again this indicates the small residual numbers who had specifically chosen to return. Two-thirds of the returnees were women, but that simply reflects the gendered composition of the nursing workforce. Among those who were not bonded, the returnees were not particularly young, but had largely returned in mid-career, suggesting their presumed ability to contribute to the workforce.

Beyond bonding, social reasons influenced return, for both doctors and nurses (see Tables 10–2 and 10–3), including the rather nebulous 'home country', but being with friends and relatives and accompanying a spouse home were highly significant. For a considerable proportion (even excluding those who were bonded), return was perceived as something of a duty rather than entirely an act of free will. Conversely, just one Samoan nurse claimed to have returned for 'higher wages and better jobs'. In other words, employment in the health sector, or good wages, were not incentives to return.

Table 10–2: Reasons for Return—by Country

Reasons for return	Nurses [1]		Doctors [1]		Total [2]	
	No.	%	No.	%	No.	%
Fiji						
Higher wages & better jobs	3	30	-	-	3	16
Less insecurity/discrimination	4	50	-	-	4	22
Home country	6	60	6	75	12	61
Due to Family members	5	50	4	40	9	50
Due to Spouse job	1	10	-	-	1	6
Due to friends & relatives	3	30	2	25	5	27
Other	2	20	6	75	8	44
Samoa						
Higher wages & better jobs	1	8	-	-	1	5
Better health and medical care	1	8	-	-	1	5
Less insecurity/discrimination	2	17	1	12	3	15
Home country	8	67	7	88	15	75
Due to family members	4	33	-	-	4	20
Due to friends and relatives	9	75	4	5	13	65
Close to retirement	-	-	1	13	1	5
Other	1	8	3	38	4	20
Tonga						
Home country	6	55	7	47	13	50
Due to family members	1	9	-	-	1	4
Due to spouse job	1	9	1	7	2	8
Due to friends and relatives	9	82	12	80	21	81
Other	9	82	14	93	23	88

[1] as a percentage of number of returned nurses/doctors of each country
[2] as a percentage of total returned respondents of each country

Table 10–3: Reasons for Return—Overall

Reasons for the returns	Nurses [1]		Doctors [1]	
	No.	%	No.	%
Higher wages & better jobs	4	5	-	-
Better health & medical care	1	1	-	-
Less insecurity/discrimination	6	6	1	1
Home country	20	25	19	28
Due to family members	10	13	4	3
Due to spouse job	2	3	1	1
Due to friends and relatives	21	27	18	27
Close to retirement	-	-	1	1
Other	12	16	23	55

[1] as a percentage of number of nurses/doctors who had returned to their countries

Migrants tended to return at key moments in the life cycle—after training for example, or when children had graduated—but at least as often when their parents had particular need of them. Thus many returned not necessarily at times of their own choosing or of their own volition, but in response to family needs or crises, influenced by the circumstances of others rather than themselves or their nuclear families. The repeated mobility of Tevai, a Cook Islands nurse, almost entirely in response to extended family needs (Hooker and Varcoe 1999, 94), is a typical if complex example of such a migration scenario, where Tevai and her family repeatedly balanced opportunities for income generation in Australia to provide economic support, with the need to be close to family in the Pacific to provide social support. Social obligations underpin this and other migration histories.

Nonetheless, those who had returned to work in the health sector earned significantly more than those who had never migrated and this was especially true for Samoa and Tonga (see Table10–5). Similarly, returnees in Tonga and Samoa, more than in Fiji, also generally received incomes that were greater than other households (Brown and Connell 2004). Correspondingly, the numbers and proportions of those who returned to Samoa and Tonga were greater. Nevertheless, these relatively high incomes are low compared with incomes that might have been, or were, obtained overseas and hence do not explain return.

Migration itself was less likely to occur where health workers owned a house or business in their home country; in other words they are well-established economically (Brown and Connell 2004; cf. Brown 1997). Likewise, returning health workers are particularly likely to establish a business on their return, having accumulated enough savings to make this possible, a pattern that occurs more widely among all returnees (Brown and Connell 1993; Maron and Connell 2008). There is, therefore, a key economic rationale for return migration outside the health sector, enabling a degree of individualism, independence and autonomy from that sector. As a result, many return migrants to the health sector become part of multiple income households.

Alongside individual choice, bureaucratic and structural obstacles may also hinder return to the health sector. Such obstacles include starting again at the bottom of the system (rather than gaining promotion by dint of new skills and experience acquired overseas) that cancel out any status or professional recognition gained from migration. Accrued benefits may also have disappeared and, even then, there may be jealousy from co-workers who have not had overseas experience (and may see returnees as seeking to lord it over them). Moreover, unless there have been changes to the health system during the absence of the migrants, the old flaws and failings are reencountered and perhaps made worse by overseas experiences had in invariably better functioning systems.

Predictably, returnees were often frustrated with the health sector, which usually compared poorly with those they had returned from and/or been trained in. Those who had been forced to start again at the bottom of the employment hierarchy were particularly frustrated. Most frustrations and complaints related to work conditions and lack of recognition of skills and knowledge, which sometimes amounted to at least perceptions of blocked promotion, though many returnees expressed satisfaction at working for the government with the prestige, reliability and stability that it provides. Others were less enthusiastic: 'I had expectations of promotion and a salary rise'; 'I am better qualified than anybody in the Divisional level. Since my return from Australia, I haven't been promoted. In addition what I am doing is nothing to do with my specialised area of epidemiology'; 'I am burdened with responsibility'; 'long hours'; 'decisions made from higher levels of the hierarchy and no say from lower levels'; 'I want to upgrade my knowledge but it is too difficult'; 'this is my first year as a junior registrar and I have been appointed to a post with a lot of responsibilities and been deprived of a lot of sleep: overworked and underpaid'; and 'overwork: surely no hospital in the world can employ someone over 32 hours?' More generally 'not having normal hours' and 'little separation of work and leisure time; we are always expected to be available', distinguished employment in the health system from that in other areas. Such responses characterised the most obvious dissatisfactions though, with certain exceptions, many similar problems might also have been experienced overseas.

Many complaints were directed at a seemingly uncomprehending and uninterested bureaucracy. An Indo-Fijian doctor who had returned to a provincial posting found it not only 'boring' but also,

> the Administration is very bad, very colonial, with an 'I'm the boss' mentality that does not encourage progress nor allow things to move ahead. The boss is very stubborn and does not listen to his staff, yet he constantly talks of reform.

He could not wait to leave, either to Suva or overseas. Somewhat differently, another doctor elsewhere spoke of 'male chauvinism within the Ministry of Health', and others reflected more broadly on the 'failure of the…government to prioritise health care' or 'the communication gap between the Ministry and the workers'.

Other returnees stressed nepotism and favouritism in island health care systems, particular problems in small health systems in societies where cultures centred on kinship remain important. Stability in a small workforce where there is limited turnover (or what is perceived to be limited turnover) may discourage innovation and change; younger staff found some frustration when trying to implement change and new ideas, especially where it works elsewhere. These kind of 'crab antics', that discourage innovation and ideas, are not unusual in many workplaces in Pacific island states. One former nurse commented: 'nurses have no autonomy'. Others perceived a lack of respect and support for junior staff, entrenched in the generation gap. In many respects this is universal: in all workplaces some expectations will not be met, though there seemed to be no work climate where new innovations were valued.

Others were frustrated by a lack of adequate technology and there was a constant refrain about problems such as 'lack of equipment'; 'not enough money for medicines'; 'staff shortages' and even simply 'other nurses', all of which affected morale and were essentially related to insufficient investment. Some of the concerns of the returnees were not merely about the factors that made it difficult to do the effective and rewarding job that they sought to do for themselves and their patients, but went beyond that to issues affecting the whole practice of medical care. Many problems are generic to health systems the world over, notably inadequate equipment and medicines, night shifts and problem patients but ultimately, the greatest concerns were about what one nurse perceived as 'failures in the job', such as 'seeing loved ones die' or 'when one is unsuccessful in helping a patient to live'. By contrast, when patients survived against the odds there was the greatest satisfaction.

Somewhat less frequently, qualifications and skills are acquired overseas that are simply too specialised, notably in outer islands, small towns and in very small states such as Niue (Connell 2007, 2009), where a more general multiskilling characterises smaller workforces. Some careers and expatriate social lives are more demanding and fascinating and simply do not exist at home for 'high fliers'. Return would demand too many social and economic sacrifices and unacceptably constrained opportunities. As one returnee, who had moved out of the health sector before being attracted back, said:

> I never wanted to come back from Australia because it was not challenging enough but my husband wanted to return. It's not challenging. The case mixes are too few and it is not specialised here. I have to be a generalist and I don't like it. I'd like to go back there again.

Matching local needs and overseas skills is never easy.

Indo-Fijians tended to be the most critical of the circumstances that they found themselves in upon return, perhaps with reason; as did those who had returned to rural and regional positions, but there were no distinct national variations in satisfaction or otherwise.

While there were inevitable frustrations about work issues, many respondents were more positive and optimistic about the contributions that they had been able to make and more generally about the benefits for themselves and their families of returning home.

I never intended to stay in Australia permanently, just to go there for study. It's been good to return to work and live in Tonga—the lifestyle is better here and my family are here…I'm comfortable. It's also good to come back and help an ailing health system (quoted in Maron 2001, 71).

The knowledge that I gained overseas is invaluable. I have been able to return to work here and start establishing new changes in dental surgery. The experience that I gained overseas is good for Tonga's development (ibid, 78).

Consequently, despite frustrations with bureaucracies and facilities, there was also recognition that the health sector had some advantages in itself: 'the salary is higher than other jobs in Tonga, I gained prestige through my return and the work is appreciated by the people'. And 'I've worked in Melbourne but it seems that you are doing it for the money. Here you don't get much money but you feel that you're really helping people'. Inevitably, considerable satisfaction was attached to the ability to contribute to a more successful workforce: 'saving two lives of a mother and baby…and working as a team with other nursing, medical and non-medical staff'; 'looking after people and planning for the health of the community'. Sometimes that was directly attributed to migration, through the 'use of overseas knowledge and skills to benefit Tonga' but usually satisfaction was simply implicit in doing a good job. For one nurse, this amounted to 'the pleasure of living with my family, low expenses, working with my own people, and being able to contribute to the government, the country and the people'. It is perhaps true that, rather more than in almost any other sphere, returned health workers are able to believe, make and sustain such claims.

Yet fitting in again posed some problems. While returnees were usually able to readjust to island lifestyles the transition was not always easy: 'I had culture shock coming back into Tongan culture, but in the end I was glad to be back'. Challenges also involved the attitudes of patients where these did not fit 'western' medicine: 'frustration with elderly patients who rely on traditional Tongan medicine rather than western medicine'. Although 'my parents are here, it is more comfortable living in Tonga and the job is more flexible', that sometimes necessary flexibility was a problem for those who had acquired specialisations and disliked having to become generalists. Here, as in other contexts, some were able to readjust and reintegrate, others found it more frustrating and resented being able to use only a fraction of what they had learned and practiced overseas. Those who had returned for the sake of others were most challenged by return and envisaged future emigration.

Table 10-4: Intended Future Migration of Return Migrants—by Country

Reasons for future migration	Nurses [1]		Doctors [1]		Total	
	No.	%	No.	%	No.	%
Fiji						
Higher wages & better jobs	2	67	1	50	3	60
More education for self	-	-	-	-	-	-
Education of children	1	33	2	100	3	60
Desire to travel and gain overseas experience	-	-	1	50	1	20
Spouse can get a job	1	33	-	-	1	20
Others	1	33	1	50	2	40
Total respondents: Fiji[2]	3	30	2	25	5	28
Samoa						
Higher wages & better jobs	3	75	1	25	4	50
Good business opportunities	1	25	-	-	1	13
More education for self	3	75	4	100	7	88
Education of children	3	75	2	50	5	63
Have friends and relatives	-	-	1	25	1	13
More contact with developments in medicine	-	-	1	25	1	13
Institutional settings	1	25	-	-	1	13
Desire to travel and gain overseas experience	-	-	2	50	2	25
Research possibilities	1	25	1	25	2	25
Total respondents: Samoa[2]	4	33	4	50	8	40
Tonga						
Higher wages & better jobs	2	50	2	25	4	33
More education for self	1	25	4	50	5	42
Education of children	2	50	2	25	4	33
Better amenities	2	50	-	-	2	17
Desire to travel and gain overseas experience	-	-	4	50	4	33
Others	2	50	2	25	4	33
Total respondents: Tonga[2]	4	36	8	53	12	46
TOTAL RESPONDENTS: ALL [2]	11	33	14	45	25	39

[1] as a percentage of number of nurses/doctors (who had returned) of each country
[2] as a percentage of total respondents who intend to migrate of each country; for reasons of space categories that had no responses have been omitted.

The real pleasure of return lay in the social context. This usually had little to do with the workplace but was about a 'more comfortable pace of life' among family and friends. Many of those who had moved back emphasised the climate, safety or the more relaxed pace of life, or simply the familiarity of the home country, indicating again how crucial social, political and economic stability is to return migration.

While return migration was for social reasons, reemployment in the health sector may even have been reluctant and others may have dropped out of the workforce, there is no clear evidence that those who had returned were 'failures' (though the methodology precludes their being recognised). Rather, it tended to suggest that returnees have contributed to national development and that even if some felt that they had in some sense 'failed', many had made an effort and battled against stubborn bureaucracies and difficult conditions.

Of the returnees some 25 (29 per cent), about one-in-three nurses and one-in-two doctors (see Table 10–4 above) wanted to migrate again 'soon'. Although intent is different from action, at the very least some degree of ambivalence followed return migration, especially when that return was stimulated by the needs of others. Such a new phase of migration would be motivated by desire for better education and new experiences for the individuals and for their children, underpinned by higher wages and a better job (see Table 10–5). Poorly paid nurses tended to seek to move for higher wages and doctors for new education and training, but overall an economic rationale was significant. Even some of those who were aware that they were doing a valuable job and enjoyed it, found it difficult to balance this with their knowledge of 'higher wages and a better quality of life overseas' that presented a constant lure and temptation. Nonetheless, some strenuously denied any intention to go: 'If the worse comes to the worst I'd leave, but otherwise I'd rather stay here' and 'even in the worst situation I'd feel obliged to stay here'. Yet in the present climate of overseas recruitment and substantial demand for skilled workers, usually only older workers did not see migration, however improbable, as both temptation and possibility.

Table 10–5: Intended Future Migration of Return Migrants

Reasons for future migration	Nurses [1]		Doctors [1]	
	No.	%	No.	%
Higher wages & better jobs	7	64	4	29
Good business opportunities	1	9	-	-
More education for self	4	36	8	57
Education of children	6	55	6	43
Better amenities	2	18	-	-
Have friends & relatives	-	-	1	7
More contact with developments in medicine	-	-	1	7
Institutional settings	1	9	-	-
Desire to travel & gain overseas experience	-	-	7	50
Research possibilities	1	9	1	7
Spouse can get a job	1	9	-	-
Others	3	28	3	21
Total number reported[2]	11	33	14	45

[1] as a percentage of total nurses/doctors who had returned to their countries
[2] as a percentage of nurses/doctors who intend to migrate future

Those who intended to remain wished to stay, by contrast, because it was home and where their relatives and friends lived (see Table 10–6). In a wider sample of all health workers in Tonga, Samoa and Fiji, among those who had never gone overseas, income was even less evident as a reason for staying. This was especially so for nurses, whereas almost half of the doctors who had chosen not to migrate indicated that income was a factor in their staying, despite the fact that they earned about one-third of what they might have done overseas (Table 10–7). Alongside family ties, owning a house in the home country is a significant brake on leaving, whereas being trained overseas is a major influence on migration (Brown and Connell 2004). Returning and staying tend to be social phenomena, while leaving is an economic one; mobility is a constantly unfinished story.

Table 10–6: Reasons for Remaining—by Country

Reasons for remaining in home country [2]	Nurses [1]		Doctors [1]		Total	
	No.	%	No.	%	No.	%
Fiji						
Good job and satisfactory income	2	29	2	33	4	31
Close relatives and friends	1	15	2	33	3	23
Good house	4	57	-	-	4	31
Due to spouse preference and job	3	43	1	17	4	31
It's home	5	71	4	67	9	69
Others	2	29	-	-	2	15
Total reported: Fiji[3]	7	70	6	75	13	72
Samoa						
Good job and satisfactory income	2	29	1	25	3	27
Close relatives and friends	6	86	2	50	8	73
Good house	2	29	-	-	2	18
Due to spouse preference and job	1	15	-	-	1	9
Low level of crime and good security	-	-	1	25	1	9
Low cost of living	3	43	-	-	3	27
Many social activities	2	29	-	-	2	18
Difficult & impossible to get visa	-	-	1	25	1	9
It's home	5	71	3	75	8	73
Total reported: Samoa[3]	7	58	4	50	11	55
Tonga						
Good job and satisfactory income	1	15	1	17	2	15
Close relatives and friends	6	86	3	50	9	69
Good house	-	-	-	-	-	-
Due to spouse preference and job	3	43	-	-	3	23
It's home	4	57	4	67	8	62
Others	1	15	5	83	6	46
Total reported: Tonga[3]	7	64	6	40	13	50
TOTAL REPORTED: ALL	21	64	16	51	37	58

[1] as a percentage of number of returned nurses/doctors of the country

[2] categories with no responses have been omitted

[3] as a percentage of total respondents who intend to remain in the country

Table 10–7: Comparison of Annual Income between Return Migrants and Never-Migrated Health Workers*

	Return Migrants				Non Migrants			
	Nurses		Doctors		Nurses		Doctors	
Total no. of respondents	33		31		96		14	
	Mean	Standard Deviation	Mean	Standard Deviation	Mean	Standard Deviation	Mean	Standard Deviation
Annual income	8273	6047	22554	31194	5754	2896	16312	8026
Annual household income	17565	20039	33175	36441	12354	6978	23825	8203
Annual per capita household income	3453	4089	8374	7844	2529	1579	6929	4469
Fiji	10		8		51		11	
Annual income	6674	2556	13867	3881	5473	1933	13327	5642
Annual household income	14285	9458	23176	11786	12305	7215	21986	7668
Annual per capita household income	2488	1576	6201	3205	2794	1728	6257	3987
Samoa	12		8		27		3	
Annual income	5330	3207	18529	5641	6380	4443	27255	5561
Annual household income	10818	5569	26540	14104	12832	7028	30569	7521
Annual per capita household income	2325	1867	6530	3404	2334	1508	9392	6226
Tonga	11		15		18		0	
Annual income	12790	7854	29334	44273	5614	2195	-	-
Annual household income	27609	31046	42048	50101	11778	6539	-	-
Annual per capita household income	5474	6257	10517	10552	2074	1091	-	-

* All income data are in Australian dollars

Conclusion: To the Islands

My time overseas has made me more open-minded to new ideas and changes…and just about life in general (quoted in Maron 2001, 79).

At no time during the past quarter of a century has there been substantial return migration to Pacific island states, despite the centrality of an ideology of return. Return has been greatest where distances have been less and economic opportunities greater, and consequently, least in more remote islands and regions (Connell 2009). Limited return migration is at least partly due to the significant differences in income levels between the island states and the metropolitan periphery, but also to a host of social and economic factors.

Those who have moved back to the Pacific from overseas stressed that the factors that resulted in their return migration (other than, or alongside, bonding) included climate, safety and the relaxed pace of life, or simply the familiarity of the home country and the presence of kin, where discrimination was less likely to be a problem—indicating how crucial social, political and economic stability is to return migration. However, they were unlikely to mention economic reasons for return. Few migrants returned because of conditions in the health sector or any great desire to return to work there. Where health workers returned to Pacific island states because of perceived economic benefits—such as the ability to open a store—these lay outside the health care system, which became, for some, mere supplementary employment. Returning workers within the health sector, though willing to contribute to the sector, were likely to resent the nepotism they found (which was quite different from the meritocracy of metropolitan states and hindered promotion and innovation), alongside a range of other problems, and stay for a relatively short period of time. Many migrants find return difficult, facing lower wages and standards of living, difficulty in establishing businesses and, simply, culture shock. Their success and their return were sometimes resented, both in the workplace (where they sought to make changes and introduce new ideas, etc.) and in local society (Maron and Connell 2008). The returnees had changed but, less obviously, so too had their homeland.

The skills drain is likely to continue, especially where there have been structural reforms that reduce public sector employment, where wages and salaries remain unequal, working conditions are difficult and hierarchical, international recruitment intensifies and many kin are overseas. For the health sector, the emigration of skilled workers has been widely seen as the most dramatic and significant example of the 'brain drain' from the Pacific islands, yet many do return. While relative numbers indicate that a considerable skills drain constitutes an imbalance, return migration is greater than might have been expected, where a general 'myth of return' has been suggested and where almost all migration from the Pacific island states has been of settlers rather than contract workers. While numbers may be small, their impact is significant for both social and economic development, in terms of gains to health services (through new skills and wider experience, and simply, additional labour) and to the economy for their (partial) investment of overseas-generated incomes. Most health workers who have returned have gained substantially in enhanced skills and experience overseas. Moreover, most have retained considerable local knowledge, education and expertise and are therefore in a position to integrate their new skills into the health system in a culturally sensitive manner (though this may not always be easy). Yet many are dissatisfied (for example, with the pace of life, hierarchical structures and their own inability to implement change), and return migration may be simply a stage in a cycle of continued migration, especially in the smaller states, where opportunities are relatively few and promotion prospects poor. Return migration, particularly of skilled workers, is therefore more problematic than for most other returnees.

On balance then, even for those who have established businesses or returned to good jobs, returning tends to be a social rather than an economic phenomenon. Indeed, given that many migrants return to look after relatives and thus may not have returned at times of their own choosing, their success is the more remarkable. Return migrants may be potential 'agents of change' but conformity is usually more appreciated than change.

> More commonly, it is return migration that slowly changes islands but, wherever and however it occurs, and especially on the smallest islands, migration and change incite resentment, envy, tension and new perceptions of identity (Connell and King 1999, 18).

Return results in some degree of confusion and uncertainty about roles and identities, enhanced by the expectations placed on returnees by individuals and social institutions, their own recognition that they had changed, and their inability to meet others' expectations. Ambivalence is at the core of the Pacific 'culture of migration', where skills must be acquired overseas but dependent families remain at home. In a sense, Pacific islanders are similar to the Miskito Indians of Nicaragua who have been described as 'leaving in order to stay' and for whom migration has become a 'way of maintaining the family by leaving the family; and it is also a means of going away without leaving' (Nietschmann 1979, 20, 22). This is no less true of skilled migrants and emphasises how migrants are seemingly forever caught between two or more worlds as they strive to support their extended households while on journeys that are never complete in a transnational world.

References

Beston, J. and R. Beston. 1977. An interview with Albert Wendt. *World literature written in English* 16: 152–59.

Brown, R.1997. Estimating remittance functions for Pacific Island migrants. *World Development* 25 (4): 613–26

Brown, R. and J. Connell. 1993. The global flea-market: Migration, remittances and the informal economy in Tonga. *Development and Change* 24: 611–47.

——. 2004. The migration of doctors and nurses from South Pacific Island Nations. *Social Science and Medicine* 58: 2193–210.

Connell, J. 2004. The migration of skilled health professionals: From the Pacific Islands to the World. *Asian and Pacific Migration Journal* 13: 155–77.

——. 2007. At the end of the world. Holding on to health workers in Niue. *Asian and Pacific Migration Journal* 16: 179–98.

——. 2008a. Niue: Embracing a culture of migration. *Journal of Ethnic and Migration Studies* 34: 1021-1040.

—. 2008b. Towards a global health 'care' system. In *The International Migration of Health Workers*, ed. J. Connell, 1–29. New York and London: Routledge.

—. 2009. Bittersweet home? The return migration of health workers in Polynesia. In *Return migration of the next generations: twenty-first century transnational mobility*, ed. D. Conway and R. Potter. Ashgate: Aldershot.

Connell, J and R. Brown. 2004. The remittances of migrant Tongan and Samoan nurses in Australia. *Human Resources for Health* 2 (2): 1–21.

Connell, J. and R. King. 1999. Island migration in a changing world. In *Small worlds, global lives: Islands and migration*, ed. J. Connell and R. King, 1–26. London: Pinter.

Conway, D., R. Potter, and J. Phillips. 2005. The experience of return: Caribbean return migrants. In *The experience of return migration: Caribbean perspectives*, ed. R. Potter, D. Conway, and J. Phillips, 1–25. Aldershot: Ashgate.

Gmelch, G. 1992. *Double passage: The lives of Caribbean migrants abroad and back home*. Ann Arbor: University of Michigan Press.

Hooker, K. and J. Varcoe. 1999. Migration and the Cook Islands. In *Strategies for sustainable development*, ed. J. Overton and R. Scheyvens, 91–9. Sydney: UNSW Press.

Kingma, M. 2006. *Nurses on the move. Migration and the global health care economy*. Ithaca: Cornell University Press.

Liki, A. 2001. Moving and rootedness: The paradox of the brain drain among Samoan professionals. *Asia Pacific Population Journal* 16 (1): 67–84.

Macpherson, C. 1985. Public and private views of home: Will Western Samoan migrants return? *Pacific Viewpoint* 26: 242–62.

Marcus, G. E. 1981. Power on the extreme periphery: The perspective of Tongan elites in the modern world system. *Pacific Viewpoint* 22: 48–64.

Maron, N. 2001. *Return to Nukunuku. Identity culture and return migration in Tonga*. BA Honours thesis, University of Sydney.

Maron, N. and J. Connell. 2008. Back to Nukunuku: Employment, identity and return migration in Tonga. *Asia Pacific Viewpoint* 49: 168-184.

Naidu, L. 1997. *Contemporary professional emigration from Fiji*. MA thesis, University of the South Pacific, Suva.

Nietschmann, B. 1979. Ecological change, inflation and migration in the far western Caribbean. *Geographical Review* 69: 1–24.

Rallu, J.-L. 1997. *Population, migration, développement dans le Pacifique Sud.* Paris: UNESCO.

Rotem, A. and M. Bailey. 1999. Health personnel migration within Commonwealth countries in the Pacific region. Mimeo. Sydney: University of New South Wales.

Thomas-Hope, E. 1999. Return migration to Jamaica and its development potential. *International Migration* 37: 183–207.

Voigt-Graf, C. 2003. Fijian teachers on the move: Causes, implications and policies. *Asia Pacific Viewpoint* 44: 163–74.

Voigt-Graf, C., R. Iredale, and S. Khoo. 2007. Teaching at home or overseas: Teacher migration from Fiji and the Cook Islands. *Asian and Pacific Migration Journal* 16: 199–224.

ENDNOTES

[1] This and all other quotations are from health workers in the three Pacific island states unless otherwise stated.

11. The Impact of Transnationalism on Niue

Vili Nosa

Introduction

For many Pacific Islanders, migration is a positive opportunity for individuals to obtain higher standards of living and material possessions not available in their homelands. Pacific states, like many small countries, have come to depend increasingly upon larger metropolitan states such as New Zealand. However, this chapter shows that the consequences of individual migration decisions invariably impact upon the state of Niue, a small Pacific Island state known by its people as 'the rock of Polynesia'. Niue is one of the most extreme cases of depopulation in the Pacific region, in fact there are more Niueans living abroad, mainly in New Zealand, than on Niue. There are now real questions about whether a state with such a small population is economically and socially viable.

This chapter provides an outline of the effects of transnationalism on Niue and the Niueans who have settled in New Zealand. The reasons why Niueans have migrated in large numbers overseas especially to New Zealand is discussed, and the chapter also examines a number of key strategies currently being implemented in Niue to encourage Niueans abroad to return to their homeland.

Background

Available information about the early history of Niue is limited and the origins of Niuean society are not well documented. Loeb (1926), Smith (1983) and Thomson (1984) suggest that Niuean social structures were greatly influenced by the immigration of people from both eastern and western Polynesian cultures (including Tonga and Samoa). Later, European influences such as the London Missionary Society, early traders and 'blackbirders' were also evident. The work of Loeb (1926) and Kumitau and Hekau (1982) suggests that all of these influences have played major roles in shaping the ideologies of contemporary *faka Niue* (the Niue way). In fact, many of Niue's indigenous cultures and customs have been shaped by elements of the world view and lifestyles of the early Polynesian colonists, since even the most basic elements of Niuean society reflect influences and ideas similar to those present in societies such as Tonga and Samoa.

Niue is situated in Polynesia in the southwest Pacific Ocean and is the highest raised coral (*makatea*) island in the world. Niue is a single island housing 13 villages; the terrain is mainly steep limestone cliffs and a large proportion of the land is coral, much of it covered in indigenous forest and scrub.

In 1900 Niue became a British protectorate; by 1901 it was annexed to the New Zealand administration where the latter had a major role in governing the economy of Niue. In 1974 Niue became a self-governed state with free association with New Zealand, and Niueans became New Zealand citizens with free rights into New Zealand (Chapman 1976; Government of Niue 1982). By 1986 the population of Niueans in New Zealand was 12,501 and by 2001 it was 20,148 (Statistics New Zealand 2006). The 2006 New Zealand census states that 22,473 Niueans reside in New Zealand, comprising 8 per cent of the New Zealand Pacific population. There was an increase of 2,325, or 12 per cent, since the 2001 census. Over 79 per cent (17,667) of Niueans live in Auckland, which is an increase of 20 per cent since the 2001 census. Nearly three-quarters (16,275) of Niueans were born in New Zealand. The Niuean population in New Zealand has therefore doubled in size, while in Niue, it has dropped to only 1,788 people (Statistics New Zealand 2006).

Niuean Migration

During the mid-19th century, Niueans joined the labour trade in Samoa, Tahiti, Hawaii, Fiji, and Australia. Many Niuean men emigrated to Samoa in order to work on the cotton plantations (Talagi 1991, 119). Mining was another factor in labour migration (both voluntary and involuntary); for example, in 1868 'blackbirders' such as Bully Hayes took 60 men and 30 women from Niue to work in the phosphate mines in Eastern Polynesia (Loeb 1926). Later, during the 20th century, labour migration increased due to the discovery of guano deposits on Malden Island in Kiribati (South Pacific Commission Report, 1983, No 11 Niue). This labour migration meant that large numbers of people were living away from Niue and other Pacific states. For example, more Wallis and Futuna shipping personnel worked in the New Caledonia nickel industry (9,000) than in their own countries (7,000). The phosphate mines in Nauru also employed Gilbertese and Ellice Islanders and Chinese from Hong Kong. Niuean migrants followed these trends and employment opportunities.

Military bases in the Pacific were also a staging arena for labour migration. For example, Filipinos in Guam were connected with the American military bases there. This created a movement from the Pacific towards America as intermarriage occurred between US service personal and Filipino residents. Since the 1900s, the USA has also recruited American Samoans into the Navy and Army, leading to more international Pacific migration. The relocation of military operations from American Samoa to Hawaii and California also led to major movements, as did similar trends in New Caledonia where France has a military presence. These recruitments and transfers are important for Pacific migration and have affected Niue given Niueans' informal (i.e., individual) involvement in military matters since World War I (Rex and Vivian 1982).

Later phases of migration occurred after World War II when rapid growth in the larger states bordering the Pacific rim led to increasing demands for labour. In New Zealand, Australia and the US, employment opportunities generated larger scale international labour migration possibilities and heralded a change from migration within the Pacific to migration out of the region. It was during this period and under these circumstances that the major emigration from Niue occurred (Crocombe 1971).

The 1970s saw a trend towards major international Niuean migration. The opening of an international airport in 1971 established a transportation route that allowed easy movement in and out of Niue. Cheaper airfares in the 1980s ensured that individuals' ability to leave increased at a rapid rate. Another major factor was the process of 'internal self government' granted in free association with New Zealand in October 1974. This gave Niueans New Zealand citizenship. Between 1966 and 1984, Niue lost over 40 per cent of its population to Aotearoa. As Douglas notes, 'I would say that well over one-half of all Niueans at that point had decided to follow their impartial colonial administrators to Auckland rather than remain on the Island to be subjected to what they thought were the biases of their own people' (1987, 188). Moreover, the influence of the extended families already living in Auckland motivated other members to leave, which in turn created 'chain migration'.

The most common and significant motivations for migration from Pacific islands such as Niue are economic: the perceived rewards of employment, relatively high wages and the added bonus of a 'better' education system (Tuhega 1977). Writers such as Talagi (1991) have also suggested that a major factor in Pacific migration is the search for recreational activities such as cinemas and public bars, which become available with higher, more secure, personal incomes. Thus the features of migration from Pacific states such as Niue are complex and interlinked and we must be careful to avoid generalisations or simplifications of this dynamic phenomenon. Some factors are individualistic; for instance, Tuhega (1977) states that his parents decided to leave Niue because of land tenure problems and because education opportunities were limited for his children as only a small number of children were selected to go overseas on study scholarships. Political factors have also contributed to Niuean migration. Talagi suggests that 'the attitude of central government was that Niueans who were dissatisfied with government policies would be better off elsewhere—this was aimed at public servants in and the general population in general' (1991, 124; see also Douglas 1987).

The physical features of Niue also influence migration; Niue is a small atoll with limited resources. The physical resources of Niue are poor; available land is limited due to scrub and forest, and the high proportion of coral means that soil fertility is low. Water comes from bores and there are no running streams or rivers (Spoonley 1975; Talagi 1991). All of these factors mean that life in Niue largely revolves around the hard physical survival mode of plantation work. This involves clearing land for planting, weeding, nurturing and harvesting; all of which is done in the burning hot weather. Traditional cultivation methods are time consuming and hard to maintain. However, for many families, subsistence agriculture is a daily routine necessary to supplement the daily diet. This lifestyle is difficult and can encourage Niuean people to leave. The 'physically easier and relaxed lifestyle' found in New Zealand may be the principal 'pull factor' in Niuean migration to New Zealand (Douglas 1987). Even factory work can be perceived in terms of relative 'ease' compared with the tough life of 'bush work' on Niuean plantations (Talagi 1991).

Hurricanes and storms have played havoc with the economy of Niue. For example, Cyclone Ofa in 1990 practically devastated the island. Most homes and plantations were demolished, leaving many people homeless. The most recent cyclone that hit Niue was the Cyclone Heta in 2004, which destroyed a number of homes and land. For many, the only option was to leave. Niue's agricultural productivity is also affected by such weather patterns. In the early 1960s and 1970s, lime and passion fruit industries were developed. The 1980s saw the commercial production of coconut cream and in the 1990s taro production for export occurred. However, these agricultural ventures have not been successful for a number of reasons and Talagi suggests that morale among plantation growers has decreased, encouraging further migration (Talagi 1991). Today, agricultural production output is scarce and since only a few of the crops (such as taro) are exported, plantation growers are often frustrated by not gaining enough income to maintain a viable living. Added to this are the poor transportation facilities such as shipping services which only visit Niue once a month and air transport which occurs on a weekly basis. These problems with agricultural production may motivate international migration for landowners and non-landowners alike.

The colonial relationship between Niue and New Zealand has led to the influx of Western philosophies concerned with gaining social and economic opportunities found in Aotearoa. For example, the education system in Niue is limited in both resources and teaching facilities. Education is free and compulsory for all Niuean children, but currently there is only one primary school and one high school, and both primary and secondary curricula are based on the New Zealand system (with a few modifications). The standard education is set for the New Zealand National Certificate in Educational Achievement (NCEA). Only a few selected students are chosen for scholarships to enter New Zealand high schools. There are also the University of the South Pacific extension centre courses. For many youngsters growing up on Niue, the desire to remain at home in Niue is strongly linked to the availability of employment. For example, two young Niuean students interviewed for the Television New Zealand documentary *Death on the Rock* (Television New Zealand 1989) stated that if they were to gain employment with the government they would remain on Niue, however both suggested that the alternative was to migrate to New Zealand.

One other significant issue was the key decisions made by the first Niuean government. Funding that was allocated to particular firms did not develop to its full potential. For example, in one case, funding was given to the premier's son-in-law for projects that were not developed. One MP suggested that nepotism was a key issue at the time of funding these organisations (Television New Zealand 1989). This particular event also pushed many dissatisfied Niueans to migrate overseas.

The Niuean Disapora

During the early 1940s and 1950s, before planes could land on Niue, many Niueans travelled to New Zealand by ship. By 1974, when Niue became independent, planes were introduced, which saw a large influx of the Niuean population into New Zealand, particularly to Auckland. The main reason Niueans settled in Auckland was to be near immediate and extended family members who were already there, but as discussed above they were also drawn to what they saw as better lifestyle, education and employment opportunities, and the good weather. As already stated, there are now more Niueans in New Zealand than the on the island of Niue. Furthermore, there are more Niueans who are New Zealand-born, and there has been an increase in the number of Niueans with tertiary qualifications. Some Niueans have married members of other ethnic groups, such as Europeans and Maori, which is one factor leading to a decline in the spoken Niuean language (Statistics New Zealand 2006).

In recent years, the New Zealand economy has gone through some economic and social changes and the cost of living has become very high for many Niueans. In the past 10–15 years there has been a significant migration shift, with a large number of Niueans migrating to Australia. Even Niueans who had been living in New Zealand for the last 20–30 years have moved. A number of cities in Australia, including Sydney, Brisbane and Melbourne, have seen an influx of Niueans mainly due to higher wages, better employment opportunities and better lifestyle. Wages are a lot higher in Australia for manual factory work than in New Zealand. Housing is also cheaper and a number of young couples have been able to purchase a brand new house, which they would not have been able to do in New Zealand. The process of chain migration means that many Niueans continue to move, to be with immediate and extended family members.

Forms of Transnational Connections

There have been a few difficulties in terms of transnational connections between Niueans in New Zealand and Niueans back home. Firstly, Niue is quite isolated and there is only one flight per week for Niueans or tourists. Return flights to Niue have also been expensive. A number of airlines have not been very successful, such as Nauru airlines in the 1970s, Royal Tongan Airlines in the 1980s and Polynesians airlines in the 1990s. In the mid–2000s, Air New Zealand became the preferred airline and the weekly flights at just a quarter of the previous price have been beneficial for the economy, with a slight increase in the number of tourists. Niueans can afford to return home to see family members more often than before.

In the past, letters and telegraphs were a popular source of communication for many Niueans. The telephone has also been another form of communication but this has been very expensive. Niueans only use the telephone for urgent matters such as contacting family members, funerals, and celebrations. With the influx of new technology, email has become a popular means by which Niueans overseas can communicate with other Niueans. Many Niuean homes now have access to email. There is also weekly news on the Niuean government website, updating major events and activities. This website *Niue Ki Mua* publishes news about government business, such as overseas travel by government members and public servants, who is looking after their portfolios, and who is going overseas for courses, conferences and meetings. There is also news about workshops occurring in Niue, public events such as show days, cultural events and other social gatherings. There are also messages from the Premier about key events and issues of government.

In a global context, there is a communication chat line called the Niue Global Community. This is a forum where Niueans communicate with other Niueans around the world to discuss and debate Niuean issues. All new members must register to be part of the discussion group and must have some Niuean ancestral connection. Applicants must provide their name, village, places of residence and employment status. This is then sent to the founder of the site, Niuean Frank Sioneholo and his moderators, who look after the website. Membership is based on the management's approval. The site also advertises key Niuean community events, cultural and social activities. Photographs of events are also displayed on the website and there is strict monitoring of the topics that are discussed.

Niuean newspapers have been another means of keeping up with events occurring in the Niuean community. The first Niue newspaper, the *Niue Star,* was established in 1993 and currently has its office in Auckland. The news items include events from Niue and New Zealand such as current events, politics, sports and other cultural activities. In the last five years, two more newspapers have emerged: the *Niue Today* which also publishes a number of key Niue events, and the *Fakapuloa Tala Niue*, another New Zealand based magazine which publishes community news, social events and sports events and is also online. All of these newspapers publish in both Niuean and English.

Niuean migrants frequently send remittances of both money and goods to kin in Niue. Container loads of products such as food, appliances and furniture are often sent home to families on a monthly or weekly basis. Sometimes when Niueans visit New Zealand they shop for large amounts of products such as non-perishable food products to send home on the supply ships. There appear to be no barriers to family connections back home except the difficulties of flights which are only once a week. Given that tourism is the main source of attracting people home, this is often difficult with no mid-week flights. However, many Niueans continue to visit Niue for special occasions and celebrations.

Future Developments on Niue

A number of key strategies have been implemented to try and rebuild the state of Niue. In the past, developing food products for export was the main strategy, however, a number of attempts, such as the lime and vanilla production during the 1960s, have not been successful due to financial constraints and political issues.

Currently, a business partnership with Reef Shipping and the Niue government has developed a few business ventures to try to rebuild Niue. In 2005 the noni product was implemented and introduced into Niue. The noni (*Morinda Citrifolia*) grows mainly in the Pacific Islands and its juice is consumed for healthy skin, joint mobility, digestion, energy levels and the immune system. The noni initiative is a joint venture between the Niue government and Reef Shipping, with a noni farm located in Vaiea and local Niueans growing noni on their family plantations. Another initiative is the fish processing factory. Fish is caught in the local fishing area and processed in the local factory then exported to New Zealand, European and other large metropolitan states. This venture is trying to expand but there is a very limited labour supply to work within the factories.

On a family visit to Niue in February 2006, I also had the opportunity to observe some of the developments with a relative of mine who is the co-coordinator of the Niue Island Organic Farmers' Association. During the tour around the islands, I saw the development of vanilla production. Many of the local farmers grow vanilla on their own plantations and around their homes. The vanilla products are grown organically, without pesticides, and then exported to Europe and the USA. This venture is labour intensive because of the hand pollination of crops and the large plantation sizes.

Another venture I observed was the young farmers' project which is targeting school leavers to assist them to establish and manage vanilla plantations, piggeries and vegetable farms. The overall aim is to ensure that these young farmers are able to produce these products on a commercial basis. One such initiative, which has been implemented to encourage young Niueans to return, is NEVAT (Niue experience of *Vaka Atu Toa*). The scheme provides an opportunity for young New Zealand-born Niueans to explore the Niuean culture and lifestyle for three months. They are given the opportunity to live the Niuean lifestyle and experience the language and culture of a Niuean.

Return Migration

The issue of return migration is a contentious topic for many Niueans in New Zealand and Niue. The former Premier of Niue, Young Vivian, constantly tries to attract Niueans overseas to return home. A number of employment schemes have been developed to attract them, but they have been largely unsuccessful. The Niuean government has sent a number of officials to investigate how to encourage or entice Niueans to return home. One initiative is bank loans from the Niue bank, made available for people to renovate their homes. There are other housing schemes such as renovating houses in partnership with government, which are then rented to tourists. However, to date, these schemes have had little impact on the number of Niueans returning home.

Niueans are more likely to return for a holiday, for between one and four weeks. Elderly Niueans living on superannuation often return home for periods of two to three months then go back to New Zealand. Many elderly Niueans return to Niue during the New Zealand winter months. There is also a strong sense of family connections for many Niueans who live overseas. They often visit family members back home, particularly over the Christmas and New Year period. There are also village celebrations that occur once a month, where a number of stalls are set up to sell cooked food, raw food products from plantations and handicrafts such as woven hats, mats and handbags. This is an opportunity for the whole village to showcase and display a number of products. Many Niueans affiliated to a particular village will return for this celebration. There is a strong sense of village loyalty for Niueans overseas to attend these functions. Other important events are the family cultural celebrations such as weddings, twenty-first birthday parties, hair cutting and ear piercing ceremonies, for which many Niueans make the journey home. These celebrations are an important part of many Niueans' cultural identity and sense of belonging to Niue.

Land disputes are another major reason why there are a large number of Niueans returning from overseas, to reclaim their land. Land disputes have been a major issue for many Niueans and will continue. The economic development of land is very difficult as most Niueans are overseas and therefore there must be a consensus decision before any land is made available for development. In some cases, Niueans have returned to claim their land and some people have remained on the island to build new homes.

Despite Niue's efforts to establish jobs and opportunities in Niue, there has been little progress in encouraging Niueans abroad to return home. There are a number of key reasons for this: many individuals find it difficult to return to Niue because of the lower standard of living there compared with that in New Zealand. The cost of food in the shops is high, as are petrol prices. Another reason is pay parity and disparity of employment opportunities. There is a large pay disparity between, say, a local Niuean school teacher and a New Zealand-trained school teacher. As mentioned earlier in this paper, the difficulty of living in a subsistence agricultural economy is due to the nature of the land. The task of cultivating plantations is very difficult because of the density of coral land. Irrigation and watering of crops is also an issue, as is the problem of pests and wild pigs destroying plantations.

Access to healthcare services is another issue where services may not be adequate, therefore patients with major health complications are sent to New Zealand for further care. In terms of the education system, students who do not get scholarships often do not get the opportunity for further education so they migrate to New Zealand. For many parents, education is an important part of their children's educational development.

Despite the many factors discouraging return, a small number have returned home. Some Niueans have returned because of the stress of day-to-day living in New Zealand. For some, the costs of living have been quite high and they have had the added pressure of living in a demanding environment and surviving on poor pay. On a trip to Niue in 2006, many Niueans with whom I spoke were enjoying the laid-back lifestyle and stress-free environment. They had no immediate plans to return to New Zealand.

Magnall's (2004) thesis on the portability of returning Niueans on superannuation showed that they were only getting 50 per cent of their New Zealand superannuation. Participants in the study found it very difficult to retire to Niue. The author identified a number of key reasons why many elderly Niueans do not return home. Participants who had a home to return to, money to build a house and a spouse who was keen to join them were willing to return. On the other hand, participants who were not keen to return home had no home to go to and their spouses were not keen to join them. Those who have returned comment on the good climate and relaxed lifestyle (Magnall 2004). Participants also mentioned that the difficulty in returning to Niue was the process of upgrading their houses with modern indoor facilities such as toilets and showers. They also had to consider growing plantations and working the physical environment. The subsistence farming lifestyle is very difficult for the elderly. One result is that elderly parents also took their children and grandchildren back to Niue to help them.

On a trip to Niue with the governor general of Niue in April 2007 a group of New Zealand-raised and born young Niuean professionals met with the Niue government to explain their views on returning to Niue. Many of them highlighted the fact that they would not return to Niue because of the low wages, the high costs of living and the difficulties of raising families. However, many

Niueans still have strong family connections and a sense of belonging, making them want to return to Niue one day.

Discussion

There is a significant trend for Niueans to migrate overseas and consequently, the population of Niue has declined rapidly. Many Niueans have migrated for better lifestyle opportunities, mainly to New Zealand. There is a large population of Niueans in Auckland and there are now more New Zealand Niueans with multiethnic backgrounds. Niueans have now moved to other parts of the world, especially to Australia, as employment opportunities are better and the cost of living is a lower than in New Zealand.

Transnationalism has played an important role for many of these Niueans abroad, who are still strongly connected with Niue through remittances, reciprocal gift giving, cultural activities, land obligations, and identity through kinship ties and obligations. Many Niueans will return for important events and to visit family. However, as highlighted in this chapter, Niue is an extreme case whereby a large population of Niueans live overseas and maintaining their transnational ties has been made difficult by inadequate transportation and expensive phone calls. Today, many Niueans have turned to technology to enable them to maintain these links through emails and the use of video conference technologies such as Skype.

A number of key issues have been discussed in this chapter in relation to return migration. The government has created initiatives to repopulate Niue and in some cases, Niueans have returned to Niue because of the climate and laid back lifestyle, a stress free environment and the low cost of living. However, the problem of population decline remains and there are still a number of young people who feel that they will not return to the island because of low wages, the high cost of living and the change of lifestyle.

In the last five years, Niue has been slowly trying to rebuild its economy with the new initiatives that have been highlighted in this paper; it remains to be seen whether these are successful in the long term. For Niue to become an economically sustainable country it needs to have a strong financial base to ensure that resources are manageable and to develop the country. There also needs to be a good governance structure in place so that the economy is stable. Economic development needs to be strong so that Niue is economically viable and not reliant on overseas aid. Social services such as education and health services infrastructure also must be improved so that Niueans will have a better lifestyle in Niue and more Niueans will be willing to return home.

References

Chapman M. T. 1976. *The decolonisation of Niue*. Wellington, New Zealand: Victoria University Press and New Zealand Institute of International Affairs.

Crocombe R. 1971. The Cook, Niue and Tokelau Islands. Fragmentation and emigration. In *Land Tenure in the Pacific*, ed. R. Crocombe, 60–89. Melbourne: Oxford University Press.

Douglas, H. 1987. Niue: The silent village green. In *Class and culture in the South Pacific*, ed. A. Hooper, 186–93. Suva: University of Auckland and Institute of Pacific Studies, University of South Pacific.

Government of Niue. 1982. *Niue: History of the island*. Suva: Institute of the South Pacific of the University of the South Pacific, Institute of Pacific Studies, University of the South Pacific.

Kumitau, V. and M. Hekau. 1982. Origins of the Niue people. In *Niue: History of the island*, ed. Government of Niue Institute of Pacific Studies, 82–90. Suva: University of the South Pacific and the Government of Niue.

Loeb, D. E. 1926. *History and traditions of Niue*. Honolulu: Bernice P Bishop.

Magnall, K. 2004. Retiring to Niue. MA thesis, Auckland University, NZ.

McDowell, K. D. 1961. A History of Niue. MA thesis, University of Auckland, NZ.

Rex, L. and Y. Vivian. 1982. The New Zealand period. In *Niue: History of the island*, ed. Government of Niue, 127–39. Suva: Institute of Pacific Studies, University of the South Pacific.

Smith, S. P. 1983. *Niue: The island and its people*. Suva: The Institute of Pacific Studies and the Niue Extension Centre of the University of the South Pacific, Suva. [Originally published in *The Journal of Polynesian Society* 11 (12): 1–113, 1902–3.]

South Pacific Commission report. 1983. *Niue*. Noumea: South Pacific Commission.

Spoonley, P. 1975. Prospects for the Niuean community in Auckland: The role of gatekeeper groups in migrant adaptation. MA diss., University of Otago.

Statistics New Zealand. 2006. *New Zealand Census of Population and Dwellings*. Wellington: Statistics New Zealand.

Talagi, M. 1991. Contemporary politics of micro-state Niue. MA thesis, Auckland University, NZ.

Television New Zealand. 1989. *Frontline: Death on the Rock*. Television New Zealand Wellington.

Thomson, B. 1984. *Savage islands: An account of a sojourn in Niue and Tonga*. Papakura, New Zealand: McMillan.

Tuhega, L. 1977. Land tenure in Niue. In *Land tenure in Niue*, ed. S. Kalauni, R. Crocombe, L. Tuhega, N. Douglas, P. Pihigia, G. Leonard, and E. Lipitoa, 25–32. Suva: Fiji Times & Herald Ltd, Institute of Pacific Studies, University of the South Pacific.

12. 'Getting Out from Under': Leadership, Conflict Resolution and Tokelau Migration

Ingjerd Hoëm

Introduction: Migration and Population Trends

In the past three decades, Niue and to a lesser extent the Cook Islands, have figured prominently in the public discourse in Tokelau, in the Tokelau communities overseas, and in administrative circles, about choosing a viable political way for Tokelau. The threat constituted by the example of Niue—as it is represented in discourse in and about Tokelau—is that of a self-governing island state, most of whose able-bodied population are employed in the public service. The negative consequences of this situation are apparent: those who cannot get employment in the public sector leave and as a consequence, the villages and community life lose coherence, life and vibrancy. In addition, this kind of emigration causes village work and development projects to fail for lack of labour. (Such loss of manpower may occur independently, of course, as a result of forces separate from the question of a choice of political institutions; see Hooper, n.d.).[1] In contrast with Niue, Tokelau is represented as a unique case, and a recurrent theme in this discourse is the continued vitality, and relatively constant population figures, of village life in the atolls.

The dominant theoretical perspectives on migration have undergone a transformation over the last three decades. The model of migration as a predominantly unidirectional flow of labour from a home country to a diaspora has been challenged by the emerging configurations represented by 'transnationalism'. These configurations have in common a continuing flow of people, information and goods between two or more social spaces, and frequently crossing national borders (hence the term 'trans-nationalism'). The emotional value of these social spaces, which Lilomaiava-Doctor (this volume) has labelled 'homeland' and 'reach', may differ. A common trait for such situations, at least as they are manifest in the Pacific region, is that the different social spaces are connected by enduring and reciprocal social relationships, through ties of kinship and other institutional connections.

In spite of the discourse on the continued vitality and relatively constant population figures of Tokelau villages referred to above, the most recent census for Tokelau (from 2006) show an admittedly small, but still significant population loss. At present, it is too early to say with any certainty whether the most recent population figures for the Tokelau atoll societies will be seen to constitute a definite trend of population decline or not. Comparative material from elsewhere in the Pacific (such as in this volume) suggests a development of continuous and multidirectional flows between different social spaces, therefore, some caution is required when interpreting the most recent population figures for Tokelau.

A useful place to start is to identify the social processes that underlie such figures. This is important, given the population size (see below for figures). The small population leads to a vulnerability in terms of ongoing viability, but also to a capacity for transnational mobilisation, when faced with events that have great potential social impact. As mentioned above, at the end of 2006, an increase was apparent in emigration from Tokelau. The emigrational pattern seems to have particularly affected the 30–50 age groups. Some people had also moved to Tokelau, but in smaller numbers. The latest Tokelau population census shows a decline of 20 per cent in comparison with the 2001 figure. In 1991, the population numbered 1,557 people; in 1996, it was 1,487 and in 2001, it was 1,449.

The total number of people living on the atolls has never been high: approximately 1,700 at most.[2] What we do not know as yet, is how many people who actually move between the atolls and the outside world between the censuses. This work still remains to be done, and the population figures hide the degree to which the people counted on the atolls might not be the same. However, it is possible to carry out a preliminary exploration of the social dynamics of the most recent population decline; in particular, it might be of interest to ask whether the population situation in the atolls can be better understood from a transnational perspective. This following exploration is based on my own fieldwork observations.

Reasons for a recent increase in emigration include: easier access to the outside world afforded by the introduction of a fortnightly charter that runs between Tokelau and Apia in Samoa; an increase in salaries in Tokelau so that more people can afford to leave; a marked increase in serious health problems and a lower standard of education. Together, these are strong motivating forces for further migration. A headline in the New Zealand newspaper, *The Dominion Post* (of 14 November 2006), hints however that there may be more sinister motives and forces behind the most recent population decline. The headline reads in eye-catching tabloid language: 'Sex and self-government blamed for population fall'. In this chapter, I present some thoughts on what I see as the social dynamics behind events that have resulted in such headlines and relate them to the transnational patterns of interaction between members of the various Tokelau communities in New Zealand and Tokelau.

The Transnational Field of Pacific New Zealand

In contrast with the policies followed by, for example, Chile or France as colonial powers in the Pacific, New Zealand has opted to follow relatively closely the policy laid down in the United Nations' Decolonisation Charter (see Angelo 2001, 259 n 43).

Transnationalism is a useful concept because it points to the existence of a particular kind of social field with inherent characteristics that set it apart from other social fields of interaction that emerge as a result of regional interaction. Some of these characteristics have been mentioned above: the perhaps most important one is the increased frequency of contact across national borders, by multiple media, and on many different levels from the personal to a state apparatus. My use of the term thus differs from those who use it as a general label for all contact between island communities in the region, including precolonial ones (e.g. Spoonley 2001, 95). To take this stance is not to deny the point made by Marshall Sahlins in his polemic article addressed to Lévi-Strauss' civilization-pessimism, 'Goodbye to Tristes Tropes', where he draws a connection between earlier forms of migration in the Pacific region and contemporary migration (Sahlins 1994). He argues that contemporary networks and flow of goods, gifts, persons, rights and obligations perpetuate patterns that were present in earlier forms of regional interaction. Camille Nakhid, in her discussion of the applicability of theories of transnationalism to the particularities of the Pacific makes a similar point when she argues that transnational relationships in the region are typically characterised by reciprocity (this volume). In the same vein, Sahlins' perspective is important, especially as applied to Oceania, as much research has tended to perpetuate an image of historical discontinuity between the (exotic and interesting) pre-contact past and an (acculturated and uninteresting) present. In order better to understand situations such as that represented by contemporary Tokelau configurations—in and outside of the atolls—we need to develop perspectives that allow us to explore such long-term continuities represented by networks of social reciprocity. At the same time, they allow us to examine how nation-states may influence relations between Pacific communities in qualitatively different ways. In this respect, transnationalism has much to offer. It forces us to go beyond one location and one community and look for connections that create new divides but also bridge distances.

Over time, New Zealand's relationship with the Pacific region has changed. At one time the Pacific represented as a golden opportunity for New Zealand to establish a 'pan-Polynesian' empire while at the same time sever the strong political ties binding it to Britain—in order to establish itself as a nation with its own, independent political profile (Hoëm 2005). As is commonly the case with such visions, it was not realised as it was originally conceived. Also, and because of Pacific peoples' greater familiarity with social conditions in New Zealand brought about by the wave of migration commencing from the early 1960s, the country does not figure to the same degree as the 'Promised Land' for prospective migrants. For example, Australia and the USA came for some time to be perceived as more promising destinations for people in search of work. Restrictions on migration also have been tightened. For example, the population (born after 1948, see NZ laws on citizenship) in what was then called Western Samoa lost their rights to New Zealand citizenship after Samoa became independent in 1962. At the same time, a new system of quota regulations for immigrants from Samoa was established. This system has, with certain modifications, remained to the present day. Today the quota is up to 1,100 immigrants per year (in addition to those entering New Zealand under ordinary immigration arrangements), granted that the prospective migrant is between 18 and 45 years of age and has a job offer. People from other Pacific nations, such as Kiribati, Tuvalu, Fiji and Tonga may enter under the 'Pacific Access Category'. New Zealand receives only a few hundred immigrants from these nations each year. Only the population from Cook Islands, Niue and Tokelau still have unlimited access to the country. (See the New Zealand Ministry of Foreign Relations and Trade web page for a fuller description of these policies.)

The Modern House of Tokelau: A House Divided?

Beginning in 1993, the process of transferring executive and legislative powers from the New Zealand administration to the National Assembly or the General Fono of Tokelau commenced in earnest. The Tokelau public service, under the authority of the village councils of elders, the *tapulega,* was only truly established once the New Zealand run State Services Commission was decommissioned. In documents from 1998, the processes of establishing the institutions for internal self-government and the previously non-existent national level in the atolls were described together under one heading, as building the 'Modern House of Tokelau'. The metaphor of a house resonates with traditional ideas of governance and leadership in Tokelau. The formal address of the respective atolls is *Falefitu* or 'seven-house' (Atafu), *Faleiva* or 'nine-house' (Fakaofo) and *Falefa* or 'four-house' (Nukunonu). These forms of address refer to the atolls' former division into large kin-groups, occupational specialisation (such as warriors, priests, etc.), to village areas and, at least on Fakaofo, to men's houses (see MacGregor 1937; Huntsman and Hooper 1996).

Local perceptions and opinions on this exercise in governance—placing all under 'one roof', so to speak—were varied. Most agreed with the plan to relocate the Apia-based Tokelau administration and put it directly under the control of the elders. To make the three atolls work together as one nation was however not so easily achieved. A major difficulty emerged with respect to inter-atoll relations and the principle that the new political infrastructure should be based on Tokelau culture. A solution had to be found to what was unofficially called the 'problem of rivalry'. This complex pattern of behaviour harks back to the 'days of war', a period when the people of Fakaofo ruled as overlords of the two other atolls (Hooper and Huntsman 1985). Fakaofo's dominance was contested and it is still the case that an atoll's or other social group's claims to a position of ascendancy is likely to be challenged by others.

The major obstacle to implementing the new infrastructure was the issue of the location of the head office of the Tokelau administration. This presented a particular difficulty, as to choose a permanent location would be effectively to place the chosen island in a position of permanent ascendancy. No unanimous agreement could be reached between the three atolls. The only choice left was to rotate the head office between the three atolls and this was implemented from 1994. It was discontinued in 1997, due to the personal costs to the public servants who had to move home every year. The national head office was therefore moved back to Apia, although recently there has been pressure to return it to Tokelau.[3]

Forms of Sociality

Tokelau forms of sociality resemble patterns common to other Polynesian societies, in that they have fostered what I have described elsewhere as a 'sense of place' (Hoëm 1999, 2004).[4] This concept refers to peoples' constant awareness of the social composition of a social situation, caused by a concern with social life in terms of social relationships (*va,* lit. the space between) and relative status positions (*tulaga, nofoaga,* see also Tcherkézoff 2008). All significant social groups, such as extended families or kin-groups (*kaiga*), the villages (*nuku*) and the atolls have their own gatherings or meeting fora, the *fono*. In such gatherings, the place to be seated (*nofoaga*) is determined by status position (*tulaga*) and the congregated group traditionally used to sit in a circle along the posts (*pou*) that uphold the roofs of the open-walled houses.

Determining who is eligible to occupy a position depends on the nature of the congregation. In village councils, only older men and family heads are eligible participants. In a family gathering, other principles are followed. Male elders in the villages as well as the senior men and women in extended families have the privilege of deciding how the lives of their dependants should be ordered. The elders can, for example, place a restriction (*lafu*) on plantation areas on the outer islets across the lagoon, thereby pronouncing them off-limits for a period. In other words, they control peoples' access to their land-holdings. They may also ban individuals or families from the villages for improper behaviour, or order them to go overseas for more positive reasons such as to take up a scholarship. The moral universe is heavily influenced by Christianity, but the regulation and assessment of actual behaviour is also and ultimately carried out in terms of such notions as *noa* (free, unbound, improper) and *tapu* or more commonly *ha* (or *sa*) (off limits, restricted, forbidden, or sacred), (Cf. Hoëm 2004: Tcherkézoff 2008: Valeri 2008).

This brief description of mechanisms of inclusion and exclusion is presented in order to provide an illustration of how the villages are ordered; on the one hand, in terms of concepts of interlocking groups that ideally exist as a harmonious and well-functioning (*teu, maopoopo*) whole and on the other hand, how the actual processes of composing groups in terms of matching persons and positions are also commonly characterised by fierce competition and social exclusion.

Some Consequences of Establishing 'the Modern House' on Tokelau

The difference between the amount of time spent on communal work for the villages and the value placed on it, as compared with the situation as it was only ten years ago, is striking and points to the speed at which changes in the economic basis of Tokelau society have occurred. 'Subsistence time' and 'office time' activities are a case in point. 'Subsistence-time' includes those centred on production (including fishing and other food-gathering activities), distribution and consumption of food. 'Office-time' activities are those that involve working in the various departments of the Tokelau public service. The two systems conflict in several respects and there are many signs that they have opposing consequences with respect to social reproduction. In short, whereas subsistence-oriented activities are geared towards reproducing large extended families and a network of inter-family cooperation, monetary based activities tend to produce smaller, more independent units that do not contribute in the same way towards village cooperation. This trend is visible in the atoll landscape as a result of the so-called housing scheme, which has resulted in a near total replacement of the traditional, thatched, open-walled houses by two-storey, concrete-floored modern housing with water catchment roofs. These houses allow smaller family units than previously to live together, and not least important, the walls provide a previously non-existent sense of privacy.

The monetary sphere is also intimately connected with demands for more frequent inter-atoll and national cooperation on a formal, institutional level. The emergence of certain conflicts between different systems of production and reproduction is clearly attributable to the UN and the New Zealand administration's project of establishing the local infrastructure deemed necessary for political independence. In other words, the contemporary rhythm of village life plays according to a different score from previously. Where in the 1960s, three months around Christmas were reserved for competitive games and festive activities, followed by more labour-intensive periods, now, work and leisure activities are more evenly distributed.

In addition, the past few decades have seen the rise of socio-economic divisions that have their basis in wage employment in the Tokelau public service. Whereas earlier there were differences between extended families in terms of the size of land areas they possessed, the ownership of land did not in itself make for prosperity. The prerogative to command able-bodied persons to gather and process food seems rather to have been the critical factor and this control was ultimately in the hands of the elders. In other words, through most of the period since the abolition of the kingship system in 1915, Tokelau has not experienced marked variation in the material status of its inhabitants. These days, such material differences are present, however, and socio-economic differences are easily detected when comparing the two-storey *palagi* houses containing satellite-discs, DVD or video players, freezers, microwave ovens and other consumer goods with other, more modest abodes with no such amenities. Thus, one may say that competing for honour has moved into new arenas.

Furthermore, and importantly for my discussion of possible factors that may influence emigration, there are signs indicating that the 'rivalry' or competition for honour that was an integral part of older political life in the atolls, have moved into the new arenas and institutions of the new administration, previously referred to as 'the modern house of Tokelau'. A slight shift in the sites of political life, or rather, its expansion into new arenas, reproduces the traditional dynamic in the villages where one 'house' or encompassing group is pitted against other 'houses' or groups on a regular basis. The qualitative change lies in the fact that this rivalry now also occurs within the administrative institutions, and its associated arenas and media.

As mentioned above, local perceptions and opinions of the last decade's exercise of governance have been varied. Most have been in agreement with the plan to relocate the previously Apia-based Tokelau administration to the atolls. The political rhetoric of the modern, or as it became in Tokelauan, the new (*fou*) house of Tokelau, was perceived by some as a bid for power by a particular group of public servants and elders, and it was challenged on those terms. This, in particular, was (and still is) done by one fraction of village leaders among those who have no or little previous background in public service positions. This faction prefers to play what may be called the 'card of tradition'.

The main issue underlying the contemporary elections to political positions such as the *faipule* (minister of external relations) and *pulenuku* (village mayor), and in deciding issues during the General Fono is the question of whether people with allegiances beyond the atoll village ('nationalists') can be trusted at all, or whether people's allegiances should be with those who have kept to one village and gradually built up their power base from their extended family and outwards ('traditionalists'). As of today, the latter position seems to have ascendancy, as Tokelau, in its first national referendum (in February 2006) the vote against a treaty with New Zealand granting political self-determination in free association with New Zealand, fell just short of the required two thirds majority stipulated by the Genenal Fono. A second referendum was held in October 2007 and again although coming even closer to the two thirds majority, the result was still to remain what some may call a New Zealand colony.

Conflicting views as to how life should be lived in the communities, in Tokelau and also overseas, run deep. Underlying such stances, I have argued, is a common form of sociality or way of relating to a larger social body to which one feels a sense of belonging. This common form of sociality is expressed in the term *alofa* and other concepts of sharing and cooperation but also, according to my analysis, in ways of competing for ascendancy and control over local and extraneous resources.

Getting Out from Under?

Prior to the 2006 referendum, delegates from Tokelau met with Tokelau communities in New Zealand and Australia in order to explain and discuss the contents of the proposed treaty between Tokelau and New Zealand. Members of the overseas communities were surprised and greatly disappointed to learn that they, as non-residents, did not have the right to vote in the upcoming referendum. The consequences of migration had never before been made so clear. As a Tokelau leader put it at one of the meetings in New Zealand, 'you have already self-determined [i.e. you have chosen not to stay and share our lot]. Now it is our turn to determine our future.' (Ulu, personal communication).

This situation caused some people to think that if Tokelau opted for self-government, they (in New Zealand) would lose their New Zealand citizenship. This unfounded fear led to strong feelings against self-determination among some (an apparent confusion between independence and self-government). As a result, relationships between overseas communities and Tokelau were activated, with some members from the overseas communities taking an active role in influencing the outcome of the vote, through nation-wide radiobroadcasts, as well as newsletters, visits, and telephone and internet contact with family members who were in the atolls. Thus, the existence of a Tokelau transnational community became manifest as a political reality influencing issues in the homeland.

The local circumstances associated with the second referendum, held in Atafu in 2007, were markedly changed. In order to explain an observed shift in allegiances, that took place between the first and the second referendum, I shall turn to the events behind the newspaper headline asking whether 'Sex and self determination [is] to blame for recent [population] trends?' Firstly, this case clearly demonstrates the extent to which new forms of media have become an integral factor in political life in the atolls and overseas. Secondly, the 'sex' part of the news story refers to a much-publicised event involving a pastor who had a sexual relationship with an adoptive daughter, then 12 years old. At the time, he was made to leave Atafu by the council of elders. He returned after some years and, following the traditional method of conflict solution, went to the elders and abased himself by asking their forgiveness (*ifoga*). The elders seemed to accept his apology, but subsequent events demonstrated that the council was divided on this issue. When the man subsequently took up the position of pastor again, the dissidents, about half of the council of elders, stopped going to church. On 3 August 2006, the *New Zealand Herald* reported that 'church boycotters lose village council jobs' over this issue.

Both to boycott the church and to expel members of the village councils in this manner was unprecedented and unheard of in Tokelau. The dissidents in this case were soon nicknamed Al Qaeda and became the victims of overt, violent attacks against themselves and members of their extended families. This also unprecedented and culturally unacceptable overt violence caused quite a number of people to relocate to New Zealand. These exiles continue to await further developments in the hope of a possible return when more harmonious (in local terms, *maopoopo*, signifying togetherness and stable leadership) village conditions emerge. Members of this group have also pleaded their case in New Zealand newspapers, demonstrating once and for all that the scale and media of Tokelau political debate have expanded beyond the atolls.

A significant factor that links this case to the processes of implementing the infrastructure deemed necessary for an act of self-determination is the delegation by New Zealand administration of its powers to the local councils, the Council of Faipule and the General Fono. As a result of this delegation or transfer of administrative powers from New Zealand to Tokelau, there is a feeling of a loss of third party appeal to New Zealand and of being at the mercy of local power politics. However, those who feel this way are in this case left with 'modern' arguments, having to appeal to the human rights charter and principles of democracy, which do not hold as much authority in the villages as the more traditional ways of conflict resolution (*ifoga*) do, In consequence, those who feared loss of third party appeal shifted their votes: from the first referendum where they voted for national unity and political self-determination, in the second they chose not to place themselves 'under' the sole authority of the local leadership,

In sum, the conflicts between opposing views as to how life should be lived in the communities, in Tokelau and also overseas, run deep and have long histories attached to them. Underlying these stances however, are the very real issues of conflict and rivalry about positions of leadership in the new national government: in particular the positions of *faipule* (and *ulu*), but also the *pulenuku*, and senior administrative positions. The position of *faipule* has become increasingly powerful, at the expense of the family (*kaiga*) representation and social security granted previously by the consensus-based village councils. This social security (expressed in the values of *maopoopo*, cooperation, and *alofa*, love, generosity and compassion) was the basis of the legitimacy of the *pule* (power) of the village councils of elders.

During the last decade, an increasing number of people reject the dominant new form of leadership. They may have lost their faith in the *taupulega*'s authority to ensure that their *kaiga*'s voice is heard. As a result, some think that it is vital that NZ, the UN or other external institutions mediate. They see themselves facing a situation where they might risk being left with the current unstable and unpredictable local leadership.

Conclusion: Containment of Conflict and the Transnational Context

The traditional leadership structure associated with the council of elders is challenged in many ways and an increase in violent and overt conflicts has ensued. Previously, overt expressions of conflict were strictly controlled and kept in check by the village councils and the recent events point to the elders' loss of absolute control over the *faipule*, *pulenuku* and the *aumaga*. At present, the situation can be described as one exhibiting a certain loss of legitimacy for both the traditional and the new leadership structures. The question of which principles should inform the present leadership configuration (democracy, titles, age or other factors) remain open, and I suggest that the difficulties that people experience at present because of this lack of legitimate leadership explains the most recent wave of migration.

As the voice of the council for the ongoing government of Tokelau itself stated, in its 2007 New Year message, 'The Tokelau Census result has also been the target of the outside media…Tokelau is a mobile and young population.' This statement can be read as a further example of the role of media in forging transnational connections. From the role that the Internet and radio broadcasts played in the recent referenda we see that events in the atolls and in the Tokelau communities overseas are currently intertwined and this transnational field clearly includes political life in the atoll communities. In this sense, the analytical perspective associated with the single-location traditional community study is no longer applicable. The New Year statement also points to an important fact which is often hidden behind population figures that tend to link people to specific locations; i.e., that people who inhabit the various social spaces that constitute the Tokelau transnational community are transitory. They are highly mobile and are likely to continue to be so, moving in many directions.

The social networks that constitute the Tokelau community have expanded to become truly transnational. However, the size of the population and the manner in which its patterns of sociality are constructed are such that the shapes and directions of peoples' life-trajectories are highly vulnerable to social conflict. In conclusion, I consider it likely that the issue of conflict resolution will have the possibly greatest impact on future patterns of migration (both to and from the atolls). How leadership handle conflict is intimately connected with its social legitimacy, and hence it greatly affects its social standing (*tulaga*), respect (*ava*) and its capacity to act (its *mana*).

References

Angelo, T. 2001. Establishing a nation—A second look. *Revue Juridique Polynesienne* 1: 235-50.

Hoëm, I. 1999. Processes of identification and the incipient national level. A Tokelau case. *Social Anthropology* 7 (3): 279–95..

——. 2004 *Theatre and political process: Staging identities in Tokelau and New Zealand*. Oxford, New York: Berghahn.

——. 2005. New Zealand og stillehavsøyer: livet i forhandlingssonen. *Norsk antropologisk tidsskrift* 16 (1): 85–96.

Hoëm, I. and S. Roalkvam (eds). 2003. *Oceanic socialities and cultural forms: Ethnographies of experience*. Oxford, New York: Berghahn.

Hooper, A. n.d. Against the wind: Tokelau 2001–2006. Unpublished ms.

Hooper, A and J. Huntsman. 1985. Structures of Tokelau history. In *Transformations of Polynesian culture*, ed. A. Hooper and J. Huntsman, 33-49. Auckland: The Polynesian Society.

Huntsman, J and A. Hooper. 1996. *Tokelau. A historical ethnography*. Auckland: Auckland University Press.

MacGregor, G. 1937. *Ethnology of Tokelau Islands*. Bishop Museum Bulletin 146. Honolulu, Hawaii.

Sahlins, M. 1994. Goodbye to tristes tropes: Ethnography in the context of modern world history. In *Assessing cultural anthropology*, ed. R. Borofsky, 377—93. New York: McGraw-Hill.

Spoonley, P. 2001. Transnational Pacific communities: Transforming the politics of place and identity. In *Tangata o te Moana Nui. The evolving identities of Pacific peoples in Aotearoa/New Zealand*, ed. C. Macpherson, P. Spoonley, and M. Anae, 81–96. Palmerston North: Dunmore Press.

Tcherkézoff, S. 2008. Hierarchy is not inequality—In Polynesia for example. In *Hierarchy. Persisting social formations in the modern world*, ed. K. M. Rio and O. Smedal, 299-330, Oxford: Berghahn.

Valeri, V. 2008. Marriage, Rank and Politics in Hawai'i. In *Hierarchy. Persisting social formations in the modern world*, ed. K. M. Rio and O. Smedal, 211-44. Oxford: Berghahn.

Wessen, A., A. Hooper, J. Huntsman, I. Prior, and C. Salmond (eds). 1992. *Migration and health in a small society. The case of Tokelau*. Oxford: Oxford Science Publications.

ENDNOTES

[1] Fieldwork for this project was carried out in the periods January–February 2002, July–August 2003, October–January 2005-06, in Tokelau, Samoa and New Zealand, and was funded by the Norwegian Research Council.

[2] According to A. Hooper and J. Huntsman in Wessen et. al. (1992) the 'earliest reliable population estimates come from the records of the US Exploring Expedition', that is, from 1841. Since 1948, census data have been gathered regularly.

[3] This wish is, for example, clearly expressed in the 2007 New Year Message from the Council for the Ongoing Government of Tokelau (see http://www.tokelau.org.nz/).

[4] For a theoretical discussion and empirical applications of this concept, see Hoëm and Roalkvam 2003.

13. The View from 'Home' — Transnational Movements from Three Tongan Villages

Steve Tupai Francis

In this paper, my goal is to explore the dichotomy of 'home' and 'host' posited in studies of transnationalism. I intend to do this by examining the very different forms of migration I found in conducting fieldwork in three Tongan villages. I argue that the view from 'home' is often a missing aspect in explorations of transnationalism. This is not particularly surprising given the focus in these studies on the networked connections of diasporic peoples and communities. As is documented in this collection, Pacific Islanders have travelled far from Oceania to reside in Australia, New Zealand, the United States and other countries; they strongly identify themselves with their 'home' places; and they continue to interact socially, culturally, financially and politically with these places of origin.

There are two elements of transnationalism that are pertinent in the context of this discussion: the processes (cultural, social, economic, political) of exchange that occur between those living in the homeland and those in the place of migration; and the new forms of cultural, social and economic interaction that are created as a result of the interplay of these exchanges (Hannerz 1992).

The strength of these connections is such that migrants living in diasporic communities need never return to their homeland in order to legitimately participate in these cross-border exchanges. In fact, transnational actors do not need to have been born in the 'homeland' to identify strongly with the country of origin of their parents or grandparents, and to participate in diasporic transactions. Similarly many of those who remain at 'home' and who participate in these transnational processes, may never have travelled overseas themselves. This is the true power and agency of the transnational connections represented by family networks (Basch et al. 1994; Ong 1999).

While much work has focused on the lives of migrants and the impact of their diasporic movements and the nature of their connections to homeland, little research has focused on the transnational behaviours, movements, actions and perspectives of those remaining at 'home'.

Additionally, although transnationalism and the examination of the connections between 'home' and the places to which people move is purely the study of movement itself, theorists can be guilty of fixing people and place in time and space. For example, the focus on Tongan migration or Samoan transnational practices, in a way, does not allow for difference within and between island cultures, or between islands and villages for that matter. The reality, as always, is more interesting and complex. The ways, means and reasons for movement are not so easily fixed.

As pointed out by Nakhid (this volume), reciprocity is central to transnationalism. My concern in this paper is therefore to analyse and explain the factors that enable people to become transnational in the first place. Factors such as opportunity and quality of connections to other places are core elements in this discussion.

Three Villages in Tonga

My research in Tonga demonstrated that transnational practices can differ markedly among island nations and that patterns of movement into and out of villages can be identified. Variables such as history, origin and socio-economic context greatly affect how transnational movements are enacted and transacted. In researching transnational practices in the Pacific islands, fieldwork was undertaken in three Tongan villages: Lotofoa in the outer islands; Hofoa, which is close to the capital city of Nuku'alofa and 'Isileli, a newly created village of outer island migrants close to Nuku'alofa. A brief description of each village follows.

Located on the island of Foa in the outer Ha'apai island group, Lotofoa is characterised by other Tongans as 'traditional', a nomenclature often bestowed on all the peoples of Ha'apai. This distinction is both respectful, with an implication that the people of Ha'apai remember the old ways and keep to the old traditions unlike those who grew up on Tongatapu, and derogatory, with an implication of backwardness. According to one villager, Lotofoa was once the capital of Ha'apai and its wharf was the centre of trade and commerce in the cluster. Sailing boats called *vakalā* were used to ply the waters between Ha'apai and Tongatapu, taking produce and livestock to Tongatapu for sale. Another local indicated that trips to New Zealand were also undertaken.

The population relies primarily on subsistence cropping and harvesting of sea resources for their daily needs. Most families are able to use plantation land for subsistence purposes while a small number of farmers generate larger incomes through cash-cropping. Wage employment is a viable option for very few residents of the village due to the small-scale infrastructure of the Ha'apai cluster. While there are a number of government departments, some retail and tourism businesses, and a hospital all located in the capital Pangai, competition for the limited jobs available is intense.

Cash in the village is acquired primarily through the remittances of family living in other parts of Tonga or overseas, the sale of produce or sea harvest in Pangai or in the capital Nuku'alofa, or through profits made by small businesses such as the *falekoloa* (food/goods stores) that line the main roads of all Tongan villages. The relatively lower per capita income generated in Lotofoa is reflected in the higher proportion of traditional dwellings such as the *faleTonga* (thatched hut) in comparison to European-style housing. There is a group of entrepreneurs in the village however, who are able to generate cash surpluses through cropping and other business interests. Their success derives primarily from the ability to combine an understanding of basic business principles and cash generation with access to farming equipment such as tractors and ploughs.[1] Much of this equipment was purchased through savings acquired during work in overseas factories or through remittances from Tongan relatives living in Pacific Rim countries. These capital purchases have enabled these farmers to cultivate larger tracts of agricultural land and sell the resulting agricultural produce in the markets of Nuku'alofa (as distinct from the local markets of Ha'apai) where higher returns may be obtained. Finally, the population of Lotofoa has been decreasing for the past 100 years. This general observation masks the more complex movement flows that are taking place in the village.

Situated on the central northern coast of the main island of Tonga, Tongatapu, Hofoa is a medium-sized long-established Tongan village. Encompassing an area of approximately one square kilometre, the population live on *'api kolo* 'town allotments' clustered along the central road leading through the village. From informant accounts, it appears that Hofoa was not originally established as a fort in the manner of other villages; rather, the area was plantation land later claimed by the royal family and transferred to the government.

The proximity of Hofoa to the capital allows young people of the village easy access to the superior secondary school system of Tongatapu.[2] As a result, Hofoa has a relatively highly educated population and consequently, many are employed in the government bureaucracy and the service sector, as well as operating small businesses or participating in the trades. Located in an arc surrounding the village, most families in Hofoa have access to or own an *'api uta/tukuhau* (bush/plantation allotment). Cash-cropping is relatively rare, with most households growing small amounts of subsistence and ceremonial foods to supplement other subsistence and income-earning activities. There are some small-scale practices that earn cash to supplement wages, including the selling of surplus produce from gardens or fish caught on the nearby reef locally, through word of mouth or in a roadside *falekoloa* or in the markets of Nuku'alofa.

The people of Hofoa could be characterised as prosperous in comparison with other villagers of Tongatapu and certainly when compared to those in the outer islands. There are many indicators of this status in the village, including the high proportion of per capita car, truck and boat ownership as well as a predominance of well maintained, European-style housing. Five village churches (of various Christian denominations), four *fale koloa* and four church halls, which also become *kava* clubs several nights a week, serve as the primary sites of village social interaction and activity. The *fono* (village meetings) and social/life-stage events that take place at these venues continue to be announced to the community in the traditional way as the *'ofisi kolo* (town officer) strides up and down the main street heralding the events in a loud voice.

Many villagers have travelled and lived in Pacific Rim countries and many households receive remittances from kin living overseas. Hofoa is also subject to a constant flow of population into and out of the village, as kin living in other parts of Tonga and overseas visit their relatives and friends in the village.

The densely populated, recently established community of 'Isileli on Tongatapu is situated on land reclaimed from the swamp to the north-east of Hofoa, approximately 2.5 kilometres from Nuku'alofa. The area was designated as a resettlement zone by the Tongan government in 1983 for people whose houses and villages were destroyed by Hurricane Isaac. Bounded in the west by the road leading to Hofoa from the ocean and southern fringe of *'api uta* owned by the people of Kolomotu'a, the area in which 'Isileli is situated has never previously been used for human habitation.[3] Constantly flooded after heavy rain and suffering poor drainage, the village population has steadily increased following the original emergency settlement. Subsequently, migrants from all island clusters of Tonga targeted 'Isileli and the nearby village of Sopu as a point of settlement. The proximity of these villages to Nuku'alofa offers residents easy access to the education, employment, family and lifestyle opportunities offered by the capital.

The area is designated as *tofi'a puleanga* (government estate). As a result, *'api kolo* (town allotments) are allocated and distributed by the Department of Lands. The land on which 'Isileli is situated was stabilised by rock quarried from coral deposits in the south of Tongatapu and transferred to the land allotments purchased from the government. These blocks tend to be much smaller than the average *'api kolo* found in older Tongan villages. Large, empty sections of low-lying land on the outskirts of the village await the arrival of new settlers. This leads to the somewhat incongruous sight of small houses rising out of the swamp like islands surrounded by as yet unclaimed *'api kolo*.

The government considers neither Sopu nor 'Isileli as a village in its own right. Incorporated within the larger and older district of Kolomotu'a, is home to most of the Kingdom's nobles, these communities do not have their own town officer. Despite the fact that both villages have developed identities separate from Kolomotu'a, administrative and governmental structures have not kept pace with these developments.

Unlike Hofoa however, there are no plantation lands accessible to the population as all available arable land has been under cultivation by the people of Hofoa and Kolomotu'a for a number of generations. This has limited the ability of 'Isileli residents to grow subsistence crops. Some householders in 'Isileli from other parts of Tongatapu are able to use the land of friends or family in the area. There are also some *toutu'u* (collective garden) groups in the village, although that land is situated in another area of the island. For most people however, food is purchased from the market in Nuku'alofa.

As a village of migrants, there are few kinship connections between the residents of 'Isileli. Intravillage ties tend to be established through religious affiliation or via village or island-of-origin links rather than through kinship or marriage. As a result, the village has a very different 'feel' from others in Tonga. Important factors contributing to this difference include the combination of tenuous cross-cutting kinship ties and the constant arrival of new residents.

The people of 'Isileli are also more reliant on the modern monetary economy of Tonga than the populations of other Tongan villages. Lacking plantation land for the production of subsistence or cash crops, families must rely on the accumulation of capital through unskilled wage labour, small business, the bureaucracy, trades or professions. As a result, there is an uneven distribution of wealth within the village, with some very poor families (often with low levels of education, poor health and poor living conditions) and some very well-off families (usually business people, entrepreneurs and professionals). Housing is the marker of this disparity: small shanty-like dwellings constructed from drift wood and 'found' materials sot next to large multistorey American kit homes. Also reflecting the mobility of those living in the village, a large number of villagers have travelled extensively within Tonga and throughout Pacific Rim countries. Consequently, a high level of remittance is also apparent.

'Isileli is a place of dualisms, of 'haves' and 'have nots', of those who have travelled extensively and those who have not, those who receive regular remittance income from overseas relatives and those who do not, those who access wealth and those who do not.

Travel and Distance: Comparing Three Tongan Villages

In order to draw out the variations and differences in transnational connections and movements that can occur even within ostensibly 'culturally bounded' island societies, this section compares the different ways and means by which Tongans move through time and space.

The journeys undertaken by people from Lotofoa primarily involve movements between the Ha'apai and Tongatapu clusters. For example, in one year I found that 96 per cent of those departing the village for a location in the Kingdom of Tonga travelled to Tongatapu; 23 per cent of the total village population made a total of 180 journeys to Tongatapu; in approximately 76 per cent of households, at least one member made a journey to another island cluster of Tonga.

A distinctive feature of movement in Lotofoa is the frequency of short-term movement. A comparison of the data reveals that the people of Lotofoa (n=187) made more than three times the number of journeys within Tonga in comparison to those in Hofoa and 'Isileli. For the people of Lotofoa, travel is an essential requirement for completing certain tasks, journeys that are unnecessary for those living on Tongatapu. These journeys are most often short to medium term, and primarily focused on Tongatapu.

Religion has played a key role in facilitating journeys made by the people of Lotofoa. Religious affiliation has enabled exchange visits between church groups in Tonga and overseas, travel by church choirs to and from Lotofoa to other sites, and journeys made to attend meetings of church organisations such as the *kau akonaki*, the women's assembly of the Free Wesleyan Church of Tonga, the Monarch's church. For the people of Lotofoa, *religion* was the primary reason for departure from the village for 33 per cent of those not present at the time of the second census in this village, one year after the first census. Most of these absentees were attending the *Konifelenisi* (religious conference) celebrations of their churches in Nuku'alofa on Tongatapu. Other villagers from Lotofoa were also overseas, in New Zealand, as part of an *evangelio* (evangelist) contingent of young people spreading the Christian gospel.

The importance of *education* in fostering movement is evident to anyone present in Lotofoa during school holidays or the Christmas period. The population doubles in size as school-age children and their parents or other guardians return from Tongatapu following the conclusion of the school term or year. Over 10 per cent of those departing the village left for education purposes, and correspondingly, 11 per cent of those returning to the village cited *home after education* as the reason for their return.

Selling produce was also a key factor for those departing (7 per cent) and returning (6 per cent). While there is a small market in the Ha'apai capital of Pangai, the produce market in Nuku'alofa (Tongatapu) is the primary site for selling cash crops because of the superior prices paid to growers. A number of farmers and their families transported their crops on the weekly inter-island ferry and sold them in Tongatapu. Most stayed with family while in Tongatapu, undertaking other activities while there. These included processing visas for overseas stays, purchasing goods unavailable in the outer islands as well as *'alu 'eva pe* (going for a visit).

The following case study is a useful example of these forms of movement out of and in to Lotofoa. In one Lotofoa family of two parents and six children, the male head, Semisi, was frequently absent. A minister in one of the poorer village churches, he travelled to New Zealand at the time I conducted a household survey. He was working and visiting his brother for three months to try to improve the family's finances. He also attended the *Konifelenisi* of his church earlier in the year.

During the month of the survey, with the head of the household in New Zealand, the family faced a daily struggle to address basic subsistence needs. These were eventually met through the sale and exchange of *lalanga* (woven mats) made by the female head and sold in the village, access to subsistence produce (basic root vegetables) grown in a church *toutu'u* as the family did not have a plot of their own, and the generosity of family, neighbours and parishioners in the village who donated food and produce to the family. While Semisi's sojourn overseas did result in his returning to the village with a small amount of cash savings, the impact of the overseas movement on the family was quite negative in the short term.

In comparison with Lotofoa, the movement of people from the village of Hofoa has much more of an 'international' focus. For example: 51 per cent of people departing the village travelled to an international location; in 40 per cent of households, at least one member made a journey overseas; 10 per cent of the village population made a total of 109 journeys to international locations; New Zealand was the country of destination for 61 per cent of those making international journeys. The range of international sites available to people from Hofoa are significantly greater than for those living in Lotofoa or 'Isileli. Residents of Hofoa had a greater proportion of parents, siblings and children, in particular, residing overseas. These close ties mean that activating connections is easy.

Hofoa is a conduit for international movement in that population flow involves inward moves to Hofoa from the outer islands, return movements from overseas and external moves from Hofoa to international destinations. A key factor is the number of family members from Hofoa established in international sites, who provide a larger range of available close kin ties (i.e., parental, sibling, children) of which these villagers can take advantage.

Socio-cultural factors are the most important motivators in encouraging movement among villagers from Hofoa. Visiting family or attending life-stage events such as weddings and funerals are key motivators for movement out of this village. This is also underscored by the primacy of these factors in the movement of villagers from Hofoa to other parts of Tonga. A useful example of this type of movement is demonstrated in the following case study. One household visited frequently in Hofoa comprised a woman and her four children, her friend and her friend's child. Living in a two-room shack on the *'api kolo* of her father, Mele, the female head of this household, was the only adult member of her immediate family who continued to reside in Tonga. All of her close kin lived in New Zealand, including her partner, her eight siblings, parents and their siblings. Only one year later, Mele and all her children had moved to New Zealand, leaving the *'api kolo* to her friend.

During this time, two of Mele's children moved to live in New Zealand with their grandparents. Meanwhile, her mother also returned to Tonga for two months when Mele fell ill. Mele's father also returned for two weeks to attend a particularly important *putu* (funeral) upon the death of his *fa'e tangāta* (mother's brother).

The story of this household is dominated by the impact of movement in the context of maintaining the social, cultural, and ritual responsibilities associated with being Tongan. With all her family living in New Zealand, Mele was obliged to facilitate, organise, participate in and contribute to all life-stage events and other cultural obligations on behalf of her family. In other words, in the context of mass out-movement, she assumed the burden of *kavenga* (ritual obligation) on behalf of her entire family. In one 30–day period, I recorded the following activities:

Mele attended and contributed to six *putu* including a week in 'Eua and extended participation in a funeral that required a week living in the household of the deceased.

In a car paid for by family in New Zealand, she daily transported kin and neighbours to town, to the market and to the *tahi* (ocean) to fish and do the shopping, and pick up packages at the wharf or post office.

Mele continuously ran errands and tasks during the extended chronic illness of a close extended-family member. She was involved in purchasing groceries, cooking food, transporting kin of the relative to hospital to have a baby, and ferrying other family members to and from the airport, a two-hour round trip.

She frequently organised, through international phone calls to her parents in New Zealand, for money to be sent to purchase the requisite *koloa* (traditional valued goods) for the funerals attended. Money was continually funnelled into the household from New Zealand to pay for these gifts and other expenses associated with the funerals she attended.

When I commented that she was very busy, Mele stated that she was having to deal with *fua kavenga*, meaning 'a lot' of *kavenga*, a 'heavy' *kavenga* burden. She was not bemoaning the fact that she had to fulfil these responsibilities; that is simply a given in Tongan society. Rather, she was commenting on the fact that the movement of her family overseas had greatly increased the movements she had to undertake within Tonga in order to sustain relationships on behalf of the family.

The characteristics of movement associated with the village of 'Isileli was very different to that of Lotofoa and Hofoa. Over a one–year period: 75 per cent of those leaving the village travelled to a location within Tonga; in 35 per cent of households, at least one member made a journey to other island clusters of Tonga;

15 per cent of the village population made a total of 109 journeys to locations within Tonga; Ha'apai was the destination for 61 per cent of these people.

One of the factors in this movement was the relatively recent arrival of most people living in the village. A distinctive feature of households in this village is the way in which many of the *'api's* (houses) in the village were used by groupings of family as a base while they maintain multiple homes in other places, including the islands and villages of origin as well as overseas. This process reflected the fact that 'Isileli homes were primarily established, without cash-cropping land, as an access point into the stronger economy, educational institutions and movement opportunities provided by Tongatapu and the capital Nuku'alofa. As a result, short to medium term movements of outer island residents to 'Isileli households were common and frequent.

The origins and history of 'Isileli, with its population of recent arrivals from the outer islands and distant villages of Tongatapu, underscores the character of movement into and out of this village. As a result, movement often involves a general inflow of short and medium term movements to the village from other places, but also a reciprocal and frequent movement of people from 'Isileli to other places in Tonga. 'Isileli may therefore be characterised as a 'transit zone', a bridge for long-term movement elsewhere.

The maintenance of links to the village of origin plays an important and continuing role in these movements. This is particularly important in the context of 'Isileli as a village without *'api uta* on which to grow cash and subsistence crops. The importance of maintaining connections to *fonua* (people and place of origin), as well as connection to family is therefore quite apparent, making it a predominant factor in movement. *Education* is also an important factor in movement to the village. The process involves young people from the outer islands but also distant villages of Tongatapu staying with family or kin in 'Isileli while going to one of the major secondary schools of Tongatapu. Conversely, for those leaving 'Isileli, *work* was cited as a reason for movement out of the household. In the main, this involved accessing employment opportunities within Tonga and overseas.

A useful case study illustrating the types of movement prevalent in 'Isileli is represented by a family of six, two parents and four children (two of whom attend secondary school), residing in four locations: in 'Isileli; in an outlying district of Tongatapu; on a remote island in Ha'apai; and in a southern state of America. At the time of the first census survey, the family structure and location of members was as follows: Sālote, the female head, who was working as a housemaid for a *pālangi* couple, and one daughter attending secondary school, were living in the house in 'Isileli; Aleki, the male head, the eldest daughter and her new husband, were living on the family *'api* on an island in Ha'apai, tending the production of cash and subsistence crops on the family *'api uta* 'bush allotment'; Siale, the eldest son had '*alu hola* (run away) from his school class during a fundraising trip to the US and was currently living (without a visa) with a family of his *kāinga* in Arizona; the youngest son was boarding at one of Tonga's secondary colleges.

This arrangement reflected the focus and situation of the family at the time. The flexibility inherent in the organisation of Tongan families however, allows for changing configurations as circumstances change. Eight months later, the family was arranged in the following way: Sālote and the youngest daughter were still living in the house in 'Isileli. At the end of the school year, the youngest son left his boarding school and joined the household. This segment of the family also travelled to the '*api* in Ha'apai for Christmas; the eldest daughter and her husband continued tending the crops on the '*api uta* in Ha'apai; Aleki, who had spent a short time in 'Isileli, travelled to the US to work and attend the marriage of Siale to a Tongan woman with permanent residence. Then, just five months later, the following configuration existed: Aleki joined his youngest son and daughter in the house in 'Isileli following his return from the US after six months with Siale and his new wife; the eldest daughter and her husband continued tending the cash and subsistence crops on their '*api uta* in Ha'apai; Sālote travelled from 'Isileli to spend six months in the US with Siale and his new wife.

This case study demonstrates the flexibility and frequency of movement, and consequent impact on family configuration, associated with households in 'Isileli. It also highlights the need to maintain kinship and *fonua* links in the place of origin while also supporting the establishment of new nodes overseas. The case study also emphasises the importance of education as an activating agent for movement.

Conclusion

This paper has sought to demonstrate that the study of transnational connections is enriched when it accounts for local diversity in the type of connections and movements that can occur both in the country to which migrants travel as well as for those who remain 'at home' (for the time being at least), in the countries from which migrants have travelled.

As the case study has demonstrated, the nature of transnationalism is mediated by a range of factors that impact on the ability of people to move from one place to another. These factors include opportunities represented by the physical location of the village, access to education, employment, ability to undertake agricultural activities and proximity to local and international transport. Hence, there are differences in the opportunities available for transnational interaction for those living in outer island villages of Tonga such as Lotofoa in comparison to those living in a village such as Hofoa, located on the main island and close to the capital.

Additionally, the case study seeks to dispel the notion of those remaining at 'home' as powerless individuals. Rather, as theorised in the structuration approach developed by Giddens (1984), migrants act are 'knowledgeable agents' who operate within *migration institutions* that regulate, operate and facilitate transnational interactions (Goss and Lindquist 1995, 331). As identified for Tonga, the migration institutions are founded upon kin, religion and connection to place (*fonua*).

In analysing transnational migrants and their interactions, migration studies have tended to forget about exploring the diasporic aspect of the lives of those who reside at 'home'. This study of Tongans has sought to provide a different perspective on these local transnational actors.

References

Basch, L, N. Glick-Schiller and C. Szanton Blanc. 1994. *Nations unbound.* Langhorne, Pa: Gordon and Breach.

Giddens, A. 1984. *The constitution of society: Outline of the theory of structuration.* Cambridge: Polity Press.

Goss, J. and B. Lindquist. 1995.Conceptualising international labour migration: A structuration perspective. *The International Migration Review* 29 (2): 317–51

Hannerz, U. 1992. *Cultural complexity.* New York: Columbia University Press.

Ong, A. 1999. *Flexible citizenship: The cultural logics of transnationality.* Durham: Duke University Press.

ENDNOTES

[1] Extra cash is generated as farm equipment is hired out to local farmers at critical points in the agricultural cycle.

[2] Hofoa is approximately three kilometres from Nuku'alofa. Most villagers drive cars, hitch lifts with a neighbour or friend, or catch the local bus that makes a round trip to the city every hour.

[3] 'Isileli is situated in the area commonly referred to as Sopu, which is the western extremity of the town of Kolomotu'a.

Conclusion: The Concept and Circumstances of Pacific Migration and Transnationalism

Camille Nakhid

Introduction

Many of the perspectives, processes and outcomes of contemporary Pacific migration and transnationalism resemble their traditional forms, including kinship, food, remittances, work, gifts, interactions, space, territoriality, home, attachments, sustained contact, relationships and inequities. Ka'ili (2005) claims that transnationalism in the Pacific can be traced back to Hawai'i and the god Maui, with Maui being widely represented in the cultural history of most of the Pacific islands. Maui's ability to sustain 'relationships with many of his relatives who were dispersed yet connected across distant physical spaces' is reminiscent of the current practices of Pacific transnationalism (Ka'ili, 2005, 2).

The diverse case studies presented in the chapters in this book suggest that Pacific transnationalism as a concept, and as a predictable series of circumstances connected to the process of migration, eludes a complete and finite explanation. While the chapters are connected in theory and focus they are distinctly individual in research and unique in direction. The complementary examples used by the authors describe their understanding and concept of Pacific migration and transnationalism from differing perspectives and contrasting approaches.

These studies make a significant contribution to theorising about the concept of Pacific transnationalism and help us not only to associate specific practices and processes with Pacific transnationalism, but also to distinguish between Pacific transnationalism and the traditional forms of transnationalism. The complexity of defining Pacific transnationalism is because it does not entirely bear out those definitions and images of transnationalism with which we have become acquainted and accustomed. Although the authors begin from traditional definitions of transnationalism they have made it clear from their chapters that this is not enough to explain Pacific transnationalism and that such an explanation requires its own specifically Pacific perspectives, research and framework.

In spite of the diversity of the chapters, it is inevitable that there is some common ground, some connecting threads which reveal the commonalities of Pacific transnationalism. As the authors clearly illustrate, almost all aspects of life are affected by Pacific transnationalism—migration, identity, work, kinship, food, gifts, even the return journey home. These seemingly ordinary human interactions that occur in the process of transnational activity are unique in their link to the cultural traditions and customs of the Pacific and, as the chapters show, distinguish these interactions from those carried out by transnationals elsewhere. In this conclusion I focus on the concept and circumstances of transnationalism which, although inevitably connected with migration, are of particular value when exploring the relationship between migrants and their homelands in the Pacific.

The Pacific region is the most linguistically complex in the world, with significant cultural differences within and between the different island groups. There is also considerable variation in political organisation; the Pacific is home to the world's smallest monarchy, and in some of its islands only tribal chiefs can be elected to parliament. Yet many authors and Pacific communities refer to a 'Pacific way' when discussing fundamental similarities in values underpinning family relationships, respect for elders and community. There are also ways familiar to the Pacific which are less commonly talked about such as domestic violence, sexual abuse and alcoholism. How do Pacific migration and transnationalism help us to understand the Pacific and its place in the world? We cannot underestimate the effect of these processes on the Pacific, and it is important from where we gain our insights into and our understandings of them. Is it 'the Pacific' that should concern us or Pacific peoples? Islands do not migrate although island ways, like those mentioned above, do. We can gain our understanding of Pacific transnationalism both from the perspectives of the people that have become Pacific transnationals or from the countries where Pacific transnationals reside. We can also explore transnationalism from the vantage point of the Pacific Islands that have been affected by the migration, behaviours, attitudes and actions of its Pacific transnationals or from the experiences of the people of the Pacific who have remained behind but are no less influenced by these transnational movements. Like the Pacific sun, Pacific transnationalism casts its shadow over all. Its effects are not limited to those that one considers Pacific transnationals nor are its impacts unidirectional. The case studies in the chapters show that we need to examine Pacific transnationalism from all of the perspectives mentioned above: the migrants, their host nations, those who remain and, of course, the 'homeland' that is inevitably affected by all of the complex elements of transnationalism.

Definitions of Transnationalism

The terms 'transnationality' and 'transnationalism' are considered by Jackson, Crang and Dwyer (2004, 4) to be trend words in the social sciences, though they believe that the ties and interactions that embody these terms have been in existence for a long time. Al-Ali and Koser (2002, 1) question whether any new developments have occurred since researchers first began describing 'international migration as "transnational migration", international migrants as "transnational migrants", and their activities and identities as examples of "transnationalism"'. The attention given to the subject of transnationalism is ongoing. Yet it is unclear what status is given to those individuals, groups of individuals or communities considered to be transnationals and what it means to the wider society that someone is a transnational.

If transnationalism is about maintaining ties to a homeland or culture, then a distinction between a migrant and a transnational is possible on the basis of the contact that a migrant has with the homeland or culture and whether that contact is limited to other migrants in the host country. Migrants, unlike transnationals, maintain involvement in only one space (Rouse 2004, 28). To a transnational, relationships, connections, and families occur across boundaries though not necessarily involving the mobility that we might expect of a migrant. Transmigrants claim or are claimed by two or more nation-states, one of which is their state of origin (Glick Schiller 1999). This argument is supported by Basch, Glick Schiller and Blanc (1995) and Al-Ali and Koser (2002), who say that transmigrants are immigrants who develop and maintain economic, social, religious, and organisational relationships that span borders. Pacific transnationals, like those transnationals described by Glick Schiller, operate in social fields that transgress geographical, political and cultural borders. Van Amersfoort and Doomernik prefer to keep the term 'transnational community' to refer to those 'that have kept their cultural identity and whose members are still guided by specific cultural norms in important areas of behaviour' (2002, 59).

Understanding Pacific Transnationalism

Pacific transnationalism is evident in a number of practices, for example, support for families through remittances, young people studying overseas, sports persons playing for other countries, soldiers in overseas forces, expatriate political support or protests against a particular government, church-building in the islands through financial support from diasporic communities, and billeting or hosting villagers. Governments in Pacific countries encourage these transnational connections as they provide opportunities for economic benefits through remittances, export of home products to those living abroad and investment in poorer villages and regions left behind. Transnational practices and linkages are significant in their contribution to sustainable development at home (Connell and Conway 2000), though remittances, in particular, can lead to uneven development in the home country. Kennedy and Roudometof (2002) point to the fact that transnational communities arise out of social injustices, poverty, global economic restructuring, economic and social uncertainty, discrimination and oppression, and provide opportunities for empowerment of underprivileged groups.

Pacific migrants create transnational spaces when they maintain a set of multi-related social relations that bind and connect them and link their countries of origin with their countries of settlement (Glick Schiller, Basch and Blanc 1995). A sense of longing for and attachment to country of origin or an ancestral homeland becomes part of what it is to be a transnational. For some Pacific peoples, the 'myth of return', as defined by Walton-Roberts (2004, 80, 92) exists when transnationals balance the desire to return with the reality of their settled life. Although at times the desire or longing for home is only emotional without any involvement or interaction, perhaps due to circumstances such as the threat of danger to oneself or family, or from being exiled, it is unlikely that we can regard those who find themselves in this situation as transnationals because of the absence of reciprocity. On the other hand, can we consider as transnationals those who, though they may interact with others in the homeland, feel no attachment to the home culture or lack the desire to return?

Lee's opening chapter tells us that the patterns of movement which saw Pacific peoples move and settle from one place to another was integral to their survival, particularly given the disproportionate comparison in size between the seas and the lands. Pacific transnationalism is a way of life, first emerging with the onset of colonization and always entailing a disparity in socio-economic status between the colonized and the colonizer. Lee correctly argues that we cannot understate the value of remittances to the life of Pacific transnationals. However, we should be aware of the extent to which such an interest in and attention to the use and sustainability of remittances deflects and diminishes our recognition of other features of Pacific transnationalism. How we judge the impacts of other characteristics of Pacific transnationalism as to their influence and significance depends, of course, on whether the impact is being evaluated in relation to the migrant, the Pacific transnational, the country, the host residents or the home residents.

A strongly ethnographic approach is taken by the authors to understanding Pacific transnationalism and their chapters are graced by many relevant accounts of people's experiences of migration and transnationalism. The historical salience of oral traditions in the Pacific make this an appropriate approach to understanding Pacific transnationalism through a grounded interpretation of cultural processes.

Identity, Relationship to Homeland and Reciprocity

Identity and relationship to homeland are two factors central to defining Pacific transnationalism. The principle of reciprocity—a necessary practice within identity and relationship to homeland (see figure below)—distinguishes Pacific transnationalism from other classifications involving negotiations across boundaries such as migration and globalisation, and highlights what is expected of a Pacific transnational.

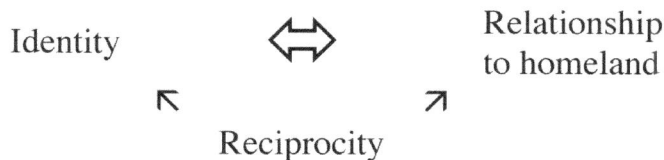

$$\text{Identity} \quad \Longleftrightarrow \quad \begin{array}{l}\text{Relationship}\\\text{to homeland}\end{array}$$

$$\nwarrow \qquad\qquad \nearrow$$

$$\text{Reciprocity}$$

Identity

It is to be expected that expressions of identity will be different for established and new Pacific transnationals. Recent transnationals are likely to display more obviously the home culture and be more familiar with its current practices. They will also be more readily identifiable to the home community than older Pacific transnationals. Researchers Roudometof and Karpathakis (2002, 41) have found this to be the case with Greek Americans and it influences how and to what extent Greek Americans identify with the home country. The difference between generations is also significant for migrant identity 'as those who grow up in different locations than their parents may have less (or different) interests' in their homelands (Armbruster 2002, 19). Similarly, there are those 'who believe they belong to the same community as their relatives abroad, but who do not, or cannot, engage in transnational networking with them' (Al-Ali and Koser 2002, 19). Transnationalism has different meanings for different peoples at different times in their lives and one outcome is 'the development of new identities among migrants who are anchored (socially, culturally and physically) neither in their place of origin nor in their place of destination' (ibid., 1–4). Ley and Walters (2004, 104) say that migrants who arrive at a new place without really leaving their place of origin turn the 'linearity of migration' into the circularity of transnationality.

Pollock's use of food as a marker of Pacific transnational identity brings home to the reader how the processes of transnationalism simultaneously maintain cultural identities and transcend cultural boundaries. Pollock's argument that food globalises at the same time that it localises allows for transnationals to reinforce their identity while sharing those foods and gastronomic habits which identify them. But compared to the presence of Pacific foods in transnational communities, there is a much greater variety and quantity of Western food found in the Pacific Islands though there is not a similar influx of North American or Western transnationals in the Pacific to accompany the presence of these foods. This can be attributed largely to the economic disparity between the two regions. Other transnational foods such as those belonging to the Chinese (egg foo young and chop suey) and Indian (roti and curries) cultures have made their way into the gastronomic identities of some Pacific communities to the extent that these foods are now considered local fare by both the home residents and the Pacific transnationals.

The way in which a host society accepts transnational communities has a major influence on how these communities shape their identity. For example, the exclusion of Palestinians from Lebanese society reinforces their ethnic identity in what Portes (1999) calls reactive ethnicity and is an underlying cause for the maintenance of their transnational identities. In a similar way, New Zealand's rejection of Pacific nations' transnationals during its recession in the 1980s led to a resilient Pacific community whose support came from its strong cultural networks and the presence and maintenance of a dominant Pacific identity. The chapter by Evans, Reid and Harms demonstrates that Pacific communities do not have homogeneous identities, and that there can be considerable variation both within and between migrant and homeland populations. Although they show that true Tongan-ness for Tongan transnationals depended on those factors discussed by the other authors, including kinship, work, respect and reciprocity, their respondents placed differential emphasis on these factors, influenced by a range of variables that did not fall neatly into a migrant/non-migrant dichotomy.

Relationship to Homeland

Pacific peoples, utilizing the concept of transnationalism as it covers place, landscape and space (Brah 1996) have managed to 're-territorialize' themselves in places away from home, and create opportunities for their local goods and services to appear where there are Pacific transcommunities (Jackson, Crang and Dwyer 2004, 8). The geographical and historical spaces held by these communities become 'constitutive' (ibid., 1–4) of Pacific transnationality. As the Pacific diaspora continues its global spread and transnational communities develop and grow away from their home communities, the concepts of space, attachments and distance are 'reconfigured' (Brah 1996). Gabriel Sheffer (in Dorai 2002, 88) identifies three main criteria for a diaspora: a common ethnic identity, internal organisation and a significant level of contact with the homeland. Portes (1999) believes that diasporas and transnational communities differ in the nature of their relationship with the homeland. According to Portes, the relationship that diasporic communities have with the homeland is symbolic whereas for transnational communities, the relationship is real. This may be because as transnational communities become subsumed into the diaspora, ties to the homeland weaken as the bonds to other transnational residents strengthen and a common homeland becomes for the diaspora, a symbol of its relationship with its former home. On the other hand, transnational communities within the diaspora maintain a relationship to the homeland through their transnational activities and are essentially the drivers and keepers of Pacific transnationalism.

Although reciprocity, kinship, ties and relationship are significant components of transnationalism, none of these begins the process of transnationalism in the way that 'home' does. It is axiomatic that without the origin of the homeland, there can be no migration or consequent transnational communities. The relationship to homeland for the increasingly migratory Solomon Islanders, as a consequence of social catastrophe, is necessary in order to 'reinforce aspects' of their traditional culture (Gegeo 2001). Gegeo sees this relationship as an expression of place rather than a move away from home. The concept of space is central to Tongans' understanding of transnationality because people and things move and flow within and across spatial boundaries (Ka'ili 2005). The expansive spread of the Pacific Islands has led to the establishment of 'far-reaching exchange and social networks' (Ka'ili 2005, 3). Pacific communities can no longer claim to be organised locally and completely around a single village but instead exist transnationally between different countries (Dorai 2002). The building and maintenance of kin-based communities 'assures the availability of emotional, spiritual and material support' for Samoan transnationals on what Burns McGrath describes as 'long, modern-day voyages' (Burns McGrath 2002). As Pacific communities continue to live and work between their countries and those that permit multiple residence and dual citizenship, they are, in a sense, developing local transnational communities in their own countries (Dorai 2002, 89).

Transnationalism involves the construction of homelands or localities in a mobile world (Kempny 2002, 126). Portes, Guarnizo and Landolt (1999, 219) add that transnationalism is the 'occupations and activities that require regular and sustained social contact over time across national borders'. As activities that significantly affect the relationship between transnational communities and communities in the countries of origin intensify across national boundaries, this intensification reflects the growing interest and influence of transnationals on the affairs of their home countries. The pro-democracy protests in 2005 by the Tongan transnational communities in Aotearoa/New Zealand can be said to have prompted the local demonstrations in Tonga in 2006 for higher wages and a more equitable standard of living.

As Pacific transnationals begin to turn their thoughts to returning home, questions turn to their status as transnationals. Even though Connell and Nosa note that the reasons for returning home are complex and diverse, one wonders whether Pacific transnationals ever return home completely or whether 'home' no longer is clear in meaning and place for them as they cast continual glances over their shoulders to the lands they have left. Does their return home cancel out their initial departure so that they are no longer transnationals or do the ties to their once adopted homeland permanently make them transnationals? For Connell's educated health workers, the dilemma is not eased by their educational status and many will re-migrate after a period of return 'home'. For Nosa's

Niueans, the incentive to return home is initiated largely by the government although the limited economic potential for them makes the return migration unattractive even when family ties remain strong.

Francis' chapter explores the diversity of international and local movement for the residents of three different Tongan villages. The reasons for these movements, which include socio-cultural factors, religion, education and the selling of produce, are influenced in a significant way by the economic and social status of its residents. Hoëm's chapter about the physical and cultural construction of home in Tokelau reminds us that transnationalism exists because of the connections that transnationals maintain with home. Her illustration of the 'modern', two-storey, concrete floor homes that cater for smaller independent families as compared to the traditional thatched homes shows how this has changed the configuration of Tokelauan life by including a sense of privacy within the walls and a competition for economic status among Tokelauans. Her disturbing account of the sexual abuse by a pastor of a twelve year old reveals the conflict that exists between the political situation of the transnationals and the influence they wish to have over what they may see as the incestuous and closed practices of the home country.

As political agreements between countries allow older island-born Pacific nationals to return home to retire after living and working overseas, retirees maintain their links to their families, children and grandchildren back in their adopted countries and to the friendships and interests that were built and developed there. Burns McGrath (2002) says this circular migration is characteristic of Pacific Islanders and has to do with their relationship and ties to the land and sea. These transnationals can be thought of as reversing their transnational status on their return home as they create collective 'homes' around themselves and have multiple identities grounded in more than one society (Wong 2002, 170–171).

Reciprocity

According to Vertovec (2004), transnationalism is the interactions that link people and institutions across nation-states. It is about having a place where one was born and another place to which one has ties. In whatever way it takes place, identity and relationship to homeland must be reciprocated between the transnational community and the place and persons with whom these connections are made. If reciprocity is not part of the process, then transnationalism cannot be said to exist.

Tongans see reciprocal transnational exchanges as nurturing the 'socio-spatial ties with kin and kin-like members' or *tauhi vā* (Ka'ili 2005, 5). Small (1997) refers to the transnational family where members live in different countries but maintain close links with each other, and where reciprocity is important to maintaining these links. According to Hau'ofa (1994 cited in Ka'ili 2005, 4), these reciprocal exchanges involve relatives abroad sending back money and resources such as appliances and clothes, while the home-based kin send local goods such as mats, tapa, and taro, and maintain the home for the returning traveller. Reciprocity also occurs in links with other diasporic communities, even through the internet as we search for and receive responses about information and news of people, place and the homeland to which we belonged. For some Pacific transnationals, reciprocity is in the giving up of their land in exchange for the opportunity to be educated abroad, thereby increasing their ability to send back money and resources, while others give up the opportunity to travel overseas in exchange for taking care of the land and maintaining the culture for themselves and those who may return one day (Gegeo 2001).

Francis highlights the inequity and imbalance between the activities that 'home' residents must undertake to maintain the cultural traditions and the reciprocal and compensatory gifts accorded these residents by their transnationals for doing so. Addo and Lilomaiava-Doktor discuss gifts as an important ritual of Pacific transnational life because of the process and values system that accompany it. For Addo, the question is whether cash can be a modern day substitute for traditional gifts among Tongan transnationals. She is concerned about how Tongan families will continue to provide for each other as expectations of money in exchange for traditional gifts become the norm. This can be answered in part by Lilomaiava-Doktor's analysis of home (*i'inei*) and reach (*fafo*) for Samoan transnationals as they leave behind what were once familiar practices of home to reach out for those practices in their new places—practices that seem more pragmatic, appropriate and acceptable. These changes are not limited to money and remittances but include education, relationships, and even chiefly titles. As Pacific transnationals persist with changed practices that have the potential to change the traditional practices at home, we may be looking at a reversal of home and reach so that the *fafo* becomes *i'inei* and vice versa.

In cities across Aotearoa/New Zealand, Australia and the USA, interactions take place not only between the city's Pacific transnationals and the home country, but also between earlier and newer transnationals. Reciprocal exchanges occur as the more established group shares information and provides networks that assist the recent arrivals to resettle, while the new transnationals share their more recent knowledge of the customs and practices of the home country with the earlier arrivals. The Macphersons and Alexeyeff argue that kinship, the co-dependence between home and migrant, is key to being a Pacific transnational, and if kinship changes, so does a Pacific transnational. Alexeyeff says that the expectation within traditional home practices such as the *tere pati* (travelling party) which have now crossed transnational boundaries is for the exchange of economic sustenance for the upkeep of agenda, obligations and emotions of Cook Islands' social relationships. As Pacific diaspora populations grow as large as or larger than the home populations, the issue of power—a seldom discussed feature of Pacific transnationalism—arises as we observe the significant difference in human capital between transnational and home residents which has the capacity to influence and alter traditional practices and relationships as well as increase pressure on the transnational communities to provide for those at home. The contemporary practices of *saofa'i* (title conferring ceremony) in Pacific diaspora communities appear to be a kind of truce in this power dynamic which subtly dictates that these communities will attend to the affairs of their Pacific transnationals while home residents attend to theirs. This does not mean that the reciprocal contacts between the home residents and the transnationals become obsolete but rather that there are changes to the way that this reciprocity occurs. It takes place in the agreements between the resident and the transnational *matai* (chief) of the different communities and an acknowledgement of each other's status and roles while maintaining and reinforcing the migrant-home kinship ties, ties that the Macphersons explain have been key to the establishment and maintenance of transnational Samoa.

Permanence and Transition

Pacific transnationalism can be temporal and fixed or shifting and continuous. At any moment, the circumstances of transnationalism can exist for any group of individuals or community of people. They occur when boundaries are crossed, and connections and links are made back to the country of origin or by their community. The patterns of transnational activities then become part of the community and of the lives of those with whom these contacts are made. It is not uncommon or difficult to identify certain communities as transnational communities or to regard certain practices as transnational. Yet it can be difficult to say when a particular activity that involved contact between two places of different national origins is *not* an example of transnationalism or to identify when the process of transnationalism stops. Kennedy and Roudometof (2002, 57) believe that transnationalism is sustained so long as new immigrants continue to join these communities, and people remain transnationals for the time that these links are sustained. Al-Ali and Koser (2002, 14) note the 'permanence and resiliency of transnationalism' and believe 'that individuals can become transnational, and also stop being transnational'. Transnational communities that become inactive in terms of transnational practices may once again decide to revive and resume these practices. Although the formation of transnational communities has accelerated in recent years, so too has the unmaking of these communities as they regroup or move back to their country of origin or integrate into their host countries (Al-Ali and Koser 2002, 7). However, it is the continuous wave of transnationals, as each new individual, groups of individuals or communities make similar crossings over similar national boundaries and maintain similar contacts, which give transnationalism its permanence.

As second, third and subsequent generations of Pacific nations' migrants are born, transnational practices tend to diminish. Although van Amersfoort and Doomernik (2002, 56) believe that, over time, the boundaries and social positions become 'more diffuse', they admit that not all groups develop in this way. They also believe that it is difficult to say at what point the process of 'immigrant absorption' draws to a close but agree that the initial processes lose their impetus and strength after about three generations.

It is possible for communities to lose their transnational identity, though it cannot be certain at what point this loss occurs. It could be when communities or individuals no longer make connections with the homeland or wish to do so. These connections do not always need to be to people but also to the ideas, cultures and customs of home. Cultures, like people, migrate and lead to 'communities of "taste", shared beliefs or economic interests' (Kennedy and Roudometof 2002, 13). However, if a Pacific transnational identity can cease through a lack of identification with the homeland, then it can also resume as new arrivals or even older members seek to re-establish links and ties. A transnational identity is usually viewed as arising out of a community. Gegeo (2001) claims that identity is a quality that is 'built in from birth' but to which 'one can add other identities', suggesting that the adoption of other identities is an individual process even though it is influenced by external or communal factors. This allows an individual, at least, to regard herself as a transnational even though she may not be seen in that way by the community in which she lives.

Kennedy and Roudometof (2002, 14) argue that differentiating between older disaporic transnational communities, and second and third generation global communities, is dangerous and misleading because of the close connections and dependencies between the localised second and third generations and the initial globalised transnationals. Communications technology and mass transport have allowed transnationals to maintain links with their homeland and have made it easier for second, third and fourth generations to sustain these links even when it appears that they have moved towards assimilation in the host country. This would not necessarily bring an end to Pacific transnationalism but does indicate that the reasons for Pacific transnationalism vary according to the circumstances of each group that migrates outside the Pacific Islands and changes in nature over the time of each successive generation. Transnational communities will vary in the extent to which they carry out or portray the ideal of transnationalism, depending on their desires, needs and expectations of both themselves and the communities from which they come. Transnational communities are heterogeneous with respect to their home communities and among their members, and some transnationals may 'share a lifestyle and personal aspirations' (Kennedy and Roudometof 2002, 15) closer to that of the dominant host community than to members of their own migrant group. Allegiance to their migrant community and home country may shift over time, depending on factors such as new friendships being made, and as the prospect of returning home grows dimmer.

Countries constantly redesign their immigration laws in order to regulate and monitor the nature and flow of migrants. Most countries require migrants to meet certain criteria related to skills, country of application, reason for application and family members if they wish to migrate. Asylum seekers must also meet specific requirements and quota restrictions upon application for refugee status. Upon arrival in a host country, a range of community and government services and organisations are made available to both migrants and refugees to assist their successful integration and resettlement into the society. In contrast, there are no government policies, state organisations or community services for those persons defined as transnationals. In fact, there appears to be no obvious constitutional benefit to an individual or community to be classified as a transnational. This may be because, as Wong (2002, 175) points out, they are regarded as *de facto* citizens of more than one nation-state rather than *de jure* ones.

Work, legal or undocumented, has made transnationals out of people—from the seafarers of Kiribati, as described by Borovnik, who intertwine their travel with the prospect of procuring remittances for their kin at home, to the Fijian fruit pickers in Griffith, Australia whose circumstances have been brought to attention by Schubert. In Schubert's account, like that of Lee's, one recognizes that moving, travelling on, seeking circumstances more favourable than the ones left behind, are central to Pacific peoples' existence. It highlights a people nomadic by necessity as often their transnational pattern involves not only one movement, but several, as Nosa illustrates in his chapter about Niueans who moved first to Aotearoa/New Zealand and then on to Australia.

In Pacific communities in Aotearoa/New Zealand and Australia, an important matter in transnationality is who forges and maintains the links with the home islands. Key members of both communities—pastors, politicians, sports stars, journalists and chiefly elders—have crucial roles to play in upholding the processes of transnationalism. They are needed to communicate with the home community about the affairs of its transnational host community, to inform the latter about events in the home country, and to make the host country aware of its transnational community. Transnational institutions work to help their nationals survive and improve their opportunities in the host country (Amersfoort and Doomernik 2002, 56). Churches, according to Lee (2003), are significant to 'the organization of social spaces' in Tongan transnational communities and to maintaining kinship connections and relationships. Church communities for Pacific transnationals, though not an exact replication of a village, provide the space and place where Samoan customs are enacted and their values reinforced

(Burns McGrath, 2002). Transnational links are forged not only through cultural identities but also through sports, leisure and lifestyle, and Kennedy and Roudometof (2002, 1) agree that accounts of transnational relationships should be extended to include other social trends that shape peoples' lives such as associations, clubs, and informal networks.

Dilemmas

Is it possible to be a transnational without having ever left home? The literature on 'home' reveals the tension between the physical place of home and the symbolic space, and home is seen not only as a territorial attachment but also as an adherence to 'transportable cultural ideas and values' (Al-Ali and Koser 2002, 7). In the Pacific nations, countless numbers of residents are involved in preparing members of their family to make the voyage to join other diasporic communities in other countries, while the same residents remain at home and send local products to home-sick transnationals, collect returning travellers from airports, maintain the family and the village at home, and share news and information. Those that remain are exposed to, engaged in, and are as much a part of the transnational experience as those who leave; they are in fact essential to its existence although they may never have left home. The knowledge and exchanges in which they are involved change how they see themselves and the rest of their world and differ significantly from those individuals that do not have similar relationships.

As new relationships develop and new circumstances arise within Pacific communities, both in and beyond Pacific nations themselves, the concept of Pacific transnationalism is challenged in its attempts to describe and reflect these phenomena. West Papuans, for example, can be regarded as 'enforced' transnationals as they fight to reclaim their land, their sovereignty and the retention of their culture from Indonesia. For some Pacific nations' peoples, the notion of being 'landless' transnationals is a reality and transnationalism becomes critical to their survival as they witness the disappearance and destruction of their islands. For example, the Fangataufa and Mururoa atolls have become radioactive and uninhabitable due to France's nuclear testing; in the Solomon Islands, tsunamis have destroyed villages forcing the government to consider resettling the locals; and in Tuvalu, climate change is causing erosion, spoiling crops and affecting the islands' fresh water. In these instances, identity and relationship to homeland may exist only in memories, and oral and recorded histories, and reciprocal exchanges between communities, as they relocate to different countries, will be necessary to sustaining these memories and histories.

Understanding Pacific transnationalism with accuracy and relevance is not nearly as important as first understanding ongoing change within the Pacific due to factors such as political instability, struggling economies, climate change and social upheaval. This book is a collaboration between those authors whose research has taken them into the Pacific and the Pacific diaspora and those for whom the Pacific is their *gafa* (genealogy) and *fanua* (land) and this allows for intersections to be made in theorising about Pacific transnationalism. For those familiar with what they observe and theorise as Pacific transnationalism, there is an acceptance that these observances are likely to change in concept and circumstance for the next observer, researcher, or writer of Pacific transnationalism.

References

Al-Ali, N. and K. Koser (eds). 2002. New approaches to migration? *Transnational communities and the transformation of home*. London: Routledge.

Armbruster, H. 2002. Homes in crisis: Syrian Orthodox Christians in Turkey and Germany. In *New approaches to migration? Transnational communities and the transformation of home*, ed. N. Al-Ali and K. Koser, 17-33. London: Routledge.

Basch, L., N. Glick Schiller and C. Szanton Blanc. 1995. *Nations unbound: Transnational projects, postcolonial predicaments, and deterritorialized nation-states*. New York: Gordon and Breach .

Brah, A. 1996. *Cartographies of diaspora: Contesting identities*. London: Routledge.

Burns McGrath, B. 2002. Seattle Fa'a Samoa. *The Contemporary Pacific* 14 (2): 307–35.

Connell, J. and D. Conway. 2000. Migration and remittances in island microstates: A comparative perspective on the South Pacific and the Caribbean. *International Journal of Urban and Regional Research* 24 (1) 52–78.

Dorai, M. K. 2002. The meaning of homeland for the Palestinian diaspora: Revival and transformation. In *New approaches to migration? Transnational communities and the transformation of home*, ed. N. Al-Ali and K. Koser, 87-95. London: Routledge.

Gegeo, Welchman D. 2001. Cultural rupture and indigeneity: The challenge of (re)visioning 'place' in the Pacific. *The Contemporary Pacific* 13 (2): 491-507.

Glick Schiller, N. 1999. Transmigrants and nation-states: Something old and something new in the U.S. immigrant experience. In *The handbook of international migration: The American experience*, ed. C. Hirschman, P. Kasinitz and J. DeWind, 94-119. New York: Russell Sage Foundation.

Glick Schiller, N., L. Basch, and C. Szanton Blanc. 1995. From immigrant to transmigrant: Theorizing transnational migration, *Anthropological Quarterly* 68: 48–62.

Jackson, P., P. Crang, and C. Dwyer (eds). 2004. *Transnational spaces*. London: Routledge.

Ka'ili, T. O. 2005. Tauhi vā: Nurturing Tongan sociospatial ties in Maui and beyond. *The Contemporary Pacific* 17 (1): 83-114.

Kempny, M. 2002. Cieszyn Silesia: A transnational community under reconstruction. In *Communities across borders. New immigrants and transnational cultures*, ed. P. Kennedy and V. Roudometof, 116-28. London: Routledge.

Kennedy, P. and V. Roudometof. 2002. Transnationalism in a global age. In *Communities across borders. New immigrants and transnational cultures*, ed. P. Kennedy and V. Roudometof, 1-26. London: Routledge.

Lee, Helen Morton. 2003. *Tongans overseas: Between two shores*. University of Hawai'i Press.

Ley, D. and J. Waters. 2004. Transnational migration and the geographical imperative. In *Transnational spaces*, ed. P. Jackson, P. Crang and C. Dwyer, 104-21. London: Routledge.

Portes, A. 1999. Conclusion: towards a new world—the origins and effects of transnational activities. *Ethnic and Racial Studies* 22 (2): 463–77.

Portes, A., L. E. Guernizo, and P. Landolt. 1999. The study of transnationalism: Pitfalls and promise of an emergent research field. *Ethnic and Racial Studies* 22 (2): 217–27.

Roudometof, V. and A. Karpathakis. 2002. Greek Americans and transnationalism: Religion, class and community. In *Communities across borders. New immigrants and transnational cultures*, ed. P. Kennedy and V. Roudometof, 41-54. London: Routledge.

Rouse, R. 2004. Mexican migration and the social space of postmodernism. In *Transnational spaces*, ed. P. Jackson, P. Crang, and C. Dwyer, 24-39. London: Routledge.

Small, C. A. 1997. *Voyages: From Tongan villages to American suburbs*. New York: Cornell University Press.

van Amersfoort, H. and J. Doomernik. 2002. Emergent diasporas or immigrant communities? Turkish immigrants in the Netherlands. In *Communities across borders. New immigrants and transnational cultures*, ed. P. Kennedy and V. Roudometof, 55-67. London: Routledge.

Vertovec, S. 2004. Foreword. In *Transnational spaces*, ed. P. Jackson, P. Crang, and C. Dwyer, 78-103. London: Routledge.

Walton-Roberts, M. 2004. Returning, remitting, reshaping: Non-resident Indians and the transformation of society and space in Punjab, India. In

Transnational spaces, ed. P. Jackson, P. Crang, and C. Dwyer, 78-103. London: Routledge.

Wong, L. 2002. Home away from home? Transnationalism and the Canadian citizenship regime. In *Communities across borders. New immigrants and transnational cultures*, ed. P. Kennedy and V. Roudometof, 169-81. London: Routledge.

www.ingramcontent.com/pod-product-compliance
Lightning Source LLC
Chambersburg PA
CBHW061244270326
41928CB00041B/3414